Unfinished Agenda

Junius Williams in front of the building of his community organization, the Newark Area Planning Association (NAPA), 1968.

UNFINISHED AGENDA

Urban Politics in the Era of Black Power

JUNIUS WILLIAMS

Foreword by Tom Hayden

North Atlantic Books
Berkeley, California

Published by
North Atlantic Books
P.O. Box 12327
Berkeley, California 94712

Cover and book design by Brad Greene
Printed in the United States of America

Unfinished Agenda: Urban Politics in the Era of Black Power is sponsored by the Society for the Study of Native Arts and Sciences, a nonprofit educational corporation whose goals are to develop an educational and cross-cultural perspective linking various scientific, social, and artistic fields; to nurture a holistic view of arts, sciences, humanities, and healing; and to publish and distribute literature on the relationship of mind, body, and nature.

North Atlantic Books' publications are available through most bookstores. For further information, visit our website at www.northatlanticbooks.com or call 800-733-3000.

Library of Congress Cataloging-in-Publication Data
Williams, Junius, 1943–
 Unfinished agenda : urban politics in the era of Black Power / Junius Williams.
   pages cm.
  ISBN 978-1-58394-722-7
1. Williams, Junius, 1943- 2. African Americans—Civil rights—History—20th century. 3. African Americans—Politics and government—20th century. 4. Civil rights movements—United States—History—20th century. 5. Black power—United States—History—20th century 6. Community organization—New Jersey—Newark—20th century. 7. Newark (N.J.)—Politics and government—20th century. 8. African American civil rights workers—Biography 9. African American lawyers—Biography. I. Title.
  E185.97.W728A3 2013
  323.092—dc23
  [B]
                                                              2013008255

3 4 5 6 7 8 9 UNITED 18 17 16 15 14

This book is dedicated to my parents, Maurice Lanxton and Bernyce White Williams, who started me on my way. They nourished and supported me with ideas and opportunities, and in their own way saw to it that I became successful. They have passed on to Glory, but their spirit is with me always.

This book is also dedicated to my younger brother Johnny (John Williams). We have always been there for each other; certainly he is there for me today whenever I need brotherly love and support.

꙳

Acknowledgments

This book was bound to happen, but it took a long time. I wrote on paper napkins, on church bulletins during church services, and on yellow legal pads. I have about forty seventh-grade "Compositions" notebooks, filled with notes and rough drafts. I wrote whenever and wherever I was inspired. During that time, many people came into the life of my beloved manuscript, and to some of them I feel grateful and indebted.

Diane Patrick, Deirdre Cross, and Jed Bickman edited the manuscript, helping me to shape and refine my chapters. They gave me confidence about the value of the book and helped me eventually attract the publisher.

Unfinished Agenda is what I call in the Introduction "a historical memoir," and so I didn't trust my memory and judgment alone. I cultivated my own voice as I was instructed to do, but other people helped provide the glue that holds my story together from chapter to chapter. I interviewed many people to get their recollection and opinions about the way things happened. I want to say thank you to the following: Phil Hutchings, George Fontaine, Ray Trent, Don Melafronte, Stanley Aronowitz, Louise Epperson, J. Harry Smith, Wyla McClain, George Richardson, Mary Darden, Dudley Christie, Jim Walker, Tom Parks, Alma Perry, Gus Heningburg, Juliet Grant, Roger Smith (Newman), Derek Winans, Eulis "Honey" Ward, Terry Jefferson, Earline Provit, "Ma" Jackson, Carl Sharif, Betty Morse, Sandy Gallanter, Rita Williams, Joe White, Joe Scrimmager, Ramon Rivera, Alphonso Roman, Jerry Chambers, Donald Harris, Verner Henry, Sally G. Carroll, Richard Cammerieri, Wilhelmina Holder, Professor Michael Nash, and Charles Geyer. (Stanley Aronowitz and Phil Hutchings gave me interviews as early as 1989.)

Still others helped me when I read their books and other writing, or when I listened to them speak at community forums or in my class when I taught political science at Rutgers University–Newark as an adjunct professor (1992), or at Abbott Leadership Institute classes between 2002 and 2012. Some people gave me little snippets of information or insight in private conversations. Thank you to Amiri Baraka, Tom Hayden, James Forman, Larrie Stalks, Calvin West, Carol Graves, Clem Price, Claude Brown, Rev. Levin West, former mayor Ken Gibson, Senator Ron Rice, Judge Clarence Faines, Bob Curvin, Kwame Ture (Stokely Carmichael), "Tiny" Prince, Carol Glassman, Reuben Johnson, Jill Hamberg, Steve Block, Corrina Fales, former mayor Sharpe James, Marcia Brown, Kabili Tayari, Eugene Campbell, John Crump, Komozi Woodard, and O.T. Wells.

I want to thank my friends in the Student Nonviolent Coordinating Committee (SNCC) for teaching me street survival skills and giving me the Movement credentials I needed to move from the South to the North; those in the Students for a Democratic Society (SDS) and in the Newark Community Union Project (NCUP) for teaching me how to organize. I want to thank my friends and comrades in the Newark Area Planning Association (NAPA) for letting me be their leader, and backing my "play" on so many occasions. I want to thank my friends in the National Bar Association, who let me be their president at the age of thirty-four, and have cheered for me in whatever endeavor I have undertaken after that one year in office. And then there are the musicians and friends in Return to the Source: Guys, you saved my life, turned me completely around. I thank my classmates in Richmond, Virginia, from the class of 1961 at Armstrong High School who have supported me through the years—and those of you who went to Maggie Walker as well! We started on our way. Then there are the members of my church families at Greater Abyssinian Baptist and Bethany Baptist Churches. And last but not least, I want to thank my parents, community activists, teachers, and students in the Abbott Leadership Institute (ALI) for letting me be myself again and again and again. You get me ready and excited for the next round. Without the people in these groups and organizations, there would be no story worth telling.

During the writing stage, each month my manuscript kept growing and growing, until my wife, Annie, a.k.a. Dr. Antoinette Ellis-Williams, told me "You got more than enough for any one book, so why don't you just *stop.*" One day I took her advice and found out I had 1,100 pages (double-spaced). She supported me with love that was full of humor and compassion. I couldn't have written the book in a home where there was an absence of these vital ingredients. Thank you, and I love you.

And then there are my four children, who love me but enjoy roughing me up with their jokes, challenges, and irreverence for the little excerpts I gave them from time to time. I kept writing anyway, even when they wouldn't read the unfinished *Unfinished Agenda* that was left casually strewn around the living room in the hope that I would get some feedback and encouragement. Thank you and much love to Camille, Junea, Junius, and Che.

Getting a publisher in today's market is not for the faint of heart. But eventually, I am a "published author" today because of the openness to new ideas of Richard Grossinger and the folks at North Atlantic Books. They took me in and made me a part of the family. I want to thank them all. Much appreciation to my new editor, Jessica Sevey, who knows how to move a project.

Finally, I want to acknowledge the people of Newark, New Jersey. Sometimes you are the rock, and at other times the sinking sand, upon which I stake my claim to manhood right here in this book and beyond. I couldn't have made it without you, one way or the other. And I wouldn't have it any other way.

Contents

Foreword

This book is a must-read for that small but prophetic minority who, in each generation, try to apply their gifts to lifting the weight of poverty and despair from the souls of the poor.

All too often such efforts end in selling out or burning out. Junius Williams has navigated between these dangerous shoals of ambition and despair all his life, faltering but never falling. Looking back, he concludes, "I have been accustomed to being the outside player, the man left alone, respected and listened to but never embraced." We learn the important lesson that it's been worth it: "I am as happy as I can be to be who I am." Could anyone ask for more than a life well-lived filled with fights worth fighting?

I think I met Junius around 1965, at a time when it was easier to be hopeful. If he had come along forty years later, he might have been Barack Obama. But he instead became one of those gifted young black leaders who invested their lives in creating the conditions for Obama's future. Junius is correct that I recruited him to a Newark community-organizing project on the basis of his charisma and talent as an Amherst College activist. I was twenty-four years old, about two years his "senior." We were going to change the world from the bottom up.

While many of us chose between lifetime commitments to our utopian dreams versus careers within the institutional status quo, Junius was smart enough to choose both worlds: he came to Newark's slums and was accepted at Yale Law School the same year. It would be a lifetime of balancing between what he calls "the streets" and "the suites." This was not about an expedient hedging of bets. It came from his intuition that community-based movements without allies in power were as inadequate as their opposite, attempting to leverage

XIII

social change from corporate law offices far above street levels. His book is an excellent narration of how his youthful intuition became a sophisticated strategy of reform.

In 1964–65, we were God's fools. Outsiders, mainly white university graduates, we descended on Newark's ghetto like disciples of St. Francis, taking vows of voluntary poverty (except on some weekend lapses in the Village), knocking on doors, trying to draw people out of their well-deserved cynicism, cultivating new leadership out of dead zones of poverty, knitting small block clubs into a neighborhood assembly, taking direct action on grievances we heard from local people: rats, roaches, high rents, police abuse, crooked grocers, callous bureaucrats, a lack of services that completed a culture of disenfranchisement—Junius recounts the story well. "The soul," he learned, "cannot find heaven here on earth without first coming to a meeting." Junius received no salary, only $25 per week from his mother. It didn't seem to matter because "NCUP provided a daily drumbeat to awaken the people to resistance. . . . It was a blessing to have been there and at work during those times."

I dwell here on Newark 1964–1967 because those were the "blessed" years I spent with Junius. The rise of Black Power, out of the failed hopes of the early civil rights period, and the four days of insurrection, burning, shooting, killing, and mass incarcerations in July 1967, altered the course of our hopes and history. The Vietnam War, begun in August 1964 and raging by 1967, finished off any remaining prospects for turning America around.

Some of us, myself included, left Newark at that time, while Junius dug in deeper. He could have sailed the affluent seas from Yale to Wall Street, or to the Higher Circles of Power, but he stayed in Newark as a matter of choice. By 1970, as I had predicted when I was recruiting Junius, Newark had elected its first black mayor, Kenneth Gibson. It was a heady moment, a high point in retrospect, an "age of federal programs" not seen since Reconstruction, largely an official response to the uprisings sweeping urban America. Mayor Gibson appointed Junius the director of his Model Cities Program, a top-down and much expanded version of the anti-poverty programs we had labored to make real five years before. Junius was moving up, the youngest Model Cities director in the country. It was a "gift to the militants from Gibson," he reflects now. Junius had shown his effectiveness in forging a coalition to hammer out the Medical School Agreements, which brought 1,000 units of housing and hundreds of construction jobs to Newark. His ability as a bargaining agent for the poor and unemployed however did not endear him to everyone.

Without the organized power of the streets protecting him, the Powers That Be, including the mayor, could not tolerate an independent threatening the patronage purposes of the Model Cities program. The budding empire of Amiri Baraka (LeRoi Jones) fell before the power structure as well, destroying "one of the most effective political black organizations" that had created Gibson's electoral base. Junius was blamed for a fiscal audit though no wrongdoing was proven against him, and was fired by December 1972. He more than survived, becoming a community-based lawyer and rising to lead the National Bar Association in the seventies at the still-precious age of thirty-four. He moved that association of up-and-coming black lawyers to lobby for sanctions on Rhodesia at the United Nations, where he presented a paper on behalf of the organization—and at home, when he led the fight for affirmative action and welcomed speakers like Louis Farrakhan.

Destiny seemed to require that Junius run for mayor of Newark himself, questing perhaps to achieve the full potential of the original strategy of organizing. In 1982, he was overspent massively and beaten badly, getting 4,996 votes to Gibson's 21,000 and Earl Harris's (another old ally of NCUP) 11,500.

Junius kept going. He ran the Newark Legal Services Project as a "law firm for the poor"; fought for low and moderate-income housing when the four colleges in Newark sought to expand their land holdings; litigated a historic court decision to bring single lever voting to the state of New Jersey, making it possible to cast one vote for presidential candidate Jesse Jackson to get all his delegates; became chairman of the Greater Abyssinian Baptist Church trustees; and formed a continuing training institute to empower parents to fight for their children.

The list is long and could be titled: Battles Won, Battles Lost, Battle On: The Life Story of Junius Williams.

Through it all he somehow remains faithful to lessons learned long ago. For instance, at his Abbott Leadership Institute, he writes that his purpose is "to help people who have been mired in self-blame, distrust, and disorganization by putting them in touch with our historic roots and with each other." Looking back, he realizes that "the collective memory of independent organizations grew more and more faint" as the "Black Political Class rose in power." "We had no class analysis to go along with racial analysis. None of the black mayors ever sought to organize their local constituency as a fighting force." He says of current Mayor (and would-be presidential candidate?) Cory Booker, that he is "just as closed in his dealings with the community" as past mayors.

Perhaps most revealing is his belief in "making other people [simply] learn to think" about their own power, the first rule in community organizing. "People who plant and cultivate ideas, and perpetually force or negotiate these ideas forward into the consciousness of the public, we last forever."

I wish Junius had written more about the pivotal years of the Newark rebellion and its aftermath. Those wanting an account might read my *Rebellion in Newark* and Ron Porambo's amazing *No Cause for Indictment*. Some of us fantasized in those days that we were on the brink of revolution, while almost everyone assumed that the violent shocks would force massive concessions from the business and government establishments. What happened instead was the rise of the black mayors presiding over a swath of cities even more impoverished, with budgets for policing and prisons on the rise, and an exodus of whites and black professionals who could afford the migration to the exurbs. Corporate investments followed the migration too, out of the cities and often out of the country itself. The costs could be written off.

What happened in Newark and scores of American cities those many years ago explains the paradox we confront today: the presidency of Barack Obama, which none of us imagined possible in the 1960s, coupled with increasing poverty, dispossession, and incarceration among the poor in general, and blacks in particular. In his narrative, Junius said, "Someone would have to organize to redirect the politics of City Hall to fight Reaganomics and the forces of globalization that were consolidating to consume the world."

One can only wish that Junius Williams had risen in power. But at least he has stayed and not been moved.

Tom Hayden
May 2013

Introduction

WHY I WRITE THIS BOOK

Change! . . . makes you wanna hustle;
Change! . . . things won't be the same.

—DONALD BYRD, "CHANGE"

People who write political memoirs believe in the power of their own story to educate, to fill in the gaps; to paint a picture with words that will prescribe the future. I am such a believer, and so I have written about lessons learned in my quest for power for black people, primarily in Newark, New Jersey. Such a journey in the name of a group can be deceiving, even illusory. And so my book is also a personal reflection on my life in politics—the personal costs of chasing power to the edge of endurance. This is my answer to many friends who ask, "Why did you do it, and in Newark, of all places?"

But there is a third theme in my book. This is also a story about the call-and-response nature of any movement for power. We made demands, and "the Empire" struck back. What is the "Empire"? The collective interests, both economic and political, that control America. Mine is a personal testimony of the power of black people to organize, build effective community-based organizations, and grab power through the politics of confrontation; only to confront the power of the Empire to quell and misdirect our voices by keeping us divided and still under its control. Carter G. Woodson said this could happen because of the power of "miseducation," and saw it as a more effective and long-lasting means to control black people under slavery and later under Jim Crow. Sometimes rather than using whip and gun, the Empire simply dumbs us down. But in fact, one of the permissible

1

conclusions from the evidence I present of the Empire's manipulation of its message and the people they create or suborn as leaders, is that they have miseducated all Americans, not just black folks. Because of our varying states of miseducation, the Empire controls by keeping Americans divided and unclear about what we have in common as members of what the Occupy Wall Street Movement calls "the 99 percent." My memoir is about how that happened in the empowerment quest for one community—the black community—using my life story as the means of exploration of principles and practices that are useful for any people who want to take power in America, no matter what color, or social or economic standing.

The Power of Stories

One way for the Empire to miseducate is by telling its stories, over and over, which can only take root absent stories of our own.

Too few of us from the Black Power generation and the movements to take power in cities through the election of black elected officials have told our stories. Hence there is very little understanding of the agenda for change we outlined for black people and America in the 1960s and early 1970s. We wanted self-determination, an end to racism, and economic security. It is an agenda that was never fulfilled, and hence the title of my book, *Unfinished Agenda*.

What does my story have in common with the untold stories of the others in that movement? First of all, we all confronted or accommodated Jim Crow racism in the South and the North. Then, we formed or joined small, unpredictable grassroots organizations and larger coalitions that moved from confrontations in the streets, combining direct action and professional technical expertise, to campaigns to elect black people to city government. These city elections created a new black political class, which unfortunately took greater pleasure in imitating its white predecessors in office than in pursuing a more radical goal of seeking inclusion of more people at the table: younger leaders, people with different backgrounds, with new ideas for community development; people heretofore left out of the leadership development process; people who were leaders in confrontation politics. This has resulted in the elimination of collective memory of the politics of confrontation that catalyzed and energized the movement to elect "the first black mayor" in Newark as this new black political class sought to justify its existence and solidify its power on terms it found more acceptable, such as its membership in the Democratic Party.

So there is a perspective on power that is not often entertained by many people coming of age now, who simply have no idea it exists. There are almost two full generations who stand upon the shoulders of my generation, and, for better or worse, who owe their position in society to us. But they don't really know to whom the shoulders belong. Some of those that do know thank us for our sacrifice but proclaim that the playing field has changed so much that our services are no longer needed, while others have learned our history and the history of those before us and continue the struggle the best way they can.

The newest generation of urban advocates sees the election campaigns of black and brown officials as models to emulate. How much of what they call "power" today comes from imitating the narrow, one-sided electoral scramble choreographed by the two-party system in America? They know very little of the most important building block of our triumph in controlling these mean streets, namely independent community organizations pursuing the politics of confrontation, coupled with eventual negotiations at the boardrooms and back rooms of private industry and city halls all over America, and election victories at the local level. These organizations paved the way for President Barack Obama by eventually creating an organized, disciplined voting bloc that knew what to do on Election Day. These community organizations became the foundation from which the Democratic Party collected campaign workers, city government its professionals in the bureaucracy, and local elected officials who proved not as threatening or disruptive to traditional party and economic interests as white power brokers first feared. But once in office, many of these officials forgot the bridge that brought them over, the power that can still be used to now help the president we elected to office. Most people don't make that connection, nor see its utility.

This is the position we find ourselves in, in the Age of Obama. The youth, parent activists, and politicians in places in Newark are symbolic of the members in urban communities all over the country who got together to elect a black president twice in this country. No matter the disagreement at home, we all agreed that we needed to elect and reelect President Obama. And his smart, tough campaign organization won him two victories despite a well-financed opposition that misjudged the president's ability to pull together a new majority that required only 39 percent of the white vote, the remainder coming from black, brown, and yellow people, with huge reliance on youth and women voters.

But our participation in these elections was based not on strategic negotiation with our standard-bearer. The Obama generation (those who were born in the last eighteen to fifty years or so), and those from my generation, invested in blind "Hope," proclaiming that great change is forthcoming, without having done the analysis of what really happened over the last forty to fifty years in our journey from Jim Crow to Barack Obama. Why is it we have a noteworthy black president but very little power in the black community? Why are we still unable to prosper in places like Newark, with its complex political culture built upon hope and despair?

I offer this book for the lessons I've learned, beginning with the common denominator of Jim Crow, which was America's context in the 1960s, and the overarching determinant of black people's responses at that time. It is a story of my understanding of power, starting with my upbringing in Richmond, Virginia; as it developed during my stay at Amherst College; traveling to Uganda and Kenya in an African homecoming; working in Harlem, New York; going to jail in Montgomery, Alabama; and ultimately becoming an organizer and political leader in Newark. It is my story, but it is also our story, as hundreds and, at times, thousands of people rose to the occasion and made Black Power a reality in Newark. Put another way, this is a story about what happened when the Movement came North and morphed into the quest for power by black people first in the streets, and then in the suites of city hall, and finally into the arms of the Democratic Party.

My growth as an organizer and political advocate has given me a different perspective on the advent of the Age of Obama. After reading my story, I want you to answer a question: How can all of us, no matter what color or what stage in life, become more empowered by the history that has brought us this new president?

This is particularly pertinent to those who are involved and impacted by the Occupy Movement, mostly young people, who have not been fooled and lulled into submission by the Empire's stories. My story can teach the members of Occupy much about the workings of power in this country, and what they need to do next, having taken preliminary steps toward personal freedom and justice for all people—just as we did forty-plus years ago.

How I Wrote This Book

This is a teaching memoir, and so I stay close to the historical record. I sought confirmation for all that I remember when it came to the big events in my life. My journey is framed by my personal recollection and interpretation, but made more accountable by using several sources. I read other people's accounts of the particular points or events I raise. I researched newsletters, doctoral dissertations, news articles from several local and national papers, magazine articles, other writers and storytellers, government documents, reports, my own notes, thoughts and recollections at the scene of an episode or event, and other documents, all to support and justify what I relate, conclude, think, and feel. I seek to be a credible resource, but also a lively one. This is a story, not unlike the historical narratives of African griots told in rhyme and verse, or Alexis de Tocqueville's stories about early America. Memoirs can be reliable historical resources, and make lessons come alive within the reader. It is my hope that I rise to that standard of storytelling.

I interviewed many people for this book, as far back as 1989. They told me what they remembered while the events were still fresh in their minds. I found notes I took beginning forty years ago, and collections of news articles when I first promised myself to "write about Newark." In some cases, they offer nice comparisons to how I feel now, but in other cases made me change my recollection of "the facts." Unfortunately many people I wanted to talk to are just no longer available—dead or moved away. The interviews I did add another dimension of personal relationships in my story: I get to share with you some of the people who made a contribution, making this *our* story. Some of the people have been heard from a great deal, but many have never been heard before. They are all people who made a deep impression on me. I marvel at the new breed of researchers who now descend upon Newark and seek only the insights and recollections of those who are well known and prominent as "leaders." So my use of language and my descriptions of fellow Newarkers in the struggle, or even those who were in opposition, is my shout-out to the leadership of many little-known warriors in the city, the impact they made on me, and the quality of leadership I have because of them.

It is my hope that when you read *Unfinished Agenda,* the missing pieces of the journey to empowerment for a significant group of Americans will be revealed to a new multiethnic generation, and that an honest intergenerational discourse on memory, power, and social justice will help propel our journey through the twenty-first century together, no matter who you are.

1
COMING OF AGE
IN THE '60s

There's a natural mystic blowing through the air...
If you listen carefully now you will hear.

—BOB MARLEY, "NATURAL MYSTIC"

Richmond, Virginia

I grew up in Richmond, Virginia, the "Gateway to the Confederacy."
Virginia was a slave-breeding state not known for the brutality asso-
ciated with the cotton belt in places like Mississippi and Alabama.
Richmond in the late 1950s and early 1960s was a clean city with broad
boulevards like Monument Avenue, noted for its many statues of Civil
War heroes. It had a genteel reputation for "good race relations."

But in reality, Richmond was no different than anywhere else in the
South—it just had a slicker image. As young black boys growing up
in Richmond at that time, my brother Johnny and I didn't dare cross
Brooklyn Park Boulevard for fear of being beaten by white boys our
age or older. For the first seventeen years of our lives in Richmond,
Johnny and I had no white social contacts, and our only white friends
we met during summers in the North or in the Midwest. We did have
one or two conversations with some of our white assailants who lived
on the other side of "The Ravine," another boundary in the back of my
parents' house, who used to shoot at us with BB guns. It was almost
out of a movie script: the white boys had guns, which they could use

from long distances, and we had homemade bows and arrows and spears made out of bamboo poles and slate from rooftops for tips. We couldn't get close enough to use them! Stone Age versus modern technology; cowboys versus Indians.

But we more than got by, and those confrontations were not every day. We raised pigeons in the back yard, and my father had a vegetable garden. My parents were music teachers. My father, Maurice Lanxton Williams, was the first black instrumental music teacher in Richmond, and my mother, Bernyce White Williams, the first black supervisor of music in the Norfolk, Virginia, schools, near Suffolk, where she was raised by my grandparents.

I remember being happy growing up. As one might imagine, music was a constant in my house. My mother and father liked European anthems and church music. My mother played WRNL in the morning when she got us ready for breakfast and school, listening to the Top 25 popular artists, who were mostly white, like Frank Sinatra and Peggy Lee; but some of them were black, like Nat King Cole and Johnny Mathis.

Both my parents were classically trained musicians. My mother studied at Howard University and the University of Pennsylvania, and my father at West Virginia State College. "Pop Williams," as the kids in the high school band called him, was my music teacher on the clarinet and alto saxophone. When I became proficient enough, he shipped me off to Dr. Nathaniel Gatlin at Virginia State College in nearby Petersburg. When I decided to play drums, he sent me to a professional drummer at Boykin's Music store in Richmond. My mother taught Johnny (and me, until I quit) to play the piano. Daddy taught Johnny the trumpet, French horn, and piccolo. There wasn't a day in our collective educations that we didn't stay after school playing in the Armstrong High School band or orchestra, or engaged in plays, school projects, or tennis. My older half brother, Maurice Cameron, a career officer in the U.S. Army, introduced us to bebop and progressive jazz. My older half sister Constance (Connie), who was a Los Angeles teacher before she died at an early age, taught us how to do Latin dances: cha-cha, mambo, and merengue. And because we were young, black, and living in Richmond, of course we loved rhythm and blues, later rock and roll. As children we joined Ebenezer Baptist Church, where we played our instruments on occasion and learned how to speak in public. Some of our teachers attended our church and otherwise socialized with my parents. I had a great childhood, insulated from "white people and their ways" by my parents and our middle class standing.

But despite the scarcity of confrontation with whites in our neighborhood, race and racism permeated every aspect of our lives. Our parents taught us that in order to succeed, we "had to be twice as good as white folks." We were constantly being prepared to enter a world dominated by whites. On Saturdays my mother or father sometimes took my brother and I to the movies at the Booker T, the Walker, or the Hippodrome, three run-down theaters designated for Colored Only, where we saw mostly B movies that had been hits months before in the white theaters. On those outings, we couldn't eat downtown at the restaurants reserved for Whites Only. When we went on vacation to Atlantic City each summer to be with my father's family, we left real early in the morning and carried bags of cold fried chicken to eat along the way. Between Virginia and Delaware, there was nowhere for us to stop on the highway, even to relieve ourselves.

Being black in those days was the suppressed anger at a saleswoman's callous whine when she finally got around to waiting on us: "Can I help y'all?" Sometimes we would laugh at the crackers, but never to their faces, so the bitterness was kept inside, the satisfaction only partial. All of us who managed to stay out of trouble in those days had to bite our tongues at some point. For some colored people, it became a habit. Being black was growing up with the knowledge that white is power, and uppidiness had its consequences.

9

That's why black people loved the blues. The blues spoke of love and lost love, money and no money, travel and arrival and leaving again: sometimes we were "Going to Chicago," and we were "Sorry but we can't take you." Then again, we might be "Movin' to the outskirts of town," because we didn't want "Nobody always hangin' 'round!" We loved the blues because it helped ease the pain of being slighted, ignored, or slapped down by white folks. Blues singers (the R&B singers of my day) would remind us of the joys and heartaches white folks couldn't share through dance, singing, or playing a horn. James Brown sang, "Down on my knees," but he got up with a smile on his face, his conked hair just right, and some money in his pocket. Even in our middle-classness, we could understand the blues, for ours was a fragile respite, our parents just one or two paychecks from being wiped out like our neighbors across the street. "The blues ain't nuthin' but the truth," and that truth was available for all of us, poor or not so poor.

Long years of suffering brought other kinds of resistance. I saw my father in resistance as the music teacher at Armstrong High School, along with Joe Kennedy, the black music teacher at our rival black school, Maggie Walker High School. They both stood up to Mr. Sanderson, the music supervisor in the Richmond School District, when he wanted all the high schools to march in the Tobacco Festival Parade, but with the proviso that the black schools march in the back. My father and Mr. Kennedy refused. And when we did march in my senior year, on an integrated basis, we showed up cautiously at the gathering point thinking we were going to be outclassed. Because you see, the white folks had done a job on us where it hurt the most: in our belief in self.

There were four corners, with the two white bands from Thomas Jefferson High School and John Marshall High School on two corners, and Armstrong and Maggie Walker High Schools on the other two. Each band took a turn warming up, showing off their prowess on the drums. Of course, the white folks ordained themselves to go first.

We listened, and began to titter and tee-hee at the stiffness of all that John Philip Sousa, West Point, Annapolis regimental drumming. We knew what Gregory Coleman and the drummers of Armstrong were capable of, and although we were rivals through the years, Walker's drummers came from the same source. So when it came our turn, each of the "colored bands" proceeded to blow them away with all that African syncopated fatback and cornbread, polyrhythmic, pre-Funkadelic, back-beatin' New Orleans Mardi Gras soul we had been waiting to reveal at this moment in history. In short, we rocked their world, shocked their falsely held belief that they were the best because they were white. White bands have precision, but black bands can strut—which requires precision *and* soul. It was on that corner that a mighty myth was shattered, before young eyes of both races. That day we marched so gloriously I could see it in my father's eyes how proud he was of us. And in the applause we got from blacks and whites alike along the parade route.

Another day of resistance came when my mother told us to break the law in a 5&10 cent store in Suffolk, Virginia. On one of our visits to see our grandparents, we went into the store to buy a few things. The Colored Only water fountain was rusty, and my brother couldn't get the water to rise. Not too far from it, the Whites Only water fountain, all shiny and new, was working just fine. Seeing our dilemma, my mother told my brother and I, "Go on and drink the water, boys," referring to the Whites Only fountain.

Just at that moment, a white saleslady came by and proceeded to berate Johnny and me, telling us, "Y'all not allowed to do that . . ." She was just carrying on, and Johnny and I were stunned by her verbal whiplash. But she didn't know she had crossed the line. Our Mama Lion was on her like white on rice: "*I* told them to drink from the fountain because the other one is broken! If you want to talk about it, deal with *me*, and not my children." My mother won the argument, because the messenger of white superiority was no match for her rage, her facility with language, and her protective spirit. We were impressed, as we left the store laughing and with our heads held high.

On occasion, the outside world brought news of even greater perils and pitfalls for black people. The murder of Emmett Till and the picture of his bloated corpse after it had been thrown in a river in Mississippi brought anger, bitterness, and sorrow. And it brought an awareness of a lot of black people coming together, not just for a funeral but also to prove a point. I had no idea what fifty thousand black people passing by a casket looked like, but it sounded like a lot to me. Images of death, pain, sorrow, and protest rocked our world as young teens looking through *Jet* magazine, usually a source of entertainment and black culture.

And let us not forget Virginia's so-called "massive resistance" to desegregation in the early '60s, which among other things shut down certain public accommodations rather than desegregate them. Faced with an order to desegregate the public pools, Richmond shut down the black pool and the white pool. The black pool at Brookfield Gardens never reopened, and it, along with the tennis courts that had seen a young man named Arthur Ashe learn the game of tennis, are now the site of a massive post office complex. But in the days of my youth, the closing of that pool cost me a merit badge in swimming and lifesaving, and therefore my chance to become the first black Eagle Scout in Richmond. Did I say Richmond wasn't evil?

But it was the picture in *Ebony* magazine of Mrs. Tinsley, a senior citizen of standing in the middle-class black community of which I was a part, being dragged across Broad Street in Richmond around 1960 or 1961 by two big redneck cops that sparked the ultimate outrage in me as a teenager. She was protesting segregated restaurants along with the students at Virginia Union University and was arrested and put in jail.

"If she could do it, so could I," I told myself, on the way to channeling anger to action. But my moment had not yet come, since my parents told me the college students who organized these actions frowned on participation by high school students. "They don't think high school students can be nonviolent," my mother and father patiently explained. Decades later, I questioned Charles Sherrod, the Virginia Union student who led the 1960–1961 demonstrations in Richmond, who later became an icon in SNCC and a pillar in the Albany, Georgia, Movement in 1963. "Did you put out the word in 1960 that high school students weren't welcome?" I asked.

He looked at me and simply said, "No."

"Wow," I said to myself. "My mother and father at work again."

Protest against Jim Crow was a call to my generation, and my parents saw I was listening. So the next best thing was to get me out of town. Fortunately for them, I was a senior, and on my way north, pursuant to Bernyce's plan.

The Bernyce Williams Liberation Plan

Every family in the South had coping mechanisms for dealing with the aspects of Jim Crow in their lives. My parents decided to send us away from the South. Well, actually, it was my mother's plan, and my father supported it.

Bernyce White Williams, my mother, grew up as the only child of a well-to-do black businessman named Junius Cicero White and his outspoken former schoolteacher wife from Richmond, Annye Johnson White. My granddaddy White didn't go any farther than high school, and was one of nine brothers. He chose to stay in Suffolk to watch out for his parents, and there he sold insurance and built himself a little real estate empire. My grandmother Annye went to normal school, which was a kind of specialized teachers academy in America around the turn of the twentieth century. It was a way of getting women into the economy and a means by which to prepare the growing immigrant population for the new industrialism. Black people like my grandmother Annye were allowed in, but only to teach black children rudimentary skills. She grew up in Richmond, but when she met and married my granddaddy White, she moved to Suffolk with him.

There are family records showing that Granddaddy White and his brothers were involved in land deals in the Tidewater, Virginia, area with whites as well as blacks. He sold insurance, and at one time had his own retail general merchandise store. When I was a boy, I could stand at one end of the block on East Washington Street in Suffolk and count proudly the houses on that block that Granddaddy White owned.

So he had the money to send my mother to Hartshorne Academy, an all-girls private black boarding school in Richmond in the 1920s, then to Howard University for two years, and finally to the University of Pennsylvania, where she graduated with a degree in music education.

My late friend and famous NAACP Attorney Oliver Hill from Richmond—who attended Howard University at the same time as my mother—told me how he got arrested for a traffic violation coming through Nansemond County on his way to Norfolk to try one of the school desegregation cases that led up to *Brown v. Board of Education.* It was my grandfather White who went to court to vouch for Mr. Hill so that he could get out of jail. The white judge said, "No need to put up bail if Mr. White says you're okay." Of course, I don't know what that judge would have said if he had known what Mr. Hill was on his way to do.

My father, Maurice Lanxton Williams, came up on the rough side of the mountain. He was the middle son of three boys born to John Baptist Williams and Minnie Ann Cobb in Danville, Virginia. My grandmother Minnie had six sisters, and her mother was born a slave somewhere in southwestern Virginia. One of my proudest possessions in the family archives is a picture of my great-grandmother seated, surrounded by her seven daughters, one of which is my grandmother Minnie. It's hard to believe that my brothers and sisters and I are only the third generation in my family born "free," compared with twelve generations of enslaved Africans and African Americans before us.

To get a better life, Grandmother Minnie decided one day to move north. She told Granddaddy Williams, "You can stay in Danville if you want to, but I'm gone." She left with the boys, settling in Atlantic City, New Jersey, and he followed shortly thereafter. I remember my grandmother Minnie in a big wooden house that my father eventually bought for her on Indiana Avenue, across from the Indiana Avenue School.

Before he retired, Granddaddy Williams worked as a janitor somewhere, and at home listened to baseball games on the radio in the sun parlor at the front of the house. I can remember him now, crouched in his chair, all alone, looking out the window and listening to the Dodgers or the Giants. Sometimes I would join him, cheering for Jackie Robinson or Willie Mays. I would become a Dodger fan, because of both Granddaddy and my father. I was taught to cheer for the black athletes, no matter what. They were the first two "race men" in my life. When my own little boys were eight and ten, they didn't understand why I would root for the team with the most black players, or a black coach, or a history of better race relations. I told them about my daddy and Granddaddy, but they still didn't get it.

Atlantic City was a summer resort, and as a young man my father worked as a busboy and waiter in several of the big hotels. If you listen to some of the old-timers, gambling ruined the city. These were working-class people, my pop included, who enjoyed privileges but suffered the downside when things were bad. He was the second person in the family to go to college, on a scholarship and work basis, traveling to West Virginia State College in Dunbar, West Virginia—a traditionally black college. He was a musician, and his major instruments were the violin and his bass-baritone voice. He too graduated with a degree in music education, and went south in pursuit of his profession. In Sedalia, North Carolina, he taught music at the Palmer Memorial Institute, the creation of Charlotte Hawkins Brown, a contemporary of Dorothy Height and Mary McLeod Bethune. The story goes that he was supposed to marry the niece of Mrs. Brown until the day he came to Suffolk, Virginia, to sing at a recital. Someone recommended my mother as the piano accompanist, and the rest was romance.

And so my parents came from different class perspectives. But combined they had the earning power to allow us to live comfortably, and the skills and forethought to do some planning for their children's future. My mother's plan was dominant, and executed in stages. She groomed us from our elementary school days to think about leaving Richmond and the South as soon as we graduated from high school. Segregation and Jim Crow were poisonous, and we had to get away to the North. Although she had gone to a predominantly and historically black university, as had my father, the "good" schools were white, she instilled in our minds from as far back as I can remember.

My father was silent on the subject of which college to attend, so long as we didn't become musicians or schoolteachers. There was no money and lots of heartaches in both. It troubled him that I was inclined toward music. He knew I loved it and was good at playing the clarinet, saxophone, and drums before I was seventeen. He planted the seed, then tried to dig it up when he saw where I was headed. He wouldn't let me play in any of the pickup bands formed by my friends from school for fear of the bad habits I might bring home. I'm sorry about that part, because I missed out on some valuable experiences and some pocket money as well.

He didn't share my mother's preference for things white. Even so, he didn't interfere with her plan, but did later express to her his regret that he was perhaps too discouraging about the music.

Pop was about as down-to-earth as a person could get. He spoke to everybody who passed by the house, and liked to plant and tend to his garden in our huge back yard, which descended into woods right in the middle of the city. He didn't like the fancy bourgeoisie parties my mother longed to attend, but from which she was ostracized by the high-society black women in Richmond. He was the best music teacher I ever had, and could make a band or orchestra sing like it was one instrument. I wish I had gotten to know him better. He died of cancer at the age of sixty-seven in 1971 when I was twenty-eight years old.

And I don't know why the society ladies didn't like my mom; probably because she was outspoken, and didn't mind telling them how smart and talented she thought she was. But she really was all that. Before she died in 2004 at the age of ninety, she got some of the recognition she deserved from her church, Ebenezer Baptist, where she had created and directed four choirs.

Stage two of her plan was to get us into as many summer programs with white kids as she could. This meant somewhere in the North or Midwest, because it wasn't possible at home. She wanted to reinforce the belief in our heads that there was no difference between ourselves and white kids our own age, except skin color and hair texture. One summer we went to camp in New Jersey. Another one, Johnny went to Perdue University in Indiana for a science institute, and I went to Michigan State, in Lansing, Michigan, each in our respective junior years of high school. We both worked in some summer camp later in those same summers. The experiment worked: neither one of us came back in awe of white people.

For stage three, she prepared us at home by pushing academics. Music preparation and practice were my father's department, and academics was hers, although they both agreed on the importance of both. She took us to the library in Richmond, which for some reason was not segregated. I remember when we first went to the "white" library on Franklin Street. Johnny and I had each selected books and were standing at the front desk to be checked out. We were excited and ready to use our brand-new library cards. Said the white librarian, hard eyes looking down at us over her made-to-order librarian eyeglasses, speaking in a Southern drawl: "What y'all gonna do with all those books?"

By now you know my mother was not one to back down, and so with perfect diction and without missing a beat, she replied, "Read them. What do you think they're going to do with the books?" Her unspoken message was, "You will not burden my children with your judgment about them." Johnny and I are today both voracious readers, and in time, that librarian became one of our biggest fans. Johnny and I were the "exceptions" to her rule about colored people.

And finally, stage four of the plan was to guide and protect us in our search for college, which by then was internalized by both of us, and she wasn't going let anybody or anything deter us. My high school counselor, a black man, was on staff with my father at Armstrong High School, and a member of our church. He called me in one day, and asked me where was I was planning to apply to college. I told him I was planning to apply to UCLA and a few other white-majority schools, my top choices at the time. He told me, "You'd better apply somewhere where you can get in." This was like a kick in the groin, which momentarily rocked the confidence my parents had painstakingly built within me. That night at dinner, I casually told my mother what happened, and Bernyce went ballistic. She picked up the phone and called him that night. She told him he had no business telling "my boy that he might not get in, even suggesting it was wrong for him to try. Is that what you're doing over there at that school? Is it your job to help, or hinder these kids?" He realized he had made a mistake. He was the only teacher who ever apologized to me for his behavior, and he did it the next day.

There was a saying in the black community that went like this:

If you white, you all right
If you brown, stick around
But if you black, get back. Get back, get back.

As pernicious and invasive as racism was in all its forms and fashions, my parents were determined not to let it damage us psychologically. So we got ready to go away to college—and that meant we had to go North.

2

AMHERST COLLEGE

I'm in with the "in" crowd,
I go where the "in" crowd goes;
I'm in with the "in" crowd,
I know what the "in" crowd knows

—DOBIE GRAY, "THE 'IN' CROWD"

I was accepted at several colleges, including Howard University in Washington, DC, and Northwestern University in Evanston, Illinois. Northwestern was my first choice because of the band and music program. Despite my parents' advice, I had decided to be a musician. I saw the marching band at a Big Ten football game on television and fell in love with the school at halftime. I decided I had to be a part of that band.

However, Amherst College in Massachusetts was the only college to offer me a scholarship, so in 1961, off to Amherst I went. Amherst had very few music courses let alone a major in music performance, and thus my dream of playing music was deferred. Reuben Clay, the older brother of our childhood friend Judy Clay, had graduated from Amherst the summer before my freshman year. He told my family of its reputation as the "best small college in the country." I was proud of the reputation and sensed that my admission was not to be taken lightly. Even though I would never play at halftime in the Rose Bowl, I decided to just play in the college band.

"They do have a band, don't they? Don't all good schools have a band?" My questions went unanswered until I arrived, when I found out about the band. The "band" was about twelve to fifteen guys who played *Lord Jeffrey Amherst* on whatever instrument they had played in high school, and walked instead of marched to the football game. I had high standards, so after a couple of those walk-in performances, I put my saxophone in its case and left it there.

The band was just one adjustment I had to make. Otherwise I believed, based on my mother's teaching, that I would find the Promised Land. I had to ignore the little things I had already noted in my summers among white people my age at Michigan State and the two or three camping experiences. Amherst would be different because it was a bastion of white liberal education in the North. I could hear my mother's voice in my ear: "Study hard, son; you're just as smart as anybody else up there. Get your degree from Amherst, and you're on your way."

Amherst was to be my ticket into that other world where, implicitly, I would be accepted for who and what I was: a young, emancipated Negro from down South, selected for my ability and not for any other reason.

But she forgot to tell me about the price of the ticket to ride.

Amherst College is more than just a college. It's a name, a reputation, and a way of life. It's where the power elite send their children, but like most of the prominent schools in the Northeast at that time, they wanted to be racially integrated, so they made sure a few young black men were in each entering class. But to a young man who was accustomed to seeing only black faces, professional and otherwise, and who had been immersed in black culture for seventeen years, I was overwhelmed, to say the least, even with the summer training sessions Bernyce had made possible.

The Battle for Academic Self-Confidence

At Armstrong High School in Richmond, I had graduated as valedictorian of my senior class, with a 3.96 average out of a possible 4.0.

I did it having missed more than 25 percent of my days in school because of asthma. I had good grades, played several instruments as a musician, and was a tennis player as well.

By Amherst College standards, I didn't do that well on my SAT test. Dean of Admissions Eugene S. Wilson obviously looked beyond the SATs and focused on the other indicators of the kind of student they sought. Dean Wilson is one of my heroes, but I was part of the college's quota system, years before affirmative action. Each year for as long as anyone could remember, there were usually four black students admitted out of a class of approximately three hundred. This didn't change until the late 1960s or early 1970s.

My freshman year at Amherst occurred during the era of required freshman classes. In most colleges, everyone gets some electives; but at Amherst in 1961, there were none, except for the language of one's choice. For me, this meant physics, calculus, European history, humanities, French (which I had already taken for three years in high school), and English, which focused on writing. All of this was attendant to the stated goal of preparation of the "whole man."

Most of the courses required reading comprehension, and the volume of reading was enormous. I could read and interpret the European civilization and the humanities, and do pretty well reading French novels, but my problem in these courses was insufficient time because of the burden of physics and calculus. At Armstrong, I'd had some of the best high school teachers possible. But the extent of the math taught was trigonometry. At Amherst, I had to learn calculus from scratch, master its use, and apply the advanced concepts not only in calculus class but as the basis of physics as well. At Armstrong, my physics was certainly not based on calculus. French at Amherst was reading and speaking; French at Armstrong was mostly reading. English at Armstrong was reading, comprehension, and writing, but not based on the critical, detached style favored at Amherst. It was as if we were required to leave our values and feelings at the door, and offer critical analysis from the vantage of the highest point in the forest, never as one immersed in the trees. Detachment was the preferred style throughout all my classes. I was an emancipated colored boy from Ebenezer Baptist Church in Richmond, who loved to read and write about what he experienced. But my attachment and passion were not the most valued traits in the education at Amherst. I had a lot to learn.

Amherst College was (and is) a process, as are all systems of higher education. My problem was that I had to learn the process and master it at the same time, while my classmates had only to master it. Most of them came from middle- and upper-class prep schools or public schools where calculus and calculus-based physics were taught at the secondary school level. Therefore, for many of them, the college-level calculus was a review and the physics a stretch but certainly more manageable. Excluding time in class, I spent an average of six hours per day studying, and this was six days a week. My calculus teacher, Professor Bailey Brown, told me I needed one day off, or I would have routinely extended it to seven days.

My friends, on the other hand, spent far less time in the books and more time playing Frisbee or whatever other recreation they could muster, including chasing women at Smith and Mount Holyoke. Because I spent an inordinate amount of time on physics and calculus, my other courses suffered from lack of attention. I went for extra help in calculus, but I had the notorious Professor Arnie Arons in physics, and he quite frankly scared the hell out of me. I went for help in humanities as well, which was a kind of European philosophical-thinkers course with heavy emphasis on the Greeks, taught by an untouchable called Professor Epstein.

I asked him, "What can I do to understand the philosophical concepts a little better?"

"Mr. Williams, do you play chess?"

"No, sir."

"There you have it, Mr. Williams. You must be a good chess player to do well in this course."

I couldn't tell if he was pulling my leg or not. All kinds of images were conjured in my mind: Was he taking advantage of me being a colored kid from the South? I don't think I even mentioned this conversation to my friends in the dorm. Somebody there was always willing to help, but I was too embarrassed to tell them what Professor Epstein said. But despite all my other time pressures, I added to my load and learned how to play chess, just in case. I became a decent chess player, but I could never anticipate where he was going in his class.

So my grades were not that good. In fact, they were terrible for the first year. I never got more than a C+, and I had a double whammy of C– in physics and calculus, two four-credit courses. This was the lowest grade average I ever made in my life. But the converse is also true: I never went any lower than a C–. I was never in danger of flunking out.

The second semester was no different. No danger of flunking, but I got very close to renewing my acceptance at Howard University. I was so psyched out in calculus that on my midterm second semester test, I had the right answer and crossed it out to scribble something completely out in left field. Professor Brown saw my predicament, revived my answer with his red pen and a message that read, "You had the right answer, here!" So with his help, I got an A on my midterm in my second semester freshman year. I ran around the dorm and all over school like a big kid showing my grade from Professor Brown. My friends rejoiced. "Juny got an A in Calculus!" I was the talk of the campus, for a minute. Unfortunately, my history, calculus, and physics final exams in that semester all fell in a two-day sequence. I studied all night for physics and history, fell asleep, never woke up in time to study for calculus, and barely made it to the classroom to take the test. I was beaten down, hadn't organized what little I did know, and flunked the final exam. Therefore, what did I get in the course? Why, a C, of course! But it was better than a C–.

Needless to say, I was devastated by the end of my freshman year. I thought I was a dummy, and that plus all the culture shock had me looking for greener pastures somewhere other than Amherst. But I came back and in my second year, took some electives, and I began to pull myself up grade-wise. Sophomore year brought more C's but some B's as well. I began to get the hang of the questions and issues, and the writing style. Amherst was a process of stripping me of all the assumptions I brought to college, and replacing them with questions. Our belief systems were challenged and systematically replaced with language of analysis and critique. We learned, when in doubt, be critical. To write in as angular and detached yet creative a fashion as possible. Humor, sarcastic and biting, was allowed, and admired, in the Amherst tradition. I once got an A in my sophomore year on a paper in economics because the teacher assistant liked the title of my paper. It was an exercise of analysis of the fluctuation of farm prices in some miserable farming market, and I called it "Hogs!" I didn't argue, and took the increase from a B to an A along with the compliment.

And so in my junior year, I became a political science major. Power fascinated me, maybe because of what I was beginning to see in the Civil Rights Movement. Through the lenses of political science, English literature, and psychology, I began to see another world. I began to earn better grades in my major courses and my electives. By the end of my senior year, my improved grades spoke for themselves. In my senior year, I made Bs and As. What would I have looked like academically if I could just have eliminated the whole freshman year?

A Yellow Sweater and a Smile

Once at Amherst, I became an "exception." In 1961, most of the "Men of Amherst" in my class had less contact with black people than did Southern whites. Most of them had never known any of us socially, and in their privileged world, black people were to be ordered around, or at best encountered on the football field. All the rest of us were curiosities, or taboo. So I had to be an exception to one or more of these rules. The more moderately middle-class guys who had gone to public schools in the Northern, Midwestern, or Western cities were more accustomed to black folks and were a little more comfortable but usually surprised by my presence. Amherst College was rarified atmosphere. So how did somebody like me get there?

In my freshman year, I smiled and took it all in. I just wanted to be accepted, to fit in. I felt the best way to fit in was to be quiet and learn, and hopefully a little of me would rub off on them. But there was a perpetual fear of rejection. It showed up on campus with the young men with whom I now found myself sharing everything, from meals to classes to fun moments. And it showed up in those awkward moments when boy met girl, where I had the constant fear of having my offer to dance be refused at a "mixer." Mixers were big dances in the area because Amherst College was all men, and nearby Smith and Mount Holyoke were for women only. So periodically on the weekends, we got together in a big hall, usually at one of the girls schools, and "mixed." Then we went back to our sterile, monosexual existence. One time they arranged a date for me at a Mount Holyoke mixer with a young black woman before I got to the dance. Everybody else was assigned random dates for the evening, but they were trying to avoid a bad situation with me on a blind date with a young white woman. I was incensed that they would think this was necessary. Wasn't I in the North?

Dating was hazardous even when I thought I was in control of the situation. While still a freshman at Amherst, there was a certain sophomore at Mount Holyoke that I had seen on a date with someone else. Let's call her Lolita. I needed a date for some big weekend, and she was one of the only black women I had seen up to that time who met my homegrown Richmond standards, so I decided to call her. The results were predictable, but the reader has to understand just how bad it was. There was no telephone in my room, and so I had to line up downstairs in the freshman dorm with all the other guys waiting to call their dates on the public telephone on the wall. No booth, no privacy, just a bare naked phone on the wall and at a cost of only one thin dime. So eventually my time came to make the call. I called information and asked for the dormitory at Mount Holyoke; I dropped my dime, and I called; someone answered. I asked to speak to Lolita. Surrounded by such a cloud of witnesses I hoped she was at the library studying, or in the infirmary, or asleep or . . . just *anything*. But she came to the phone, and in her confident, educated, cultured voice said, "Hello?" I swallowed hard and let it all hang out, knowing I was being overheard by at least ten other guys in the hall waiting to use the phone or just hanging out. I started, "Hi, my name is Junius Williams, and I'm a student at Amherst. You don't know me, but I was wondering if you would like to go out with me on Saturday (to the such-and-such event)?" There was this one- or two-second pause on the other end of the line, a silence that was joined by the guys in the hallway, waiting to see how well I did. After all, I was a black guy, and they had probably never seen "a Negro" work his show. If I hit, my stock would definitely go up. Possibly become a legendary figure. Maybe they would emulate my direct, two- to three-sentence, no-holds-barred approach and capture the girl of their dreams on the first call.

But after that slight pause to get herself together, she came back with all the righteous indignation of a young black woman, learned from her mother, grandmother, and aunties in the Midwest and said, "Do I know you?" I was an audacious stranger on the other end of the line, one who dared invade her space, interrupt her time unannounced, and without portfolio. I expected the hammer to fall, but not quite so hard, and in front of witnesses with whom I didn't care to share my horrendous misfortune. I knew my goose was cooked, but I did the dance anyway. "No, we don't know each other, but I saw you, and I'm . . ." I tried to give some pedigree, I suppose, lighten the moment, create some interest from this "older woman," the object of my faint and now dying hopes for at least one weekend away from the books and with someone who looked like me. She mercifully cut the conversation short by telling me she wasn't interested. I hung up, turned around, looked into the merciless eyes of the Inquisition, and I didn't have to say a word. I shrugged and half-smiled, made my way back to the room—shot down, by a sophomore at Mount Holyoke. I never saw her again, nor did I want to.

However, most of the guys at Amherst were friendly and nice enough. Later, somebody told me they remembered me as a freshman because I wore a yellow sweater and had a big smile on my face all the time. To some, I was just a happy, yellow-sweatered colored boy. And most of the guys accepted me as such.

The smile was both my offense and defense. I didn't realize it at the time, but every day I was running parallel to the development of the Civil Rights Movement, then in full bloom in the South. I was employing the strategy of Gandhi without knowing it by wearing them down with my capacity to suffer. I wanted to show them that I was a good guy, fun to be around, and just like them in every way. I ignored a lot of things in order to get along and gain some friends. And that's how I became the "exception."

I was told on more than one occasion, "You're not like the other Negroes I know." Or, "You're not like I thought colored guys were supposed to act." Or, "We had this colored guy in my school who . . ." Tune out, smile, but keep standing there.

For those of us who went to "integrated" schools at the time, "exception" was the highest status we could achieve unless our white student friends had done some introspection on their own or came from families with consciousness.

Alpha Delta Phi and Fraternity Culture

Exceptionality led to being "the first." In 1962 I was the first to join Alpha Delta Phi fraternity. At the time Amherst was about 90 percent fraternity membership, since the frat houses were the only places men could have women in the rooms (during prescribed hours, of course). So in the spring of my freshman year, I, like most of the men in my class, participated in the "freshman rush." If we lived in the dorms, we would have no social life, and no place to go with our dates. For me it was always first a question of "What date?" but hope springs eternal. Over time and with good reason, I grew far too cautious to try to date white women, and there were only a few black women in the four-college area.

Alpha Delta Phi, or A.D., was the fraternity for the "Big Men on Campus": talented athletes, scholars, zany characters who were attractive to the ladies of Smith and Mount Holyoke. Of course there were variations of that theme: some fairly bright idiots, and some real chumps. But A.D. was considered the hardest fraternity to get into. During the rush, sophomores and juniors at other fraternities told me, "They just want you because you're black. You'll be sorry in the end if you pledge A.D." After some anxious moments and some soul searching, I took the bid and "dropped" at A.D. "I might be happy or sorry with any of you guys," I thought. I liked the profile of Big Man on Campus, even though at the time, I wasn't. Joining A.D., however, put me in the center of a lot of conversations—some that I knew about, and some I didn't: "He really belongs there" or "He's just being used." I didn't care what they said. Truth be told, during my freshman year I had come to like guys in a lot of different fraternities. So I focused on the friends I felt comfortable with, and moved into the fraternity house in my sophomore year.

I liked some of my "brothers," and others I didn't like. Being in a House meant eating with the guys at meals in the dining hall each day. These were heady times, hanging out with the guys from "the Phi," which is how we referred to ourselves when we joked about our vaunted and coveted reputation. But what about being able to have women in the house? Remember that promise? At A.D. they advertised to freshmen (and to the young women at the nearby girls schools), "Every room is a corner room with a fireplace at Alpha Delta Phi." It was true—and the fireplaces worked. It was a gorgeous mansion, sitting back on a hill. The A.D. house, as did all the fraternity houses at Amherst, had the look and feel of old money. In my sophomore and junior years I had great roommates. I enjoyed the hell out of the fireplace, but usually by myself or as the third party while one of my roommates entertained *his* date. In the basement, we had a social room where there was a keg of beer each weekend, Friday through Sunday. There I got to listen to all *their* favorite music, interspersed with some Aretha Franklin, Ray Charles, or James Brown that I managed to put on the jukebox. The white girls were just wild about the way I danced. But they were somebody else's dates. "Hey, Juny, my date wants to dance with you."

"That's fine," I thought, "but what about a slow drag?"

Please remember: at Armstrong High School I had been the guy who stayed in the middle of the crowd for fear someone would see my fumbling steps. But at Amherst College, with a couple of beers under my belt, you would have thought I was Usher or Michael Jackson.

This was a strange culture, socially attuned to the pouring and tasting of beer. Oh, you can believe I did develop a love for beer, because on those halcyon nights, when the last cars had gone to Smith and Mount Holyoke, or returned to the local hotels if the dates were "imports" from places like Wellesley or Miss Porter's School for girls, or snuck upstairs to somebody's room with a fireplace, there was still beer in the keg to be consumed. After hours, the guys got together and played "Whale's Tales," a drinking game that tested your memory, wit, and wisdom.

Echoes of barely coherent male voices shouting "Drink, Williams!" reverberate in my skull as I recall these moments of beer-soaked frivolity, up to now buried deep within the recesses of my ancient memories of eternal youth. I was one of the better players, only because I knew how much I could drink and when to call it quits.

But it was at A.D. that some guys—two in particular—often got drunk and lost their inhibitions: I got called a "nigger" whenever they got liquored up late at night after the party was over. One of them was a friend, the other a full-time jerk. On the next day, when they had sobered up, they were apologetic: "I really didn't mean to say those things. I just temporarily lost my head." I wanted to believe them, but it tore me apart. Could I ever really relax around white people? How far could I go in becoming their friend before discovering I was just another nigger to them? Was I one drink away from being the nigger they had seen all along?

But let me not be overly harsh. Living at A.D. had its other perks. My best friend at Amherst, Chuck Bunting, lived in A.D. I liked my sophomore-year roommates, Harvey Croze and Larry DeWitt, who were a year ahead of me. There were good times, and I have many fond memories and many friends. My freshman-year roommates were good matches for me. Tom Furness and Pete Pinney were natural and relaxed, and willing to help me when I had a problem with calculus or physics, which was all the time. It was important to feel comfortable at "home," and they made it possible. There was Vic Ishioka, a Japanese guy from California, who left Amherst after his freshman year; John Boe, from New Jersey; George Bassos, the Greek; Fred Tesch.

This was the way I met the Class of '66 at Amherst College, the class below me: As a sophomore, out on the quad on a chilly October night in 1962, I remember George Bassos telling the whole class of freshmen at the annual Sophomore versus Freshmen Water Fight. "I got this kid [me] who will take on any member of the freshman class and beat 'em in wrestling." He built me up as the next Primo Carnera, but I weighed about 140 pounds at the time. I swelled up and looked as tough as I could. He had those kids scared as hell because most of them were bigger and stronger than me. Basso was playing the race card: I was black, and he knew these young kids, mostly from the suburbs, would think I was some kind of tough mutha. But he was also playing with fire, because some of the freshmen had gone to public schools in cities and were not in awe of a scrawny black kid just because Bassos made me look exotic. After about a two-minute standoff, out from the crowd stepped Evan Maurer, a solid piece of muscle from some school in New Jersey who weighed about 180 pounds—a high school wrestling champion, I found out later. The only wrestling I had ever done was with my little brother, and I wasn't about to wrestle this guy. I don't know how he did it, but Bassos talked me into and out of the match and still maintained the mastery of the crowd. He was amazing. I think a lot of guys still wonder whether I could have taken Evan.

Overall, however, most times the weight of adjustment was all on me, and even the good guys never realized the burden of adaptation that I had to overcome as a person of color. Most white folks don't realize that to be white is, first and foremost, to be privileged. The norm is white. At Amherst, white people were the dominant culture, from the choice of values, the humor, the music in the frat house, to the beer that we drank each week. Blacks or any other group who are outside that mainstream had to adapt or be unhappy. In the opening years I adapted, which is why I love drinking beer to this day. So it wasn't all bad, was it?

The rhythms of life were different for a young black man from the South. First of all, being around all men was anathema to me. I had gone to coed schools all my life, and I was just beginning to feel confident with the opposite sex. Any woman on the Amherst campus was someone's date, or a student from nearby Smith or Mount Holyoke who took classes with us. The University of Massachusetts (UMass) was a mile down the street, but they had their own women.

UMass students were working-class young men and women, mostly from Massachusetts, going to a state school. Amherst College was middle- and upper-class, appealing to an international student body. Therefore, an unspoken judgment was that Amherst College students were better than UMass. I never had that feeling. I would gladly have dated at UMass if I had known any black women there who met my Richmond standards of what a fine woman looked like. I was choosy, but not based on class. Since sometime in the 1970s Amherst has been coed, and it's a much more natural environment because of it. But that didn't help me when I was there, when finding a date was always a horrendous experience.

Some elements of the Amherst culture were strange. There was a rule that we had to go to Johnson Chapel a certain number of times per semester, where we heard secular lectures on various topics. At chapel, some of my colleagues wore a coat and tie over a bare hairy chest, along with blue jeans or shorts and sandals. The grunge factor was always something that amazed me.

Their music of choice was the Beatles or the Rolling Stones. Black people's music was Marvin Gaye and Tammi Terrell. They liked R&B as well, but the emphasis was on the former and not the latter.

Amherst was a challenge to teach me to overcome obstacles, and I won it hands down. But in examining these events and episodes, I see the price I paid. Often "My soul looks back and wonders how I got over," as the old gospel lyric proclaims. I had friends at Amherst, and eventually at the other three colleges in the area. But there were instances of betrayal that I had to suppress in order to maintain some of those friendships. For example, some of my fraternity buddies decided to go to New York City for Thanksgiving vacation in my sophomore year. I decided not to go to Richmond that one year in order to hang out with them. When we got to the hotel room, they announced they were going out and pretty much told me I was an albatross around their neck for finding dates. I thought about it, and told them to go ahead. So they left me in the cheap room by myself. "Keep a good upper chin, mate." That's the role I accepted and was forced to play quite often. So I went wandering around midtown Manhattan, and came upon a line of people at some theater. It was an interesting mix of people, from the dark-skinned to white, and they all looked like they wanted to have fun. I had discovered the Palladium, for years the home of Latin dance in New York City. I was not about to wait in line and didn't have a lot of money anyway, and so I saw a guy carrying in drums for one of the groups.

"Hey man," I said, "I'm broke. Can I help you carry some of those drums?"

He looked at the line, sized me up, and said, "Okay," and in I went—with some *small* drums, I might add—free of charge. That night I stood on the side and watched some of the most amazing dancing I had ever seen. It was my only time at the Palladium, but it gave me a new respect for the dances my sister had taught me a few years before. Much later in my life, I would go to Latin dance clubs in New York and dance with all the love and imagination my older sister had taught me as a teenager in Richmond.

So was I upset about being left? Sure, but if I had stayed to hang out with my Amherst friends, rejected and put down at some white club with white women who didn't want to be with me, and friends who saw me as a burden, I never would have gone to the Palladium. Nothing is all bad, and nothing is all good. Precious moments come when we're otherwise lonely and feeling down and out. Amherst College was that initial experience for me. While I was there, I made sacrifices; when I went home to Richmond, I was ready to exhale.

There were social dividends. As time went by, I met people with whom I could relax and let my guard down, in the fraternity and across the campus. We got to know each other in ways that took us beyond the plastic smiles, based on common interests and compatibility of personalities. But I could not be validated in the ways I needed to be until I got around black folks, and that usually meant home. As much as my Amherst friends were friendly and supportive, it was not enough. I needed the infusion of black music, humor, language, clothes, dance, and rhythm, just to be off guard for a minute—and I could only get that around my own people.

I went to Boston on occasion, and partied at Boston University with African Americans and South Africans. There was a large contingent of South African exiles there. Of all the people in Africa, the patterns of colonialism carved into the black South African psyche were closest to those in black America. Apartheid was South Africa's Jim Crow. I loved their hot, loud parties because they partied the way we did. Oftentimes oppression is the mother of cultural creativity. Africans colonized on both side of the Atlantic were free only to express ourselves through music, dance, and humor. Those of us from the diaspora in those hot, sweaty rooms in Boston shared the multirhythmic intensity of R&B and South African music: Hugh Masekela and Miriam Makeba matched Wilson Pickett and Gladys Knight. When we got out on the dance floor, we were indeed one people.

And I listened to the South Africans' stories, I learned, and I ended up feeling very comfortable with them. We shared a common foe. During those trips I felt the need to belong to the struggle in ways they did, which got them run out of or banned from their country, sometimes just in the nick of time. And herein was the greatest need for validation: there were few at Amherst who shared my growing urgent need to be a part of the movement for change that was coursing its way through this country. I wanted something bigger for myself, and it was tied to getting rid of Jim Crow.

At Amherst, I was involved. I played squash, tennis, and lacrosse (I made the freshman team in squash and lacrosse), and became a prominent member of SRE, the Students for Racial Equality. And I was still "the guy in the yellow sweater who smiled a lot." Remember him? I gave no one any reason to dislike me, and wore on everybody's good side. Popular, and therefore "exceptional,"—even made it into the "God House," which was the not-so-nice nickname of Alpha Delta Phi. So, I really had it made. I was doing my work, I had escaped freshman year, and I was recruited into the most prominent social set. All I had to do was go home on holidays and get my batteries charged, come back, and keep on smiling. I would have whizzed through Amherst in a four-year blitz. Right?

Wrong.

Something was missing in that formula. Being the "exception" and the "first" was not what I needed to gain a sense of self-worth. That only came when I accepted the role of resistance I had to play. I could have stayed out of controversy's way by continuing to be the token. But racism would still have prevailed, in the South where I came from, but also right there on campus.

So I chose to take on racism.

The Turning Point

In my junior year at Amherst, there appeared two anonymous guest editorials in the student newspaper that were anti–civil rights. I could see that the writer was gaining momentum each time, and as a student on campus, I took offense that he was allowed to promote his racism under cover of anonymity. So I felt I had to stand up to him.

There are turning points in everyone's life when we have to fight, even if we have to do it by ourselves and in public. For me, this was one of them. In a letter to the editor in the January 13, 1964, issue of the *Amherst Student*, I called him out, condemned his attack, and called him a punk for hiding in the shadows:

To the Chairman of the Amherst Student:
On last Thursday there appeared a second in a series of recent anti–civil rights, anti-Negro articles. In this letter, the anonymous

somebody points out that all Negroes (and whites too, he adds, to make the point even more tenable), could become the 16th President and give Gettysburg addresses, because everyone in the United States has been given as much "opportunity" as Abraham Lincoln had. The point of this cogent illustration is that lack of opportunity has not been the thing holding the Negro back; it is the Negro himself.

This is not an attempt to make a rational reply to that charge; I merely want to know why this person, and the person before him if they be different, did not sign his name to his profound bits of insight and observation? If his ideas are worth expressing, are they not worth defending?

I went on for a few more paragraphs, speculating on his psychological profile. I asked him if he was scared to take a step out of the protection of anonymity for fear of being out of step with the mainstream. I offered him counseling, or a referral to others who could help him. I challenged him to use his freedom of speech in an open forum, to defend his ideas in front of everybody.

And I shut him up. There were no more articles like this from him.

This letter earned me a new kind of respect on campus. People took sides on the issue because I forced them to deal with Mr. Pseudonym, which is what I called him. Certain people on campus started looking at me in a different way. If I had no enemies before, I did now, but I had the respect I wanted on my own terms. This was far more important than being in A.D. or any of the other firsts I had accumulated.

In freshman year, one of my firsts had been to turn in the first English 1 paper to be Professor Cole's "s—t sheet." After an assignment, for analysis and criticism he would print the papers he thought were very good or very bad. This was done anonymously, but of course, I knew what I had written. My essay, written for the assignment "What is Drama?" was the first paper on the first such sheet, and he tore me apart. For the whole year, he didn't think much good could come from my pen, and I often thought of leaving school because I couldn't do anything right in his eyes.

But when he saw my editorial response in the *Amherst Student*, he wrote me a letter. He told me I was a credit to my race, he applauded the position I had taken, and he liked the way I wrote it. He spoke to me about "controlled anger," saying that I had the touch and used it with great skill. I couldn't believe my eyes. For the first time, I was more than a blip on his radar screen. I had mixed emotions at the time, because I had really grown to dislike him for his constant criticism. Yet I had internalized his standard of performance in writing—which meant he was a good teacher—and now he told me that I had in fact met his standard of writing.

I still consider his praise as one of my crowning achievements at Amherst. The thrill of that letter, which I no longer have in my possession, means more to me than any grade I received before or after, in college or law school. Even now, I smile whenever I think about it.

Because of the Movement, my life turned in a different direction on the campus of Amherst College. After that incident, those who had any doubts about the Movement stayed away from me. Those who were into civil rights elected me president of the SRE. I was elected to the student council. I was elected to the senior honor society, SCARAB. I made new friends. And lost others. Sometimes, though, respect is more important than friendship. From that point on: no more yellow sweater, and the smile came out more and more selectively.

But there were other kinds of challenges based on race that had to be overcome. My strategies were different depending on the affront.

I remember being at a fraternity party at next-door Chi Psi during Prom Weekend with my date, a young black woman in my class at Smith College. We were enjoying the music of some R&B group when I felt and heard the splash of beer. That wasn't unusual, but when I looked toward my date, I saw that most of it had landed in her hair.

I saw the horrified look on her face, and turned around to see if perhaps it was just an accident. Nobody fessed up; everyone continued talking in their little cliques. It was as though nothing had happened, and it was the two of us who were outside the Matrix looking in. It couldn't have been an accident because of the direction of the beer and the amount that was thrown; my date was drenched. But there was no one to blame, no one to fight, just groups of young, white, upper-middle-class people our own age conversing normally and naturally. We both looked at each other, and decided not to pursue it, so we just left. I took her back to Smith. Lesson learned: sometimes it's better to face the Ku Klux Klan than to face a cracker who hasn't the guts to be a man.

Stepping Forward

By my junior year, I began speaking out more about racism and the solutions I chose to undertake. In the spring of 1964 I was the featured speaker at Johnson Chapel, having just returned from spring break in Richmond, where I had done voter registration for the first time. I was inching forward at each opportunity to find a place for myself in the "real world." At twenty years of age and now president of the Students for Racial Equality, I pursued a full political agenda both on campus and off, as much as possible given my decision to stay in school and graduate. Here is an excerpt from my Chapel speech:

> In many of these neighborhoods the people who lived there have just recently come from the Deep South, hoping to find employment in the North. Nine times out of ten, they are unable to get a job. The people who have been in Richmond all along fare no better. Consequently, even in the newer housing projects, many of the people must depend on welfare checks, and were at home when we called.

In the speech, I told stories of those who would not or could not go down to city hall to register, including a woman who could not write, and a senior citizen who didn't believe there was any way to remove Senator Byrd from Virginia except by "blowing him up. That's the only way to make those white folks listen," she concluded.

"But voting," I said, "is just as effective a weapon. Your vote, counted with thousands of the Negro votes in Richmond and in Virginia, can work just as well to put a man in office that will do things to help the Negro."

One of her grandchildren, about eleven years old, had been listening to the entire conversation. He said to her, "Grandmother, why don't you go ahead and do it?"

She smiled at him and at us, but she wouldn't agree to go to City Hall. "I've been around too long," she said.

He soon lost interest and went out to play ball with his younger brother. We soon left because it was getting late. In ten more years, he will be of voting age. Ten years is a long time, too long, for by that time it will again be too late [for him].

By now a vision of the world I visited should be at least a hazy picture in your mind. It was a very hard world, an almost impenetrable world to reach into and stir things around. It was not so easily split up between old and young as my two examples might imply. Here were countless young people, young married couples, young single mothers, who all thought it just as useless to go downtown and register. Even more discouraging were those who simply said, "I'm not interested," or "I don't want to vote," and closed the door in our faces. And then there were people who just weren't able to fill out the forms.

But in all cases, even in these open-and-shut instances just mentioned, there was something in [the eyes of the people] that words can't really describe. They seemed to want to take this one little thing we had to offer them, but they didn't quite know how to do it. They seemed to sense we were offering them a chance to begin a different life, only a slightly different one, but different nonetheless. But they couldn't convince themselves that they were ready for this life, or that it was ready for them. It was too late for our single effort to make a dent in this world.

But I closed triumphantly with a voter registration success story, as any good Southern colored boy who grew up in the Baptist church knows you gotta do. Hope is all we have in this business, and I was selling the Movement as much as reporting on my activities. I received a warm response, maybe even a standing ovation? I know I wanted one.

These were prophetic words gleaned in moments of awareness of the Movement I was growing into. Richmond was not in the grip of the same fear as the Deep South, at least not openly. There was a deeper, ingrained lack of hope, lack of self-pride that percolated through those housing projects where poverty as well as racism had taken its toll. This was the combined truckload of history and present conditions that one faced in the North, in cities like the one to which I was destined to relocate a little more than one year after this speech, although I didn't know it at the time. And here it was in the urban South, in my own hometown, that I had already confronted and dealt with its symptoms, concluding correctly that no one registration effort could "make a dent in this world."

Malcolm X and the "Civil Rights Revolution"

I tried to get Malcolm X on campus. In 1964, my junior year, the SRE—in conjunction with similar organizations on the other three campuses in the area—began planning a civil rights conference titled "The Civil Rights Movement: Reform or Revolution?" to take place on all four campuses February 12 through 14, 1965. We got the support of the college administrations, including money for expenses, and began inviting our speakers. This was a leap forward for all of us bitten by the Movement bug. With SRE, we had held vigils, walked on picket lines, participated in local demonstrations in support of the Southern Movement, and did voter registration nearby. So the conference was a step up in the level of involvement.

Through somebody who knew somebody, I got the number for Malcolm X, who was the boogeyman of Black Nationalism at that time. I called his house, and *he* answered the phone. In a few short words I told him what we were trying to do. He asked me a few questions, including how much honorarium we could muster. I told him.

He paused, and told me that wasn't very much.

I held my breath, until he said, "Yes, I'll come."

I couldn't believe my ears. *Overjoyed* is not an adequate word. All the other pieces were falling in place. Our list of speakers and seminar leaders read like a who's who in resistance movements from the North and the South: Jesse Gray, the Harlem rent strike leader; Stanley Aronowitz and Tom Hayden, representatives of the New Left; Bill Strickland and Julian Houston from the Northern Student Movement; Dave Dennis from CORE, and a host of others who were conscious but not necessarily on the front line, like Bill Worthy, the editor of the *Baltimore Afro-American* newspaper.

As I look at one of the original posters that is now framed and hanging on my wall at home, I am amazed and sorry that there were no women speakers on the list.

On February 12, 1965, more than one thousand college students from all over New England and beyond jammed into the main hall at Mount Holyoke College for the opening session of the conference, to hear Malcolm X, Ossie Davis, and Michael Harrington set the tone for the three-day conference. Were we about revolution, or was this reform, like the New Deal?

Malcolm X never made it to the conference, nor did Michael Harrington. Malcolm X stayed in Europe one extra day trying to get into France, but was denied entry. That extra day kept him away from Massachusetts. Nine days later—on February 21, 1965—he was killed in the Audubon Ballroom in New York City.

Michael Harrington couldn't get to western Massachusetts because of an ice storm on February 12 in New York. Ossie Davis, who had left New York early, saved the day, because we had people hanging from the rafters in the big auditorium at Mount Holyoke, and they sure didn't want to hear from me. Mr. Davis gave Malcolm's speech, then Michael Harrington's, and then summed it up with his own. I'll always be grateful to Ossie Davis, and told him so whenever we met subsequently.

The conference was an incredible success. It increased my status and visibility, not only on campus but also off. Tom Hayden came and led a workshop, though I didn't get to hear anything anyone said. He told me later that on the basis of our achievement, he made a note to invite me to come to Newark. Although I didn't get to participate in my own conference, the planning alone was like a graduate course in "Movementology." On all four campuses, there were people who collectively educated one another about the history and current status of change in America, and who was doing what, how well, and when. I got most of the credit, but it was a team effort.

My fraternity life took on far less importance. Knowing there was an alternative lifestyle, in my senior year I moved out of the fraternity to live alone over the dining hall and associate with the little band of white and black renegades that I had met from all four colleges. We, who believed in the struggle for racial justice, had learned to be supportive of one another in the Connecticut Valley. Some of us went onto the front lines of the South, eventually. I learned that I couldn't have it all, didn't need it all. I had to decide what was more important. Being content within myself was most important. At meals I ate with the guys from the Phi, but I enjoyed my privacy afterward.

In a way, on this college front line we were being prepared and toughened for our lives ahead. It wasn't apparent at the time, but this was our Mississippi. Malcolm X once asked, "What does Mississippi have to do with Harlem?" His answer: "They're both in America." My last year was spent in contemplation, study, and activities all directed outward, toward my future goals and the state of the Movement in America. And I had some fun along the way.

Marion Wright Edelman and Crossroads Africa

In my sophomore year, 1963, there was another eventful Chapel speech for me: the one delivered by Marion Wright (soon to be married to Peter Edelman). She was a young black lawyer who told us about her experiences in Mississippi with the Civil Rights Movement. She exuded confidence. I sat spellbound, listening to her stories of people who resisted the only way they knew how, challenging the system, registering to vote at the peril of their own lives. This woman, next to my Mama, was the second most influential woman in my life at that time. She was clearly her own person, in control of her life, on her own terms. As one of only a few black folks in the audience, I was invited to meet her after the lecture at the home of Amherst's president, Calvin Plimpton. I couldn't wait to tell my mother that I had been invited to the president's house.

In her speech, she had also spoken passionately about Africa and a summer project called Crossroads Africa. I was so full of questions that toward the end of the little discussion, she asked me if I wanted to go on Crossroads.

As politely as I could manage, I told her "yes," suppressing my excitement, as a young man from Richmond, Virginia, with good home training is supposed to do. But I said to her, "I can't afford the trip." She said, "Don't worry about the money," and proceeded to get me a scholarship.

And so in the summer of 1963, I was on an Air France jet on my way to Uganda, by way of a brief stopover in Cairo. During the whole flight and afterward, all I could think was, "Take a look at me now!"

I was one of three hundred U.S. and Canadian students who went to different parts of Africa with Crossroads that summer, under the program run by James Robinson. Eleven of us went to Uganda, which was not my first choice; I preferred more well-known places like Ghana or Kenya. But I did my homework, and read some of the history of Uganda before I went. When I arrived, I was happy to be there.

Our mission was to build a fourteen-room outpatient hostel, with brick walls and a tin roof, as a part of the Church of Uganda Kisiizi Hospital, which had sixty beds, a dispensary, and an outpatient clinic serving a wide area of northern Kigezi, Uganda. Our Ugandan partners (called, of all things, "counterparts") were students from a local building trades school, along with a cast of hundreds of local Ugandans, especially when we raised the roof on the finished product. We lived in tents for ten weeks, and on weekends went on trips, including to game reserves around the country. We were hosted by a medical doctor who was part of a mission of the Anglican Church.

Kigezi District is one of the most beautiful areas of the world, with its terraced green hills and gentle people. There I met and tried my French with Tutsi refugees, expelled by the Hutus, in a forerunner of the conflict decades later. I climbed Mount Muhavura up to its 13,500 foot summit at the juncture of Uganda, Rwanda, and Congo in the fabled Mountains of the Moon. We saw the beauty of tropical vegetation and mountain flowers at the bottom, and experienced the rare treat of seeing snow fall down upon us on the equator, on top of one of the highest peaks in Africa. We thought we were on top of the world as we looked down on clouds surrounding other peaks in Rwanda and Congo. Coming down, we had to run, racing to stay just ahead of the setting sun. There are no streetlights in the middle of a gorilla sanctuary.

African Awakening

If Amherst College was responsible for my first opportunity to speak out for black people, Uganda was responsible for my awakening as an African. Being middle-class in Richmond blunted the physical attacks, and even most of the verbal ones. But nothing can completely stamp out the emotional and psychological impact of racism in America. The standards of beauty were white: "good" hair was straight and blond; light skin was preferable to dark. Our heroes, and thus our measuring stick of value and self-worth, were mostly white: We cheered for Tarzan against the "natives," the cowboys against the Indians. Our standard of fashion was European, although our African butts changed some of their designs. Does it sound familiar even now? Black kids still prefer white dolls, unless there is some kind of intervention in their lives to point them in another direction.

For many in America at that time, it was Malcolm X who sparked our consciousness about being black. But his was the nationalism associated with the Nation of Islam, projected onto the center stage of American media in a 1959 documentary produced by Mike Wallace, called *The Hate That Hate Produced*. In 1963, while many had Malcolm and his message of separation from the "white devil," I had Africa. I had "the real thang, bay-bay," and there ain't nuthin' like a little taste of Africa when you're still in your teens to help set your head straight and your priorities in order.

After the long cold winters in Massachusetts, it was wonderful to be kissed by the warmth of the African sun. It took its time getting up in the morning, and the nights are cold in the highlands of Uganda. But once up, off came the T-shirts and out poured the sweat as we excavated the land, laid bricks made from the mud right on our site, and raised beams and a tin roof, all within ten weeks. Our African counterparts, young people our age but in technical school, spoke very little English. It was music to my ears to hear them talk to each other in several different languages, going back and forth in whichever languages they had in common. What a difference to me, who spoke only one language well and struggled in French—a European language, at that.

Sheila Trammel and I were the only two blacks among the eleven Crossroaders in Uganda. Sheila was a young woman from Altadena, California, majoring in music at Pasadena City College. Both of us were taken to heart by the Ugandans, and to say it was like a homecoming would be too hackneyed, but that's what it was. For the first time in my life, we, who were black, could go places white folks weren't welcome. For example, at the time of our trip, nearby Congo was off limits to whites because of the civil war. I was told Sheila and I would be safe, but in deference to the others, we stayed with the group—not without flaunting our newfound privileges. (All of us did go across the border, so that we could honestly say we visited Congo. Climbing the mountain put us in Rwanda, and the plane's arrival and departure and other travel to Nairobi and Mombasa took us through Kenya. It was a five-country trip, when you add the landing in Egypt, and more than most other Crossroaders experienced.)

Our Ugandan friends were down-to-earth, intelligent, fun-loving people, proud of themselves as Africans. But they too were in resistance to the continuing bonds of colonialism, which had formally ended just that year with Ugandan independence from Great Britain. But its remnants were still intact right before our eyes. The doctor in charge at the hospital was the personification of a white settler: he was English, of the Church of Uganda, which was Anglican, and imposed white values on all who lived and worked at the hospital. To dance, drink liquor, and "socialize" between men and women was absolutely prohibited, because it was "un-Christian." Can you imagine Africans under the yoke of a rule that said *don't dance*? The rules, however, were meant to be broken, and I'm afraid that on occasion we were catalysts for the activities the good doctor frowned upon. Once our counterparts found out that we liked the ladies as much as they did, there was a meeting of the minds.

"Tell me," John Buwera asked with a big smile on his face, "which of the nurses do you like?"

There was a young white Crossroader from Ontario, Canada, who loved women as much as I did. Canada and I smiled back at John. "Monica," I said. Canada said, "Mary." To me it was just idle locker-room conversation. But within moments, there were Monica and Mary, blushing, smiling, and looking down the way African women were taught to do in deference to men.

Many stereotypes were broken just comparing the two of them. Monica was jet black, with a smooth complexion, curves in all dimensions, and Nilotic features. Mary was brown, about the complexion of most black people in the States, with broader features. In the States, we were taught that Africans all had big broad noses, thick lips, were extremely dark, with short nappy hair, when in fact the people of the Kigezi District were as diverse as black people in Richmond, or anywhere else in black America. Some were good looking, some were not. Monica was one of the prettiest women I met anywhere, with a gorgeous, engaging personality. She challenged my own definition of who was "pretty" and who was not.

From that point on, the students arranged for nighttime soirees at our campsite. The nurses from the hospital would sneak over to see us. Dr. John, our English host and the plantation manager, had explained earlier that the dances the Africans did were "too provocative." The Ugandans laughed and said, "You're right." Too bad Dr. John and his saintly wife never took dance lessons, because we certainly did.

But we were cool. We didn't want the African nurses to get thrown out of the hospital, or the trade school guys to get sent home. Only Canada, in his lust to score, got Mary in trouble. As expected, she bore the brunt of the shame, not him. She didn't lose her job, but was punished. After that, we accepted the limits on behavior, including dancing.

But there were other rules off campus, so to speak. Agre, who was a male health worker and assistant administrator at the hospital and was a good friend, invited me to visit his house with Monica. And one day I went to a *duka* (like a general store) up the hill from our campsite. There was a young woman there who spoke the local Ugandan languages but also spoke French. She was a "half-caste," as they called it: her mother was Congolese and her father Belgian. Her sister saw me checking out her little sister (who was in her twenties), who was just as interested in me. In French and English, big sister set up a date for me and her sister later that night, at the house behind the store. My Canadian friend was jealous, as well he should be, because this Miss Congolese was indeed a fine lady. So I made ready to go back up the hill at about 7 or 8 o'clock that night.

The only factor I hadn't considered was the darkness. I had a flashlight, but I had forgotten how dark it could be with no streetlights. And somehow that hill was longer and steeper than I remembered from earlier in the day. All around me I could hear the sounds of the forest: the insects, the frogs, the birds. And the only light was the little round perimeter created by my flashlight as it penetrated the darkness a few steps ahead. Everywhere else was pitch black. Thank you, Eveready batteries.

I made it to the duka and was announced by the barking of the dogs. There were no lights on anywhere, but underneath the porch and a nearby truck, I could see the bodies of men stirring, arising from the sleep I had disturbed. People went to bed early, I guessed. Not for me to judge—I just wanted to find my date. Suddenly a light went on in the back house, and she came out with a lantern, beckoning me to come in. I was relieved, because those guys waking up didn't look too happy to see me. She smiled; I smiled. I asked her, mostly in French, who they were. She told me they were guards, because there were bandits all about. "You are a brave man, coming up to see me," she said, visibly impressed that she meant that much to me.

All of a sudden, I didn't feel very brave. Bandits? Big sister match-maker hadn't said anything about bandits when we made this arrangement, I thought. But Miss Congolese thought I was a hell of a man, and I was already there. More importantly, I was young—nine-teen years old—and the immediate reward for my bravery occupied me for the moment. But afterward, I came to my senses: I had to go through the guards, back down that hill, and through the bandits, should they have been awakened by my little journey or by all the commotion I created upon arrival. My new friend wanted me to stay, but I knew when it was time to go. As I made my way out of the house, the guards were now ready and waiting. They knew I was no bandit, but were probably mad that I got privileges they couldn't get. There were at least four or five guys with machetes closing in on me. I tried to slow them down with whatever little Rushiga I could speak.

"Come on, guys," I wanted to say. "Don't be haters." It was dark, but I could see that life for me was about to become much more dif-ficult, and perhaps a lot shorter than I had anticipated. Just at the right moment, big sister came out of the duka and told them something in Rushiga. They didn't change their minds about me, but now they were under orders to leave me alone.

"Pass," big sister said. "Pass." And I did indeed pass, keeping my eye on these menacing protectors and wannabes, as I walked to the road.

Now all I had to do was worry about the bandits. I put the flash-light on and walked a few steps down the road. "Foolishness," I thought. Any bandit within a mile could see me, and focus on this lonely target out after hours. It was dark, but the trees made a cor-ridor down the road. Up above the trees, the dark of the sky stood in contrast to the dark of the forest. So I figured if I stayed in the middle of the outline created at the juncture of trees and sky, I could make it back to camp. All I had to do was feel for any holes in the dirt road, or any sticks, or any wild, furry thing that may have decided to cross the road just when I did, or smelled how scared I was and decided to have me for dinner. I even took a chance and ran, looking up then down. I made it back in about thirty minutes, realizing how fortunate I was to see my tent once again. Nobody was awake, and that was fine with me. It was only when I was inside the warmth and protection of my sleeping bag that I had a chance to smile and think about how good the good part of the evening had really been.

My African Friends

I learned so much from their example. John Buwera, a master bricklayer, took me under his wing. I still marvel at how he could do corners. He was the fastest bricklayer on the team, and his work didn't get torn down to be redone by his teachers, who were on site as supervisors. John was strong, very dark and proud of it. He kept a short, nubby pencil in his hair, and when he had to do project-related calculations, he wrote on the ash on his arm. I grew proud of the fact that my hair was like his, and after a few weeks in the sun, my arm was almost as dark as his. I too carried a pencil in my hair in celebration of the African I was becoming, and wrote on my arm, which was just as ashy as his. What I wrote, I don't know, because I sure as hell had no role in calculating anything to do with that construction. My mother, bless her heart, would have died at the sight of me. Bernyce would have been on the site every morning with a jar of Vaseline for my ashiness, and insisting on getting my hair cut. My hair was getting longer and thicker without me even noticing it. By the time I left Africa, I had an Afro. I looked like I felt at the time: like an emerging African living in America, and it felt mighty good.

When I arrived back in the United States in August 1963, my mother and brother Johnny gathered me up at Idlewild (Kennedy) Airport, and we made a stop in Washington, DC, to visit her best friend, Charlotte Nash. She hadn't planned it this way, but our arrival in DC was on the morning of the March on Washington. My brother and I wanted to go, so she dropped us off somewhere near the Washington Monument, with arrangements to meet somewhere later in the day.

"If I could find my way around Uganda and Kenya, I can reach a rendezvous point in Washington, Mother, so don't worry." I hadn't told her about my hitchhiking along with Canada from Mombasa to Nairobi, a journey of several hundred miles. Thank goodness for Canada: a black Kenyan farm truck driver gave us a ride just as it was getting dark. He let Canada ride in the cab, and put me in the back of the truck, where I huddled and shivered in the cold for the last hour of the trip.

At some point the cultural had merged with the political. In my tent in Africa, I had seen a copy of some European or American paper that was weeks old. In it was a picture of Danville, Virginia, the birthplace of my father and the then–hot spot for the Civil Rights Movement. Had I been at home, there is no doubt in my mind that I would have been with SNCC in Danville. When I looked at that paper sitting in my tent in Uganda, with the picture of young black people being arrested by the cops, I felt guilty. The feeling left, but when I went to the March on Washington and saw the kids from SNCC coming out of Danville, so proud and wonderfully clear, singing all the latest songs, treated with such respect by the older, middle-class union members and professionals at the march, I knew I belonged with them. I saw that their hair looked like mine: full, bushy, symbolic of pride, symbolic of a newfound lost past. They hadn't been to Uganda, and I hadn't been in Danville. We came by different paths, but we reached a point of consciousness at the same time.

The Southern Civil Rights Movement awakened young people to black consciousness and black identity through struggle. But this was only one source of my growing racial identity. My life at Amherst College, with the interplay between school and the outside world, including this incredible journey to Uganda and Kenya, was an incredible gift for me in this regard. And it was a gift that kept on giving through the hurdles and challenges I continually met and conquered on campus.

The March on Washington was a high point along the road to my Movement awareness. Johnny and I were a part of history without realizing it. With so many people around us, I had no idea what was being said "way up front" by the many speakers. I knew the great leaders in the Movement were there, but people in the back couldn't see them, and no one really stopped walking to listen to the words on the speakers. Some people sat down and conversed among themselves; others had their feet in the water of the reflection pool; people saw friends, and ran up to greet them. Most of the interesting people to me were the folks in dirty jeans and bib overalls, with T-shirts or denim shirts. These were the people who had been on the front line somewhere, and most of them were from SNCC. Of course there were people from the labor unions, and black professionals who looked just like our parents. But I don't remember what their signs said. I do remember the SNCC sign that said "Freedom Now!" People now recite King's speech as the best thing ever. To me, being there with all those people, many of them my own age, was the high point in my own personal civil rights movement.

Political Science and Professor Earl Latham

Political science at Amherst was taught by a foursome of icons in the field, known nationally and internationally for their publications on the subject. They were all hard to please, each had his own little niche in the subject matter, and I took their courses with fear and trepidation, but with advancing confidence into my junior and senior years. Professor Kateb taught international politics, Ben Ziegler and Earl Latham various other domestic variations on the subject, and then there was Professor Henry Steele Commager, who was an institution in American studies. Commager didn't like to be challenged on his narrow, white interpretation of the dawning of the American empire. I don't recall taking him on, but after I took the course, I was convinced that black folks had done more than he was prepared to acknowledge. Later, I filled in the blanks with my own research and investigation.

By far, Earl Latham was my favorite. There was a certain amount of pompousness in all of them; this was to be expected in that department. But "The Duke of Earl" was at times funny, urbane, and knew his stuff. On the other hand, Ben Ziegler was just pompous, and loved to hear himself talk. So I let him talk. In Professor Latham's class, I learned to talk with more confidence.

There was one course he taught, the name of which I forget, but it featured a textbook he called "The Mason and Beaney." Gentlemen," he intoned, "Take out your Mason and Beane-e-ey," leaving the last syllable ringing in the air for a few seconds. We swiftly complied, because he was not a man to play with. All the humor—if there was to be any in class that day—was initiated by him. I reference the book— which I still have some forty-six years later as a part of my permanent library—because it was a study of constitutional law, containing all the great cases, including the *Slaughter-House Cases, Pennoyer v. Neff,* and *Brown v. Board of Education.* We read and dissected each case, but the book emphasized the politics and the power considerations behind each decision made by a very political Supreme Court. I was fascinated, and did very well in reading and understanding the cases.

Professor Earl Latham took a liking to me, and seemed to really appreciate me for my mind. (There were others, but in my freshman year, they were mostly throwing out life vests in their conversations with me, and seemed surprised to see me still there on campus in September of the following school year.) But Professor Latham warmed up to me, and I to him, unlike most of my other classmates—if *warm* is the right word. Let's say he was less standoffish by the time I finished the second course with him.

And so he invited me to participate, for the summer of 1964, in a summer program he sponsored through his connections with government agencies in Washington, DC. Of course I said "Yes!"

My parents were thrilled; this was the kind of thing they wanted for me. But the learned reader will recall that there was something quite monumental planned for Mississippi for the summer of '64 by SNCC with the Council of Federated Organizations (COFO). It was called the Mississippi Freedom Summer. Students from all over the country, especially white students, were wanted in Mississippi to help the cause of voter registration.

I heard about the Mississippi project too late. I had already committed to working in DC, and I didn't want to cross Professor Latham, who was also the chairman of the department in which I took my major. "It's not nice to mess with Professor Latham," the slogan went. And so, like the sit-ins in Richmond and the Danville demonstrations in '63, here I was once again missing a main event in the struggle for black people's rights in the country. I was upset, but I had given my word.

Who knows why God sent Jonah to Nineveh? So I went to Washington, so as not to get eaten by the Big Fish.

Three things happened that summer. First of all, the job itself was boring. I was placed in the U.S. Information Agency (USIA) with a nice man whose name I don't remember. He was a real colorful character who wore suspenders and smoked cigars. The USIA was the propaganda arm of the U.S. government, and later I was to learn what evil lies it told: the cover-up of the murder of Patrice Lumumba in Congo, the radio broadcasts to incite insurrection in Cuba, and more. But for the moment, I knew nothing about Lumumba and very little about Castro, and so I happily went to the USIA, with "high security clearance," I might add. That meant absolutely nothing to me, and for the record, I didn't tell anybody what I read. But despite my boss's best efforts, I had very little to do except make copies and run errands.

Second, there were my roommates, all from Amherst and poli-sci majors like me. We rented an entire house in Georgetown, vacated for the summer by some rich family, next to the home of New York senator Kenneth Keating. When I arrived, they had staked out all the beds, and directed me to sleep downstairs on the floor on a mattress in the corner of the living room. I paid equal money, but got no bed? I spent my night turning off the central air conditioner. White folks, I learned early on at Amherst, liked it real cold. I would wait for them to go to sleep and then *bam!* Off it went, and the arguments began.

I could have put up with both had it not been for the national events colliding and butting heads with my values and my summer job. On June 21, 1964, Freedom Summer volunteers Michael Schwerner, Andrew Goodman, and James Chaney were reported missing in Philadelphia, Mississippi. A little over a month later, their bodies were found in an earthen dam, and Mississippi was on the map as the hellhole it was for blacks and those whites who fought alongside them for justice.

This I could not endure, sitting in the seat of government while the government did nothing to protect the rights of people I cared about. If I had been there, one of those guys could have been me.

I got mad as hell, dashed off a quick letter to Professor Latham, and didn't wait for a reply. I told my roommates and my friend at USIA that I was leaving, and got ready to go to Mississippi.

The only problem was that I couldn't go to Mississippi just like that. In Washington, to feed my need to be close to something relevant, I had made contact with the SNCC affiliate the Nonviolent Action Group, or NAG, as it was called locally in Washington. There were very few SNCC folks in town because the majority were in Mississippi. Betty D. was a young lady I met in DC, and she was connected to the NAG folks. We hung out quite often, as much as her daddy and mama would allow, since I got the feeling they didn't think I was worthy of their daughter despite my middle-class credentials, chief of which was Amherst College. (Despite my growing disdain for my class roots, I knew how to use them when necessary to impress a young lady's parents.) Her daddy, whom I never saw, was always in the back room, sending out messages of "no" through the mother, who was willing enough to transmit them to me as I tried to date their daughter. In fact, some of those proclamations may have been from her mother.

Anyway, Betty D. was political, and was as mad and upset as I was about Mississippi. She called somebody and told me SNCC didn't want any newcomers at that time. I thought it was because of safety concerns, but later found out there were a lot of government spies descending on Mississippi under the guise of newborn concern. My feelings were hurt but I understood.

So what was I to do? Clearly, I could not sit in DC and do nothing. So I remembered Julian Houston, my friend from Richmond. Julian was in Harlem, working full-time with the Northern Student Movement (NSM), specifically with the affiliated Harlem Education Program (HEP). Julian was about my age and the son of Mrs. Alice Houston, one of my favorite English teachers at Armstrong High School. Mrs. Houston, a friend of the family, was one of those gifted teachers who could make English come alive for us. Before leaving town for a private school, Julian had gone to Walker High School. And here he was, on the front line of the Movement, not in the South but in Harlem. I called and he told me they could use some help. I was relieved, but wondered: help doing what?

With my parents' grudging consent, I got ready to leave Washington, DC, for Harlem. They didn't understand why I wanted to leave a "good job." But at least they knew Julian Houston, and I suppose that was some consolation.

Harlem on My Mind

The Northern Student Movement (NSM) was an organization headed by Bill Strickland. Bill and Julian had both come to our "The Civil Rights Movement: Reform or Revolution?" conference in 1965. Strickland pointed NSM north, feeling there was a need for some black students and their white supporters to deal with the issues of poverty and race, just as Tom Hayden would suggest to me about Newark. NSM never got the publicity that SNCC received, although many of the leaders had started in the South and come up North.

The Harlem Education Program was a division of NSM and was funded to do a widespread tutorial program in Harlem. Upon reflection, his description of what he was trying to do in Harlem sounded like Tom Hayden's conversation with me a year later: the Northern ghettos were the next stage of the struggle, where racism was commanding but not always obvious, and where something else called "class" played a prominent role in what happened to black people.

Julian Houston wanted HEP to be more than a tutorial program. Aided by Andrea Cousins (daughter of Norman Cousins, the editor of *Saturday Review*) and with the help of the community, they set out to build a playground in the area of 147th Street and Bradhurst Avenue. Life at HEP was hard physical work, moving old mattresses, burning trash, chasing rats, and trying to get the city to move refrigerators and other stuff from the lot between three buildings on the block. There was a cadre of the willing, mainly mothers with the help of some young men on the block, who helped in one way or another. But the real heavy lifting was done by Julian and Andrea, a.k.a. "Pigeon," who tried to get people to see themselves as a unit, to work together, to overcome difficulties, to take on the city. In other words, HEP wanted the tenants to become organized, just as the people in the South were at this time. In the South, James Forman, the executive director of SNCC, talked about overcoming fear as the first step toward getting people organized. Here it was the distrust of the neighbor next door, the doubt directed toward self and everybody else who was black. There was plenty of new garbage thrown out of the windows each day from certain households, enough to compel the recent converts to say, "See, I told ya! Niggers ain't [do-do]!" Self-hate, anger, defeat—all of this stood in the way of our playground.

So at night, after the backbreaking, exhausting, frustrating days of clearing debris, chasing rats, and watching people still throw trash out of their window down onto the "playground," Julian Houston, Amy Cousins, John (whose last name I can't recall), and I sat around a big Riverside Drive apartment overlooking the Hudson River with barely enough furniture to sit and sleep on to talk about the bigger picture. We had wonderful discussions about the history and meaning of the Movement, and our work in the context of the struggle nationally and throughout the world.

It was here that I had my first discussions about the interplay between race and class, and my laboratory for understanding and applying the theory I learned was right there on our block. But I also learned about Castro and Cuba, Nkrumah in Ghana, Patrice Lumumba, Marcuse, and the back-lot organizing format of Saul Alinsky in Chicago. That summer of 1964 was the first time I became conversant in the implications of what certain world leaders did and how it related to what we were doing on that lot. I learned that when Castro came to the UN to speak, he insisted on staying uptown in Harlem at the Hotel Theresa. Lumumba was *elected* president of the Congo, and overthrown and murdered by the CIA. He was not a dictator, as proclaimed by the press and my friends at the USIA, but had been seen as a liberator by his people and by African and Asian nations of the world, then emerging from the clutches of European colonialism. Like Nkrumah, Lumumba believed in Pan-Africanism, or the belief that people of African descent should unite politically, culturally, and economically.

I heard my new friends use class analysis so easily to discuss what was happening in the world, in Harlem, and learned for the first time that it was time to add such an analysis to my expanding vocabulary about race.

These kids were so full of knowledge and information. I felt like a walking dummy—all I knew was "We Shall Overcome." Sometimes we would talk way into the early morning. The conversation flowed. Did Marxist analysis fit the Harlem situation? Who was this guy Frantz Fanon? And where was this playground in the context of world revolution, so demonstrably apparent in faraway places like Congo, Ghana, China, and this new place called Vietnam? Needless to say, I felt woefully inadequate. In my world, Marxism meant communism, and everybody knew the communists were bad. Just look at how they gobbled up all those countries, oppressed millions, killed hundreds of thousands in places like Hungary and Poland.

"But Junius," they may have asked me, or perhaps I asked myself, "Have you ever read anything by Karl Marx?"

I didn't know until that summer that aside from a description of the political system in places like the USSR, Marxism was a tool for political and economic analysis. That's how civil-rights-one-dimensional I was. Not because of what *I* knew, but because of the company I kept and what *they* knew, I realized beyond a shadow of a doubt that this was some radical stuff we were discussing.

And so when I went back for my senior year at Amherst that fall, I made sure I took a course from Professor Colston Warne, an aging economist who didn't get the accolades bestowed upon the laissez-faire capitalist brigade of professors, who were bright, fair-haired, and definitely mainstream in the academy. Professor Warne was a patient, intelligent man, rumored to have been called before the McCarthy committee in the '50s. It was all very quiet, and I didn't bother to make further inquiry. That was his business. I liked him a lot, and his class was small enough for some real discussion. After all, how many people wanted to take a class from someone so clearly out of the capitalist mainstream? Not exactly the course you'd need on Wall Street or in Daddy's law firm. But I got an A in the course.

In the class we read about and compared economic systems around the world. Because of him I got to read *The Communist Manifesto* by Karl Marx and *The Wealth of Nations* by Adam Smith. From him I learned that there was socialism in Norway and Sweden, but this was *democratic socialism*, as opposed to the *dictatorship of the proletariat*, which typified the Soviet Union. I learned that a democratic socialist had almost become President of the United States, and that a former head of the Communist Party in the United States was a black man named Benjamin J. Davis Jr., who graduated from Amherst College. I also saw a side of capitalism that up until then was unclear. My education with Professor Warne explained why I was having so much trouble applying the theory of supply and demand to my everyday life. I learned that quite often big corporations got together and fixed prices, so whether we "demanded" or not, prices were going up. A new word entered my vocabulary: *oligarchy*, as opposed to *monopoly*. Oligarchy typified the American economic (and political) system, and one had to learn how it operated to become a knowledgeable political scientist.

I learned a lot but concluded I could not be a communist, because putting *all* the control of the means of production in the hands of "the Party" was akin to monopoly by the state instead of the capitalists. As a young black man, why jump out of the frying pan and into the fire?

Academically, I was gaining credentials to match my civil rights experience, and fascinated with the people who were becoming my friends, who were not communists but who were unafraid to use the word *Marx*. Little did I think, however, that this new information about politics, and my better understanding of the concept of class, was in any way central and critical to my future in the Movement. Living in Harlem and cleaning out vacant lots by hand and dodging paper bags filled with garbage were not on my A-list of things to do. I wanted the Southern Civil Rights Movement as it had been portrayed and etched in my own mind: thousands of people marching, defying the Klan—all the stuff I had read about, heard about, seen on TV, listened to in conversations, but had not experienced firsthand on the front line of battle.

But I was already on the front line of the struggle in Amherst, Massachusetts, and in Harlem, New York, with opportunities for growth and fulfillment way beyond my wildest dreams. By the spring of 1965, I had done it all, except join with those my age who had dropped out or finished school or never went to college and took their places on the front lines of protest in America. I felt a call as strongly as I now feel compelled to tell this story, and neither my parents nor anybody else was going to stop me from completing what would have to be called my destiny.

It was the South, therefore, where young people like me wanted to be, to complete the process started in Amherst, Uganda, and Harlem, to learn more skills and find out where the Movement was inalterably headed.

3

MONTGOMERY AND BEYOND

Ain't gonna let nobody, turn me around...
I'm gonna keep on a walkin,
Keep on a talkin',
Marchin' up to Freedom Land

—TRADITIONAL FREEDOM SONG

Montgomery, Alabama and SNCC

So it came to pass that in March of 1965 I entered the Southern Civil Rights Movement ready for frontline duty. On our spring break, friends from UMass, Smith, and Amherst College piled into an old Volkswagen bus, headed for the Selma to Montgomery March.

My mother and father had sent me north, since there was nothing left in Richmond but low wages and Jim Crow. Yet here I was on my way even farther south, to Alabama, to place myself in harm's way. What did they do?

They never tried to stop me. But when our group arrived at my family's house in Richmond, my father took one look at the Volkswagen and said, "Here, take my car." We would be safer in his car, my parents thought, since it was a late-model Buick station wagon. We didn't know it at the time, but the Virginia license plates helped in other ways. On our way through South Carolina, with Fred Aronow falling asleep at the wheel, he must have started to swerve. A cop car moved up on us, lights twirling and siren blaring. It was nighttime, and the two black men in the car crawled into the back of the station wagon and put coats over our heads while Fred pulled over. Fred led the cop to believe we were college students on our way to Fort Lauderdale, Florida, for the annual big spring fling. The cop looked at the license plates, figured we were white college students from Virginia, told him to be careful, and let us go. We were told later that other integrated cars never made it to the march. The state troopers read the paper and were like crocodiles waiting for the wildebeests to cross the Zambezi River. Virginia plates and Fred's quick wit kept the cop away from our reverse Underground Railroad, going south to fight for freedom. I'll always be grateful to Pop Williams for the car.

"Not Selma, but Here in Montgomery"

To get to Selma, we had to go through Montgomery, Alabama. Somebody had told us to "check in" with SNCC to find out if there was any danger on the road ahead. There was always danger, but anything out of the ordinary we needed to know about. We found SNCC headquarters at the corner of Jackson and High Streets. We walked up the stairs and let ourselves in. Nobody seemed particularly thrilled to see six more college students from schools in western Massachusetts. In fact, there in the upper room, we were given a "so what, you're here" kind of greeting, wiping out any feeling we may have had of being relevant.

Stokely Carmichael, the only SNCC organizer I recognized by name, reputation, and pictures, asked us, "What are you going to Selma for? We need you here." His Trinidadian accent still sings in my mind.

Somebody explained that SNCC was opening a second front in Montgomery to put more pressure on Congress and President Johnson to pass legislation to enforce the right of blacks to vote in places like Alabama. We all had been active on our respective campuses in support of SNCC and other civil rights organizations, attending rallies, walking on picket lines, and raising money. Without too much deliberation, we decided to stay in Montgomery.

One of the SNCC veterans took us downstairs and assigned us living quarters with one of the families who lived on the same block as headquarters. We were assigned a patch on the floor for our sleeping bags and a corner for our stuff. Food was brought to us in bags, or our hosts shared their food with us. SNCC and the community were organized.

The SNCC base of operation, at the corner of Jackson and High Streets, was in the heart of the black community in Montgomery. I don't remember too much else about the city, but I'll always remember that corner. There were hundreds of young people behind police barricades of some sort. Lots of college students, some white, from up North, and some local black folks and college students. The whole Selma-to-Montgomery push, and this ancillary thrust by SNCC in Montgomery, was because on the other side of that barricade there were white folks who had shown they would stop at nothing, including violence, to protect white supremacy. A month earlier, Jimmie Lee Jackson had been killed protecting his mother after a voting rights rally in nearby Marion, Alabama, which set folks on the road to Montgomery, under the leadership of SNCC. Pictures of John Lewis (now a congressman from Atlanta) being beaten down by policemen in Selma while trying to begin the march to Montgomery had the same effect as the picture of Emmet Till in the casket. It sparked a wave of protest, and a federal judge who initially banned the march and Martin Luther King Jr. had to catch up with the people, who started coming in from all over the country. There was going to be a march whether the big folks wanted one or not.

Blood in the Streets of Montgomery

On the day we arrived, white men on horses, wearing cowboy hats and carrying long heavy sticks, were there to keep us confined to that one tiny block. We were told that these were Klansmen, brought in from the country and deputized for this special occasion to crack skulls. SNCC was determined to march on the State Capitol, which was a distance away; the cowboys were just as determined that we weren't going anywhere, and there was very little press coverage to protect us. To this day, everybody knows about Selma, but very few know about Montgomery in 1965.

As we attempted to move out, the horsemen rode into our ranks, whipping anyone and anything within the radius of their wild swings. There was panic as people ran, horses reared and whinnied, their riders hurling insults as they crashed down upon those of us unable to get out of the way. In the matter of a few minutes, bloody faces and heads could be found throughout the confines of that block in Montgomery.

I remember running up two or three church steps, to a church door, which was locked the whole time we were there; not all black churches supported the Movement. A small group of us was trapped, surrounded by motorcycle police and the horseback riders on three sides and the cold church facade on the other. Somebody started singing *"This may be the last time / It may be the last time / I don't know."* It was in Montgomery that I discovered the power of song to cope with fear. It was in Montgomery that I had to reconsider the power of God to work miracles, because truly, this was the valley of the shadow of Death—and I was scared as hell of dying at that moment.

As soon as we started singing, the cops seemed to lose their enthusiasm. Everywhere else, heads were split open, but the next charge at us didn't come, although we were helpless. Something much bigger than all of us protected us from physical harm and watched out for me throughout the days to come. Every time, I seemed to be just one step ahead of a horse and long stick. Years before, in Richmond, I had joined church, but I did so because it was expected of me. At Amherst, what little connection I had with religion and spirituality was replaced by criticism and skepticism. But here on a cold gray day on a street corner in Alabama, I had to take another look at myself in the context of God. That's the only way I can explain what happened that day in front of that church.

Later, I remember running through the front door of someone's house, a horse coming up on the front porch after us, to hear President Johnson droning on about the introduction of the Voting Rights Bill. Our presence in Montgomery, and those marching by that time on the highway from Selma to Montgomery, had been felt in Washington; but that wasn't the most important thing to me at that moment. If that doorway had been bigger, that horse would have come right on into the living room on top of us.

When horse and rider left the porch, I caught my breath and went outside to see a white motorcycle policeman tearing down the block. The crowd parted and let him through. He roared to the end of the block, and wheeled around for another pass. Some of the protestors knelt in the middle of the street, hoping to make him stop. He didn't, and going at about forty miles per hour, he plowed into a Latino demonstrator who was able to roll and take the impact on his left thigh. There were screams of horror and disbelief, and both driver and motorcycle were upended on the street. Seeing the downed policeman, the crowd, myself included, rushed forward to kick his butt. But the injured demonstrator stood up, blocked our paths, and shouted us back to nonviolence. We had all lost discipline, but he had not. SNCC didn't believe in nonviolence as a way of life. But it would not help our cause to take our pound of flesh from this one miserable excuse for a human and lose sight of the overall objective.

It had been less than a month since Malcolm X had been shot and killed at the Audubon Ballroom in Harlem, New York. I wonder what he would have said, seeing all the blood on the shirts, the bloody bandannas around split heads, and now this one act of the oppressed saving the oppressor. How long could America depend on these disciplined soldiers who eschewed Old Testament demands for revenge? How long could it last in Montgomery, let alone in the rest of America, which had not yet been rocked with outright rebellion—except in Birmingham in 1963 after the bombing of the Reverend King's brother's home? All-out urban violence, the hallmark of a people whose anger could no longer be contained, was yet to come, a wild card in a deck stacked against black people and our allies.

But personally, Malcolm was not on my mind. I felt ashamed that I let anger cloud my vision, and it took a man in great pain and with little use of his left leg to stop a crowd, which had become a mob. I learned a lesson at that moment: keep my eyes on the prize, and hold on! After that, anger never got a hold on me in the street, neither in America nor any other place in the world where I found myself in confrontation with the powers that be.

But what about the cop who did the damage and ended up in the street? He was hurt, stunned, and couldn't believe he was still alive. He struggled to pick up that heavy bike, got it upright, kick-started it, and drove off into the night, as scared (and fortunate) as any cracker could be during that entire campaign. I wonder what he told his friends?

Dr. Martin Luther King: "De Lawd" Cometh

We were still confined to that corner. More and more people joined us, some black and some white. On the second day, we awoke to learn that somebody must have told Martin Luther King that things were getting out of hand in Montgomery, because rumor had it that he left the line of march from Selma to join us in the hood. Despite myself, I was thrilled at the prospect of marching with King. I knew this was SNCC turf, and I was now with SNCC, but how can you not be thrilled with the prospect of being so close to the big man himself? Most of the people shared this feeling, especially the local black folks. "Oh, Lord," somebody said, "we goin' downtown now!" The march took on an almost festive air as we awaited his arrival.

There was an aura about King that was unforgettable. I see him now in my mind's eye: collected, peaceful, calm. He was in his element and totally in command of himself and the situation. But all was not well with our friends from SNCC. "De Lawd God," as he was often called off-camera, was clearly not welcome there, and in a few minutes I saw why. With King at the head of the procession, the police moved the barricades and we headed downtown toward the Capitol. We had no interference from the police or the cowboys, and a cheer went up from the crowd. "They were scared to touch Dr. King," I thought, and so did the rest of the crowd. He had come to town to lead the people, but only for a block or so. King, and his entourage of SCLC types, slowly marched us in a circle, right back to Jackson and High Streets, and shortly thereafter left town. Clearly, this was some kind of move by SCLC to take the heat out of Montgomery, because the Selma march was to be *the* focus. This little circle-step with King was supposed to satisfy us so that there would be no need for more bloodshed in Montgomery. At best this was a humanitarian gesture by SCLC, to cut down on the violence. At worst, it was one-upmanship over SNCC, probably with the support and perhaps even by the arrangement of the White House, since someone had clearly given orders to the rednecks to leave us alone for that half hour or so. During that little masquerade, when we turned around and went back, the cops threw peanuts at us. And after King left, we were right back behind the barricades. The SNCC folk didn't hesitate to give us their interpretation, and King's image was clearly tarnished that day. I had heard about the competition and one-upmanship in the Movement, and now I had seen it firsthand.

SNCC Raises the Ante

The next day, SNCC surprised the police and the cowboys. Instead of heading out of the intersection at Jackson and High as we had done in previous days, we went the opposite way. The cops weren't prepared for this move, and so there were no cops or horses at the other end of the block. Instead of marching downtown, we went through the neighborhood, singing freedom songs and generally feeling good about ourselves. Our destination was the historically black Alabama State College, whose campus was not very far away. The buildings and grounds weren't fancy, and there wasn't very much of a campus to see. Our mission was to enter the classroom building, where students were in class with their professors. We came in through the back door, uninvited, a throng of several hundred, over the protest of some of the administrators. But nothing could stop that freedom train as it swept through the halls, singing "Which side are you on, boy, which side are you on?" and chanting "Freedom/Now!" in call-and-response. There was pandemonium as the students broke for the doors to join us. There were some quiet smiles of approval and some looks of resignation on the part of most of the faculty. A few tried to stop the students, but there was no way to stop them or us from our appointed task of increasing our army by at least another two to three hundred students. The school was emptied out, and for the next week or ten days Alabama State might as well have been on holiday. By then we were an army over five hundred strong, supercharged to take on the enforcers of Jim Crow.

With our new volunteers, we moved downtown. The crowd was larger, more boisterous, and swelled all over the perimeters of the march route. But through the streets came the horses and the motorcycles again. King was gone, the deal was off, and it was open season on niggas and their white agitatin' supporters.

The horses were particularly vicious in the open like this, because they could be used as battering rams going at much faster speeds. In our downtime behind the barricades, the veterans had told us about ways to stop a horse, including putting a lighted cigarette on its nose. I thought this was particularly cruel to the horse, who really was only doing his job, but I didn't see anybody trying to get that close to a galloping horse to try it anyway. But what I did see both scared and angered me, as a cowboy on horseback ran over a black teenage girl, knocking her to the ground. In the pandemonium that reigned, screams rang out. From the corner of my eye, I saw a young black man, linebacker size, headed in the general direction of that particular horse and rider with a brick in his hand, crying and swearing revenge. I later heard that the young woman who had been knocked down was his sister. We were once again at the point where black rage could no longer contain itself, and this time there was no veteran to stop him. So, as he ran by me, I jumped on his back, and pleaded with him to put the brick down. In the back of my mind I saw the young man from the day before who had been hit by the motorcycle, but more importantly I knew that if my new brother here was successful, he—and now me— would be shot on the spot. All the way down the block he ran, comfortably, with me clinging around his neck. I don't know if my weight or my message got through to him, but finally he stopped, in tears, put the brick down and watched his sister get up and be led away to safety. She was okay. And so were we. *We are soldiers in the army / We got to fight, although we have to die / We got to hold up the blood-stained banner / We have to hold it up, until we die.* Years later, I would write a "Rap" about this event for my singing group, Return to the Source, using this Freedom Song and words inspired from this moment.

But we had to turn back once again, short of our goal. Too much bloodshed, too much resistance. And once more, the violence was one-sided.

James Forman

That night we went to a mass meeting at a local church. (In the North, we say "rally," but in the South they were "mass meetings.") I had been to rallies, but none like this. We were wounded, physically and spiritually, in pain for those of us who had taken the brunt of the horses, but generally down because one-sided fights like that can take the wind out of your sail. It was particularly vicious; it made no distinction between men and women, black or white. It was designed to send a message, and it did.

But SNCC had been at this for a long time, and had the balm to heal the grief-stricken soul: we had to feel the power that was within us, the power that was us, united and able to function as a group. We had to feast on the spiritual stuff that only comes from within, when the people decide that their cause is just, and that the time is now. In a church near Alabama State College, speaker after speaker reminded us of who we were and what we were all about. And we sang all the songs everybody knew. There were new songs that to this day I associate only with Montgomery and that time in 1965:

> *I read in the paper . . . shoo-doop-be-do-be-doop*
> *Just the other day*
> *That the freedom fighters' coming*
> *And they comin' this way*
> *They comin' by bus*
> *And they comin' by plane*
> *But if they have to walk*
> *They comin' just the same!*

Governor Wallace
You know you can't jail us all-all-all
Governor Wallace
Segregation's bound to fall . . . shoo-doop-be-do-be-doop

The songs opened our hearts, flooded our hearts and souls with whatever force within us resonates in times of pain, trouble, in anguish, but also, in triumph.

Ain't gonna let nobody turn me around;
I'm gonna keep on walkin', keep on talkin',
Marchin' up to freedom land!

The last speaker was James Forman, the quiet, brooding former executive director of SNCC. Forman was older than most of the hierarchy in SNCC, but had a youthful smile when time allowed him to use it. He didn't use it that night, because he gave another reminder of how late it was in the Movement. For me, it was my first campaign, but for him, how many? You could see the pain, the frustration, the fatigue, but most importantly, the accumulated anger written all over his face. That's what I saw in Stokely Carmichael and the other veterans in SNCC: the unresolved anger of having to be disciplined, to keep it in, to take the beatings and the killings, and not be able to retaliate.

Earlier in the campaign, Willie Ricks, the father of the term "Black Power" a little more than a year later, had jumped on top of a parked car at the intersection of Jackson and High and came within a sentence or two of proclaiming the end of nonviolence.

Ricks's fiery, angry rhetoric reciting the history of the violence and intimidation meted out when black folks stood up for their rights was met with the sustained cheers from the black people in the crowd. I didn't pay much attention to our white friends who were there to cast their lot with ours, but clearly, Ricks was talking black, not white. Perhaps the white people on hand felt the same way; that "We shall overcome" no longer had a place in the vocabulary of this part of the Movement. Ricks pulled us back, after coming within one or two sentences from saying "Let's get it on."

And so that night at the mass meeting, the issue of how long the anger could be contained came up again. In church, James Forman told us that he was getting tired of being on the short end of what America had to offer. He told us, "If black people can't sit at the table, then we're just gonna have to knock the f—ing legs off the table!"

There was about one second of stunned amazement, and then shouting and stomping like I had never heard before, as the crowd sprung to its feet in a mighty show of support, blacks and whites alike. So when we left church that night, on our way back to our little compound or into the blackness of the city at large, it was good that we weren't confronted. There would have been no nonviolent resistance. King and his New Testament–agape love may have been in full force on the highway, but that night, the Old Testament reigned inside Montgomery.

Looking back, here was a vision of SNCC in America in years to come: the increasing wages of conflict would not be one-sided for long.

Time to Go to Jail

The next day there was a new energy and resolve in the encampment. Jim Forman and some of the other staff went around and quietly determined which of us were willing to go to jail. I said I would. From our contingent, my good friend Posey Lombard also agreed. Posey was a young white woman from Massachusetts, and a senior at Smith College. After graduation, she would go back to work with SNCC in Mississippi, and was a Movement person until her untimely death in a motor vehicle accident in 1985.

I gave my wallet and other personal possessions to Jim Forman, so that the press and my contact people in Massachusetts could be notified. Standard operating procedure. I felt comfortable with Forman.

He had a reassuring manner about him, but you could see his nerves were stretched thin. I didn't ask too many questions, and went with the flow. By then, I was prepared for whatever came.

But the police and their henchmen must have smartened up about the rough stuff. Or heard about the mood at the rally the night before. After four or five days of trying to march, news of Montgomery was beginning to leak out into the media. There were more cameras each day. And there were more and more people joining us, mostly young black people from Montgomery, boosted by the Alabama State kids. This was a hard group to handle, even with horses, guns, and motorcycles. All the backup was on the highway, so Montgomery had to change its tactics. So as we lined up to march, and went toward the downtown area, there were no cowboys, just a solemn-faced police escort around the perimeter of the line. And we didn't go quietly; we went singing and chanting, as only Africans in the diaspora can do when we're happy, triumphant, and know we're on a roll.

All along the route of the march, black folks stood on the sidewalks, some just watching, some cheering us on like we were a conquering army. It was like the pictures of the American troops marching into Paris after the defeat of the Nazis in World War II. Tears came into my eyes as I watched the old people along the route, some of them too old to even stand up, but they were our best cheerleaders with their gentle waves. How many times had they been forced to say, "Yassa, boss man?" How many sidewalks had they been forced to vacate to let a white man and his family go by? How many lynchings had they seen, or maybe even escaped, to live in the shadow of Governor George Wallace's statehouse, still on their knees, until this day, when they could watch us march proudly by? My heart went out to them; I was marching and singing and chanting and clapping as loud as I could, for them as well as for me.

Our ranks increased steadily as more and more people left the relative safety of the sidewalk and stepped for the first time in their lives into the mainstream of resistance to injustice in America. These were mainly the young, as the old, no longer so bold, but with their eyes and the wave of their hands, just said, "Represent, son. Represent us all." If I had been back in Richmond, I would have been the talk of church the next Sunday: "Child, did you see Bernyce and Maurice Williams's son out there in that march? He was marching for *our* freedom, chile. You should have seen him—marchin' for me, and marchin' for you!"

The Capitol Building

For the first time, we actually left the black community and went downtown. I remember a big park around the Alabama State Capitol, and a flagpole on top of the Capitol from which fluttered two flags, one of which was the Confederate Army Battle Flag. On the far side of this broad plaza and this little outpost of hell was a screaming mob of white people, at least equal to the size of our group. They were yelling, screaming, cursing, waving placards, and generally portraying evil. For the first time, I was happy to see the police keeping them behind barricades. I knew that if they got loose, what we had already survived would be like a Sunday school session compared to what those folks had in mind for us.

As we prepared to picket the Capitol, the city police lined up and blocked our passage. They told us we couldn't walk on the sidewalk and would have to get into the street. When we made ready to walk in the street, the state police moved in and told us that we couldn't march there but would have to get on the sidewalk. I could see the amusement this afforded the cops, who wore different hats, but were one and the same. They had planned it this way, to see what we would do. As decisions were being made by the SNCC folk, a few of the white students came forth and said they wanted to go back. Fear was written on their faces, and they were very close to losing control. The SNCC leadership tried to explain that their only course at that point was with us. If they went back alone, they would be subject to the violence of the mob gathered on the other side of the square. Ironically, the safest spot in this level of hell was right there, under those trees, in full view of everybody and everything.

Our white student friends would have none of it, and insisted upon returning to the base of operations. These students must have thought that since they were white, everything would be all right. Later, I heard that before they had gotten very far on their journey, they had been severely beaten. They didn't understand that once they took that first step in support of justice for black people, they forfeited the right of being white. The lesson was clear: "When you come to the dance, stick with them that brung ya."

Without fanfare, the decision was made to sit down on the curb in front of the Capitol. We weren't going to give the cops, and the state bureaucrats looking out the windows, the satisfaction of trying to dance between the street and the sidewalk, so we just sat down and let them make the next move.

They were prepared. Several paddy wagons were driven up and they began arresting us one by one. Some people were dragged, but since I didn't see the political advantage of having asphalt burns on my ass, when it became my turn I got up and walked into the wagon. Looking out the back window of the van as it drove away, I was glad for the safety of being arrested. There was no way we would have all survived that mob. I wonder where those white people are now, those who were frothing at the mouth, ready to kill to preserve an old order that benefited them so little. I wonder what they did with the rest of their lives.

To this day I do not know how many people were arrested. I know there were several hundred because the city jail was overfilled, even when they packed us into the cells beyond legal capacity. I wonder how many people marched down that hill with us and got caught up in the moment, with no intention of going this far into jail. I wonder,

when they left their corner in the hood, did it change their lives forever, as it did for me?

> *You got to do when the spirit says do;*
> *And when the spirit says do, you got to do, oh Lord,*
> *You got to do when the spirit says do!*

Kilby State Prison and Worth Long

Because there were so many of us, the powers that be decided to
move some of us to Kilby State Prison. After one night of singing and
clapping and raising as much hell as possible, I was among those
transported to Kilby, which was more than one hour's drive away, if
memory serves me correctly. I remember that it was cold, which made
the ride actually seem longer than it was.

There were 150 to 200 of us transferred to Kilby. They separated
us by sex, and put each group into two big holding cells. The women
were across the hall from the men.

The psychological war began almost immediately. There were no
beds, just mattresses on the floor with no sheets or blankets. The later
it became, the colder it got. At some point in the early evening, some
guards appeared and threw in some blankets. I had found a mattress
away from the door, and turned over to see a mad scramble for the
few blankets they threw on the floor, with dust flying all over the
place. No way was I going to enter that fray, and so I resigned myself
to being cold for the night. Then, Worth Long took charge.

Worth is a short man with glasses. He looked like a stereotypical
political organizer from books by Kafka and Dostoyevsky. I found
out later that he had been with SNCC for some time, and had been
one of the field secretaries working in Selma and the communities in
Lowndes County, Alabama. SNCC had a deeper involvement in Selma
than did SCLC, despite the headlines for King in the march.

Worth got up on one of the tables in the holding pen, and got everybody's attention by yelling louder than the combatants for blankets on the floor. Once most of us were listening, he began:

"I don't know about you, but if I was a man, I wouldn't take a blanket for myself, unless there was a blanket for everybody." He paused and let that sink in.

Then he said it again, establishing eye contact with everybody in the cell. As we without blankets waited, one by one those who had scrambled for the prize came up and threw their blanket into a pile. The pile grew, and the guards who had been standing outside the locked gate to watch the niggas fighting each other for blankets, had to take a second look at the new black men that emerged from this struggle.

"One of the things they do to us is make us fight among ourselves," Worth explained. "If they can't get blankets for all of us, then we all ought to sleep cold."

"Yeh, yeh, yeh," was the reply, as we all bought into to what Worth was doing.

In less than five minutes, Worth had organized the cell. He turned a pack of individuals who were following their individual instincts for survival into a group of men who were willing to stick together.

The rednecks at the cell door caught on too, and after trying to tell us these were all the blankets they had and seeing our response, they went somewhere and got some more blankets. Everybody in both cells slept with a blanket that night.

All I could do was look at Worth and say to myself, "Wow!" Worth had defined the terms of the confrontation, and showed us how to win an immediate victory. From that point on, we were a unit, and not just a bunch of stragglers thrown into a cell together.

But this clarity was short-lived. The next day, Worth got himself put into solitary confinement by trying to integrate the prison church service. We had established a prison routine of singing freedom songs, messing with the guards, and trying to talk to the women across the hall, which was forbidden.

With Worth gone, there was a communication function that was missing. The leadership vacuum was filled by Stu House, a young man from Detroit who was the only other SNCC regular in the cell by this point, and, of all people, me! I had watched Worth, and to my surprise, when I spoke up, people listened.

As the days went by, Stu and I held the cell together, settling disputes, holding little rallies, reminding everybody to "keep your eyes on the prize; hold on." It worked—so much so that when one of the lawyers came to the cell to make sure we had everybody's name and an outside contact, he thought I was one of the "SNCC guys." To me, this was the ultimate compliment.

We decided that unless all of us got bailed out at the same time, none of us would leave. This seemed noble at the time, in keeping with the high moral tone set by Worth. However, it was impractical. Most of the people in the cell were young black men from Montgomery or the vicinity. Most of them had no Movement experience and no money. It was more difficult to get sponsors to bail them out, unlike those of us who came from out of state, most of whom were white, but some black, who came with our middle-class support kits that we didn't even know existed: parents with money, school support groups, church affiliations. There were people in the Movement who were not in jail, who knew how to work those networks up and down. I had been a part of such a support network in Amherst College. Now, I was to be the beneficiary of my own work because I was one of the first to hear that my bail had been arranged. This distressed me because I had taken the oath of solidarity. Initially, I refused to take the bail along with some others, but the lawyers reminded us that it really wasn't the way things had to be: there was money set aside, and if I didn't take it, it would go to somebody else. There were hundreds of us arrested, scattered between prison and jail, and the people working on our behalf didn't have time to keep up with our solidarity vows.

And so, after seven days, I was bailed out, along with a few others. My cellmates understood my dilemma, and wished me well. I left knowing that Stu would carry on. I often wonder what happened to my friends from jail, including Stu.

The Selma to Montgomery March

While we sat in Kilby State Prison, out on the highway the marchers were making progress towards Montgomery with much fanfare. Those of us who made bail were taken to the fairgrounds in Montgomery, which was the staging ground for the final march on the State Capitol the next day. Thousands gathered to attend a rally organized by SCLC: I remember seeing Nina Simone being escorted across the wooden planks that had been laid out as a walkway across a very muddy, rain-soaked field. And it was still raining when we got there. From the back of the stage, I saw Harry Belafonte, Sammy Davis Jr., and a host of other stars who regularly supported the Movement.

Those of us from Kilby found we had a new status: We were "those just released from prison." That status got us behind the stage allegedly made from stacks of coffins loaned by a local black funeral home, and free access to the comings and goings of the celebrities and civil rights, labor, and show business personalities. But we were in no mood to smile at our well-wishers. There were still people in jail, and we were powerless to get them out.

To me, the most impressive staff person was Ivanhoe Donaldson, a SNCC veteran who had been put in charge of logistics for this affair. He was on loan from SNCC. Most SNCC people didn't want to march with King, but Ivanhoe did, and so he was on hand with his impressive organizational skills to make things work. He had on a yellow rain slicker, and carried a walkie-talkie. He was clearly the go-to man. I made note of his style and job description for future use.

I don't remember where I slept that night, but the next day, I was among thirty thousand people who converged on the State Capitol to hear Martin Luther King Jr.'s third-most-quoted speech. After volunteering to help, I was assigned to a work detail on the first aid jeep. We were the very last vehicle to ride into town. I was too tired to walk, and glad to get the ride. I kept looking out the back of the jeep, expecting the Klan to come running up and ambush us. There were no cameras back there, and I was an open target. But I guess they didn't want me.

What Did It All Mean?

We had triumphed: a voting rights bill had indeed been introduced to Congress. And it had some muscle:

- The suspension of literacy tests in twenty-six states, including Alabama, Georgia, and Mississippi, the focal point of much of the SNCC effort.
- The appointment of federal examiners to replace local officials as voter registrars under certain situations.
- Authorization of the attorney general to intervene in cases of denial of the right to vote.
- Authorization of the attorney general to take action against four states that utilized the poll tax (the charging of a fee as a prerequisite for voting).

But what was Montgomery really all about? Would this law not have resulted from the pressure generated from the mainstream Selma to Montgomery March with the attendant violence that resulted in the brutality at the Edmund Pettis Bridge and the deaths of Jimmie Lee Jackson, Reverend James Reeb, and Viola Liuzzo (who was killed after the March was over, having carried marchers back to Selma from Montgomery)? Hadn't a reluctant President Johnson been forced to introduce the Voting Rights Act and see to its progress through Congress in a few months' time, without the violence and jailing in Montgomery?

That's a tough call, perhaps made easier in hindsight. Montgomery never got the headlines that Selma commanded, but clearly the White House knew that a bunch of students, mostly black but some white, were being beaten in the streets of Montgomery on a daily basis. If the negative appeal of bloodshed had an impact on the president, then here was some more bloodshed for voting rights for black people.

But Montgomery was more than just a sidelight to Selma. Every action SNCC took, and each confrontation we withstood, strengthened the resolve of the people by giving us the confidence to overcome fear through organization and defiant confrontation. For some of us, this was the first time. So ingrained was the fear of the white man and his authority that the basis of struggle must begin with an act to overcome fear. All around me, I saw men and women growing in self-confidence, me included, thereby increasing our usefulness as political operatives.

But more was involved than the release of a psychological chokehold. Montgomery showed the power of the Movement through organization managed by a cadre of experienced politicos who knew the strengths and weaknesses of a mass group of people, and were capable of giving it direction. I saw the clear strategy and tactics managed by the SNCC operatives, and though conditions changed from day to day, moment to moment, the people were given a clear set of goals and objectives: We were to reach the statehouse and picket for the right to vote. White resistance through violence was anticipated; nonviolence was our tactic. It was the resistance that would move the federal government from point A to point B, whether they wanted to do so or not. People Power, I learned, had to point people toward those clearly stated and agreed-upon goals, with execution in as simple a means as possible, with the opposition's moves and countermoves anticipated. This was my first lesson in building People Power in the streets of America.

Then there was the competition revealed in this game of power ball in the streets of Montgomery. SNCC set up and delivered a series of demonstrations separate from the Selma to Montgomery March to show SCLC that Martin Luther King Jr. was not the only major player in the game. How much of the SNCC Montgomery movement was motivated by one-upmanship, to get back at King and SCLC for taking control of what had started as an SNCC march? Or was Montgomery a power play within the Movement, led by radicals who believed that King and the forces around him were more likely to stand for less rather than more in the resultant voter rights law?

Willie Ricks told me later, "This was the Battle of Montgomery." Who won? SNCC was able to get local people and students from Alabama State and nearby Tuskegee University, to stand up to white terror, to tie up the city's police resources for two weeks, to bring in white student support, to fill up the jails and Kilby State Prison, to take the hardest punches Alabama could throw, and to send a lesson to SCLC about the need to share the spotlight. And it contained the anger of the masses by manipulating the threat of black violence, using it to gain the attention of the federal government and as a means of catharsis for those who were tired of ours being the only side that was nonviolent.

Later that year, the Voting Rights Act was passed, and it opened the door for thousands to register for the first time, and led to a change in the complexion of Montgomery and Alabama politics for years to come. The people had made a significant dent in the power of racist white folks who were well entrenched in their positions of authority, with their police, institutions of propaganda, and private army. SNCC and SCLC forced all of this into the open where everybody saw the dirty laundry of the Southern power structures and the Feds had to step in on our side.

Montgomery was the single most important training ground for me and for many others new to the politics of confrontation. Contrary to what our parents taught us, and our teachers, and our neighbors— all good people but primarily concerned about our safety—young people *could* make things happen with the tactics of direct action, witnessed by so many others who enjoyed vicariously what we set in motion. I didn't read about it; I saw it, I did it! I was a part of something that was growing that many white folks in power didn't want to see happen: black people comfortable with the knowledge that they could shake the foundations of America. Three years later, in Memphis, Tennessee, somebody in the white power structure decided the most well-known leader in this movement of possibilities knew *too* much, and was a growing threat beyond mere "civil rights." Hence Dr. King had to be assassinated. It was only then that I came to appreciate his leadership, and wished I had gotten to know him personally.

Beyond

With my experiences in Montgomery, I was indeed ready for the next step in the spring of 1965. I was made aware of powerful possibilities, but also made more aware of my own leadership skills. Upon my return to Amherst College, I made ready to graduate and to return to the South, more specifically to Alabama, where I intended to work with SNCC. I hadn't talked to anybody in SNCC and didn't know specifically where I would go, but assumed it would be Lowndes County, where rumor had it SNCC intended to build an independent black political organization. In fact, in the summer of 1965, Stokely Carmichael and other SNCC workers began the process of registering voters in a place where four-fifths of the population was black but where, at the beginning of the decade, not one black person was registered. It would lead to the creation of an independent political party, known as the Lowndes County Freedom Organization, with its symbol the Black Panther. This was indeed the first Black Panther Party. Without knowing any of this, I felt intuitively that this is where I wanted to be after graduating in May of 1965.

Tom Hayden and the Direction of the Movement

"What's so important about Newark?" I asked Tom Hayden. This was the first time "Newark" came up on my Movement radar screen. It was March or April 1965, my senior year at Amherst. I was enjoying the conversation, because I was being recruited. No one else had recruited me to do anything since my senior year at Armstrong High School in Richmond, Virginia, when Dean Wilson recruited me to Amherst College. I had no prospective employer, and at the time I hadn't heard from any law school. And I must admit, the urge to go to Alabama was more of a hope than a real plan.

Tom Hayden told me that he was looking for black college students or graduates to come to work at a Students for a Democratic Society (SDS)–sponsored project in Newark called the Newark Community Union Project (NCUP). NCUP was a self-described "democratic movement of the poor," and one of the crown jewels of the SDS-sponsored ERAP urban projects across the country. This was no accidental conversation. Tom Hayden sought me out, based on the civil rights conference I helped organize in the four-college area earlier that year, which he attended as a speaker. There is a note somewhere in the archives of NCUP telling people on the project that I should be a candidate to work in Newark. I didn't know this at the time.

As impressed as I was that he had gone out of his way to find me and talk to me, I thanked him but told him that I was on my way to Alabama to work with SNCC. In his own persuasive style, Tom told me that the Civil Rights Movement was over. That with the passage of the Civil Rights Act of 1964—which guaranteed blacks access to public facilities, housing, and employment opportunities—and the probable passage of the Voting Rights Act of 1965, which would protect black people's right to vote in the South for the first time since Reconstruction, this phase of our struggle had come to an end.

"What is needed," he explained, "is a cadre of young people who see organizing as a profession, who will now begin to concentrate on the much more difficult economic problems in the Northern cities: landlords and high rent, poverty, joblessness, and police brutality. And in addition, Newark is a majority black city. It is likely to elect a black mayor in the very near future."

I had no way of predicting that Selma to Montgomery was indeed to be the last great civil rights march of the era, and that anything afterward would indeed be "post–civil rights." But what really made me think about Tom's challenge was his description of the nature of the struggle to come, and his projection that the North was now more important than the South in terms of that struggle. It was an invitation to travel in a different direction. It forced me to review my experiences in Harlem in the summer of 1964 that were in the recesses of my mind, compared with the big bang that had been set off by Montgomery. I remembered how tough it was getting black people in large tenements to come together to build a playground. The enemy was not the Klan but the inside-outside lock that racism and classism had on the minds of the people: It operated from the inside through self-hate and self-doubt, and from the outside through the police, carnivorous landlords, and the welfare system. Was I up to the challenge? I told him I would think about it.

Unbeknownst to me, in 1965 a young black man about my age— twenty-one—had also been recruited by Tom Hayden for NCUP in Newark. Phil Hutchings of Cleveland, Ohio, had dropped out of Howard University in the early '60s to join the Southern movement. On a picket line in Knoxville, Tennessee, a white heckler had used Phil's cheek as an ashtray. Phil later joined SNCC and worked with the Mississippi Freedom Democratic Party (MFDP) challenge to the regular Mississippi Democratic Party for seats at the Democratic Party convention in Atlantic City in 1964.

"Tom was shameless," Phil told me years later. "He got me to come to a party in New York City, and after I had a few drinks, he told me how important Newark was, and why I ought to be there. To me, after the civil rights stage, [the power structure] was going to create Birminghams all over America, where everybody could sit on the bus wherever they wanted, eat at any restaurant, and the problem of racism would become less obvious.

"But we still have all those other problems related to class. Newark's majority black population and its size made this a place to find some of the answers for the problems of class and race."

As the higher power would have it, within a few days of the conversation with Tom Hayden, I got letters from both Columbia Law School and Yale Law School: I was accepted, with scholarship and loans included in the deal.

I was happy and relieved for another reason. Aware of my growing Movement activities, and following my pronouncement at a family gathering that I was going to be a civil rights organizer after college, my mother and father extracted a commitment from me to apply to law school. I argued, and told them that I could always go back to school, but the time for the Movement was now, and I had already put off my commitment for four years. But in the end, they prevailed. They knew how to work me pretty good, by a combination of guilt, solid reasoning, and letting me make the final decision. So at some point early in my senior year, I dutifully went through all the procedures: LSAT test, applications, and recommendations. But the compromise was that I would only apply to two law schools. No way was I going to fill out a lot of applications just so I could get into someplace I didn't want to go, anyway. "If I am accepted in one of the two," I reasoned, "then so be it. If not, I'm going South."

My parents accepted the compromise. But I don't think they knew the high stakes poker I chose to play. I applied only to Yale and Columbia, two of the top schools in the country, because I really didn't take this law school commitment seriously. "Maybe I should have," I thought later, "after all, they are your parents . . . well, it's too late now. Application time is over." Thank God I didn't have to disappoint them. And it made a lot of things fall into place.

I told my friends of my good fortune. Some of them were elated. Some just said, "Oh, yeah?" with a look that asked, "How did you get into Yale and I didn't?" This was a look I had come to expect. Many of them had better grades than me. There was no way I could have attained a sparkling academic record based purely on grades, given my first-year struggles with required courses at Amherst. So I kept my good fortune quiet for the most part. Of course, my parents and family were ecstatic.

Affirmative action had not yet been created, and therefore there was no institutional target for my white peers to direct their anger and envy upon my admission to both law schools. But it was important for *me* to understand what had happened and to accept my own place in either school.

Understanding came in the form of a chance meeting, sometime in April of 1965, with a young man from the South on the sidewalk near the dining hall on campus. He was white, and we knew each other but didn't cross paths often. It was our senior year and we were comparing notes, since he was from North Carolina or Tennessee, and had gone to white public schools. We both recollected the miserable first year experience in physics and calculus, and I was surprised that his grades and his experience were just like mine. I learned too that his high school didn't teach calculus or advanced physics the way our friends at Amherst learned them in private or public schools in the Northeast.

I thought I was the only one who felt like a dummy—until that moment, when I learned that Armstrong High School, and other black schools of the south, were not the only ones without the advanced courses. I had personalized the teaching gap in my high school and assumed that black schools were the only ones deficient, when in fact, most of the Southern public school districts were not as advanced as the traditional feeder schools to Amherst. Instead of beating myself up with self-doubt for three and a half years, I should have congratulated Junius Williams for doing as well as he did.

It was this conversation that helped me understand what a great job this young man and I had done in being able to overcome. Mrs. Diamond, my favorite math teacher at Armstrong, hadn't let me down. Armstrong hadn't let me down. I hadn't let myself down. I wasn't dumb, and he wasn't dumb. Some of us just hadn't had the same preparation and indoctrination as the kids in Connecticut and New York. And to be able to learn enough calculus at Amherst College to get a C by the end of my freshman year, and to do the same in physics, which required calculus as well, was an academic feather in my cap, and not an indication of deficiency in ability.

Nobody ever told me, but I think the law schools must have credited me with that first year as an academic high point, and not the low point my grades would indicate. My effort was an indication of my ability to overcome. They had reason to see my progression as an ever-improving track record that brought me to B's and A's in my senior year, along with the letter of recommendation from Professor Earl Latham. I learned later that over the years, Yale had grown to trust his judgment.

I recite that bit of history because lots of young black men and women today believe the hype when they're told they are "not qualified" because they don't have the identical scores of white people in their peer group. Had I gone to some of the elite prep schools or prestigious public schools as my peers at Amherst, and had I been prepared to take tests and configure my reasoning in such a way as to master the assessment process as they had for many years, there is no doubt in my mind that I too would have been at the top of my class at Amherst College. But I succeeded in another way: by *learning,* then *mastering* the skills at the same time, at Amherst. They had sixteen years, and I had only four. Thank goodness there were people at Yale and Columbia (and other schools like them, both yesterday and today) who were willing to look beyond the obvious and recognize an alternative assessment of talent and ability.

I wrote Tom and told him I was coming to Newark in June. I wrote Yale and told them I was coming in September. I wrote Columbia and told them, thank you, but I'm going to Yale. And I told my mom and pop that they had won. They were the happiest of all, I think, and the biggest winners in this derby. They just wanted me to be a lawyer. I was hopeful but unsure whether I could convert my enthusiasm for the Southern Civil Rights Movement to Newark, hopeful that I could manage Yale and manage my commitment to protest and struggle, hopeful that I would like Newark enough to call it at least a long-term base, that I could help bring some change, and that I could eventually become an attorney for unpopular causes.

Making Sense of the Amherst Years

As memories began racing back to fill these pages with detail, I was interested in assessing the interplay between Amherst College and the outside world, both of which had some bearing on my relationship to the decision I made about my political direction.

The "whole man" at Amherst in many ways was an uncomfortable fit. It produced young men who were analytical and critical, but who believed in very little except themselves and their unchallenged position in a world of privilege created by their forefathers and mothers. And yet by the point of my senior year, I too had mastered the techniques of dominance through writing, debate, and political awareness. I could have been a very good surrogate capitalist.

But unlike most of my peers, I had something that was bigger that went way beyond me: I had the Civil Rights Movement. And I had something to believe in that I would recognize as the God force working within and outside of me, something that led me to that point, at that time, and beyond.

It was Amherst that gave me the challenges I needed to overcome, and helped me to gain the confidence that helped make me as useful as I potentially was to the Movement. I had to overcome the racism endemic to the North—subtle, therefore more devastating, and if not confronted could have left an indelible scar on the psyche that says, "You, young black man, are not as good as they are." I triumphed, beginning with the "Mr. Pseudonym" articles in the *Amherst Student*. While other kids my age were on the front line somewhere in the South or in the ghettos of the North, I was on the front line at Amherst, and without that challenge, there would have been no opportunity. Without the opportunity, there would have been no victory.

The scars left by Jim Crow in my upbringing were young, and more easily healed than they were for others. By my senior year, I had gained confidence in my ability to compete. I enjoyed the platform Amherst gave me for debate with my classmates or any other takers about the demands for black people for equality in this country. I discovered I was quite good at it. I could write, talk, and think on my feet. I even knew about vectors from physics class, and more than enough about Hammurabi's Code in ancient Babylon. And I could play chess, dance, and play lacrosse as well. Not bad for a middle-class newly emancipated colored boy from Richmond, right?

Amherst means so much to me in another sense because it made me appreciate the value of skills, and took me to new heights in the definition and refinement of my talents and abilities. There were so many other things that enabled me to grow as an advocate, skills and resources I developed that have traveled with me down through the corridors of my life—skills that I use even today in enrichment of the only consistent profession that straddles all aspects of my life: I am an organizer and an advocate, and the world I began to see came from these formative years. In those years, I just followed my nose and led with the skills I had learned: analysis of problem, assessment of resources, articulation of both sides of an argument; and communication of choice and direction, through the spoken and printed word. All of that started in Richmond, but was taken to a new level at Amherst College. Some of it was in class, but most of it was from the give-and-take with my fellow students who challenged or supplemented my worldview through constant discussion and argumentation, and the out-of-college adventures Amherst made possible, like Crossroads Africa, the civil rights conference, and Montgomery, Alabama.

In addition, I began to refine my racial identity because of Amherst and in spite of it. Amherst told me through its useful contradictions that I could have white friends, but I was not white; that I could be engaged in white institutions, but I must leave my own mark upon them; that I could have a good time, but I must do so as a black man, and not a white wannabe. I believed in something bigger than me, and thus I was connected in a way most of my peers were not: to a force that emanated from the South, but had a Northern and an African antecedent as well. Without the Movement, I would have been adrift, set up for a big fall, a black man with the credentials to function in white society, but no real sense of who I was. Without Crossroads Africa at age nineteen, I would have been without an early reference of where I came from and who I was, in the global sense. Without Harlem I would not understand the intersection between race and class. Without Montgomery, I would not understand how to deal with fear. And without Amherst, there would have been no fertile ground upon which to connect them all.

So who was I? In racial and cultural terms, who was Junius W. Williams? If I were to look at myself in terms of my parents' generation, I was "the exception" and I was the creator of many "firsts." This is what my parents planned and sacrificed for me, and for my brother at Princeton, to achieve. But we, as the recipients of that mandate and standing upon the shoulders of these giants who preceded us, had to look beyond their horizons and find our own answers. Who was I, in my own terms?

The law school acceptance and my decision to stay North left me with a clear and rejuvenated spirit. My last memory of Amherst College in that period of my life was not graduation, but packing my last few bags and heading down the highway with two of my best friends, Merble Harrington and Alice Gloucester. My parents and brother, Johnny, came up for graduation and took most of my luggage with them. Johnny was the second and final installation and manifestation of the success of my mother's plan: he had finished his junior year at Princeton. My parents were in seventh heaven. I was so happy to please them, to give them both reason to be proud of me, and to let them bask in the sun a little bit, because as you can imagine, I wasn't too keen on marching in a cap and gown. After all, I was going to Newark.

They went back to Virginia in the same station wagon that took me to Montgomery with the car full of stuff. But they were happy to be crammed in, big smiles on their faces. I needed to stay and tie up loose ends. Merble had graduated from Smith at the same time, and Alice was a graduate student from Hampton, Virginia, who had only been in the area for about one year. In my senior year, the three of us, all Movement-oriented, became a tight bunch. Within a day or two of my graduation, I got a ride in Alice's car with Merble, heading south, eventually to Newark and a brand new life.

It is hard to recreate that moment, riding in the car, windows down on a sunny day in May, with two fine black women, radio blasting with the music of *our* choice. *"I'm in with the 'in' crowd / I go where the 'in' crowd goes."* I looked out the window of Alice's car, seeing the landmarks I had come to know for the last time as an Amherst College student passing by swiftly on Route 9, as we headed from Amherst to

Northampton, in the direction of Smith College and the great highways beyond. There was Chi Psi fraternity house, where somebody white once threw beer on my date; across the road, there was Phi Delt, where I sat in on drums with Taj Mahal, then a student at UMass; then Theta Delt, the house I almost joined, and the Amherst football field where I had once *walked* onto the field carrying my saxophone, which was now safely stored in my parents' home in Richmond. Last seen through the back window of the car was the steeple of Johnson Chapel, the tallest point on campus, slowly receding into the distance, punctuating a sea of memories at Amherst.

The song continued, just as it plays in my head at this moment. *"I'm in with 'in' crowd / and I know what the 'in' crowd knows."* I had never felt so happy, so relieved, and so comfortable with my life as I did at this moment. I dwell on it now because it was such a feeling of completion, and perfection, and I don't know if I've ever felt that way again. At peace, at rest; just complete. Amherst College gave me so much, and I gave so much in return. The contract had been completed, the quid pro quo fulfilled. We were both moving on, and I was going *where the "in" crowd goes.*

4
NCUP: MY FIRST SUMMER IN NEWARK

Look out, baby, 'cause here I come
And I'm bringing you a love that's true
So get ready 'cause here I come

—THE TEMPTATIONS, "GET READY"

Arriving in Newark

After graduation from Amherst I went home to Richmond for a few days and then came to Newark to work for NCUP. Upon arrival by Greyhound at Penn Station in Newark, I was told to take the local bus to the corner of Bergen Street and Clinton Avenue. Someone would meet me and take me to the project house.

In transit, the bus went through the intersection of Broad and Market Streets, the retail and commercial center of Newark. Richmond had a lot of black people, but I had never seen this many black folks downtown except in Nairobi, Kenya. Newark reached black majority status before Washington, DC, making it the first major "Chocolate City" in America. The white folks I saw were largely professionals, and came from one of the many office buildings all within a three or four block radius of that intersection. Seven years later I would take my place in that hustle and flow when I opened my law practice at one of those buildings, at 24 Commerce Street.

The black people were mostly working-class men and women, changing buses, walking across the street, shopping, talking to each other in the warm weather of June. Young women were dressed in the fashions of the '60s: Jackie Kennedy hairdos—as close as they could get to it—short skirts, jeans, colorful tops. I didn't notice the men as much, but they were probably checking out the same women I was.

And nobody took much notice of me. Clearly, I was just another face in a sea of black, brown, tan, and beige. Coming from four years in western Massachusetts, where I always stood out, Newark was truly a refuge. Little pleasures like blending in—pleasurable if you like being black. It seemed like Newark was grinning at me, giving me more comfort as each mile clicked off. I had a feeling I was about to enter a world where politics would become the Supreme Being in my life for a long time.

Introduction to Newark

I arrived at the corner of Bergen Street and Clinton Avenue, and got off as instructed. To my surprise, there was a demonstration going on across the street in front of a local bar called the PON, a place I would come to know quite well. I crossed over, not knowing anybody. I must have looked like the newcomer since I had a small suitcase. Somebody came over, introduced himself, took my bag, and asked me if I wanted to get on this picket line protesting the police killing of a black man. I said, "Yes," and so within five minutes of arriving on Clinton Hill, I was in my first demonstration.

It was small but noisy, about equal numbers of middle-class whites and working-class blacks. A few more men than women. I was introduced all around. This was a CORE demonstration, and the Newark Community Union Project (NCUP) was there in support. We picketed with signs in a little circle. People were passing out leaflets that explained how a police officer named Martinez had shot an unarmed young black man in the back earlier that month. People were chanting their displeasure and singing freedom songs. I felt comfortable and in my element.

At some point, Bob Curvin, the CORE leader, called off the demonstration for the day, but the NCUP people wanted to stay. A few words were exchanged; Curvin took his sound equipment and put it in his car, but the NCUP people stayed on the corner, just as loud as they were before. I remembered the conflict in Montgomery between SCLC and SNCC. Sometimes, the good guys don't always see eye to eye. I could live with that. I stayed with my new friends in what had now become an NCUP demonstration.

Allies and Adversaries

The Students for a Democratic Society did a "Prospectus for a Newark Organizing-Research Project," which is undated but probably done in late 1963 and early 1964. Three factors stood out: a black majority, a white exodus, and an overall population decline, all linked to the suburban expansion. The white people who could afford to move took jobs and wealth with them, leaving black folks, a growing number of Puerto Ricans, and white folks too poor or too stubborn to leave.

In fact, NCUP was established because of the convergence of these three factors. NCUP decided to organize in Lower Clinton Hill after its break with the Clinton Neighborhood Council (CHNC). CHNC was a liberal advocacy group formed by whites back in 1953–1954. By 1964, CHNC had a diminishing base because of the white exodus, with an increase in black residents as tenants in the houses once occupied by white homeowners. CHNC invited SDS to come to Newark to inject new blood into the organization. But there developed an ideological split between the young students and the older more established CHNC. So SDS left CHNC and moved down the Hill to organize poorer tenants, most of whom were black. They organized around landlord-tenant conflicts, police brutality, unscrupulous retail store owners, and urban renewal—not around unemployment as had originally been planned. The people involved in the breakaway organization called themselves the Newark Community Union Project, or NCUP.

In the summer of 1965, NCUP was at the peak in its mission to empower poor people to fight for themselves using the tactics of direct action inherited from the Civil Rights Movement. NCUP was a mix of white and black college dropouts or graduates and local black people from the neighborhood, some poor and some working-class.

Two slogans still come to mind, like verbal logos in any conversation I heard that first summer and throughout my association with NCUP for the next two years: "Let the People Decide" and "We have no leaders." Democracy was the calling of the SDS "students," which was what the local black residents called the white organizers. These urban projects created by SDS were dedicated to the idea that decisions were made in a group, in discussions sometimes going on into the early morning hours. It was designed to keep one person (or a few people) from having all the power. And many in SDS felt it was the last chance for an integrated movement, where blacks and whites could work together despite differences in race and class. The students were mostly white and from the middle- or upper-class strata of American society.

NCUP built a base of about fifteen block groups, with 250 people loosely affiliated in one way or another. Work in the Movement was not always confrontational. In fact, most times it was folks planning the next action, or people having fun, or resolving some personal issues. But the underlying tension between NCUP and the local white political and economic power structure was always there, and eventually led to some form of confrontation.

Congress of Racial Equality (CORE)

NCUP was not the first to fight for justice for Newark's growing majority of black folks. CORE, or the Congress of Racial Equality, was the most consistently vocal civil rights group in Newark in the early 1960s. The racially integrated Newark chapter of CORE was formed in 1961, with Bob Curvin, Newark native and Rutgers University graduate, as its head. Before NCUP, the chapter sponsored demonstrations for hiring black workers at Barringer High School in coalition with black labor unions and white clergy, and negotiated with twelve major companies for jobs for minorities in Newark and other locations in New Jersey. CORE raised charges of police brutality; it generally opposed City Hall for its insensitivity to the rights of black people.

CORE and NCUP were allies, despite that disagreement on the corner in the demonstration on my first day.

Moving into NCUP

At some point that afternoon after the demonstration we went to the "project house," where I was to stay with a number of other NCUP folks. When I got to the apartment on Ridgewood Avenue in the Clinton Hill section of Newark, there were just too many people in one space, mostly white college types (some for the summer, some permanently), and a few black folks, mostly from the neighborhood. I didn't like communal living. The next morning, Tom asked me how I was doing, and I didn't complain. But he must have seen the unhappiness on my face.

Phil Hutchings told me later that Tom treated him and me differently. He saw me staying in Newark and becoming some kind of leader, and Phil was "more like Tom," an organizer who would one day move on. I was one of the people to be nurtured and developed. Tom moved quickly to find me another place to stay. No doubt I would have left the project if I had to stay in that apartment.

The next day, I went to my first community meeting at the headquarters on Bigelow Street, two doors down from the Third Precinct of the Newark Police Department—close enough for the cops to watch us all the time. Tom pulled me to the side. He said he wanted me to meet Vickie, who had agreed to let me stay in a room in her apartment. I expected some older, stout woman with glasses and a big Southern smile who smelled like fried chicken. Instead, Vickie was young and fine.

Vickie

Vickie was twenty-eight years old, a single mother with four children, ages about ten to three. She had on a wig that night, piled high on her head, and was dressed like she was going somewhere important for the evening, with heels, a fashionable dress, and makeup. I felt she couldn't possibly be just coming to our meeting, but there she was. I said, "Hello, how'ya doing," and other small talk one uses when he is meeting his new fine landlady for the first time. She was checking me out, and I her, in the midst of all the coming and going in front of the office, but probably for different reasons, since she had kids and a stranger was about to move into her home.

I moved in the next day. Didn't take much time because all I had was a suitcase. Steve Block, a Williams College graduate, and Phil were on my case. "Look at him; he's living with the foxiest woman on the project." Of course this was man-talk; they didn't project their fantasies and their envy to the white women on the project, some of whom had black men from the neighborhood or were romantically involved with other SDS organizers on the project. Some didn't have a man, and others didn't want one. But it was up to me to downplay my obvious good fortune, to play it off like, "It ain't nuthin', man, I'm just staying in the house. I got a job to do and I'm here to do it...."

And that *was* the way it was, for several reasons.

First of all, Vickie was older than me. I was only twenty-one, and when you grow up in Richmond, the older girls let the younger boys know that they had larger fish to fry. I wasn't in their league, even if I dared to get interested. I remembered very well what happened to me over the phone when I dared asked the lovely Lolita for a date when I was at Amherst. She let me know I had overstepped my boundaries, so I wasn't too happy about the prospect of being shot down again by making a move on Vickie.

And then there was propriety, and discipline. I didn't want Vickie to think I was moving into the house of someone nice enough to accept a stranger, and try to "hit on her." And I didn't even know how to begin the conversation, truth be told, because I was such a lame! Going to Amherst College had not tightened my game, which was really nothing to speak of in high school. You know about "game," don't you? It's the gift of presentation; the knowledge base women want and need to hear in order to make their choice. My experience in high school was limited, Amherst was slim pickings, and even though I had dated some women, there was nobody like Vickie in my experience before.

So I kept my distance. Went out to do my work on the project in the morning, came back in the afternoon or early evening, socialized within the parameters of the project with my friends, and closed the door at night to my little room. Vickie had the large bedroom with her four children, all in a double bed. I felt bad taking this extra space, which surely would have been utilized by her family, but she assured me it was okay. This was the Movement, and this was her sacrifice. It worked out fine that way.

Vickie didn't go to many NCUP meetings because she didn't have time for "all that talk." But whenever she participated, she watched and didn't miss a beat. She was an intelligent woman who knew how to survive.

Learning How to Organize

Work on the project started for me the second day I arrived. I paired up with one of the senior women organizers and went to a block NCUP had previously organized.

My partner and I were canvassing the block trying to get people to come to an NCUP meeting that night. We had the usual number of brush-offs, and a few insincere instances of, "Yeah, I'll be there." I wasn't annoyed by the brush-offs or false promises, having done voter registration in Richmond and Springfield, Massachusetts. I walked up on the porch of one house and saw an old man. He looked like a farmer from down South, just sittin' and rockin' in that chair. It was my turn to make the pitch, so I asked him to come to the meeting. He told me, "No, 'cause comin' to a meeting ain't gonna do no good." He went on to tell me how sorry "Negroes" were, and I told him things were changing. "All we have to do is stick together, and just remember, the Lord helps them who help themselves." For the first time, he looked at me. My Biblical reference opened a new relationship between him and me. My new friend and I went back and forth, our conversation interlaced with Bible verses I remembered from Sunday school in Richmond or Vacation Bible School in Suffolk. After about fifteen minutes, the SDS lady and I decided it was time to go on. We left him with a smile on his face, and extracted a promise to come to the meeting, which was about police brutality or something. He didn't come, but I knew I had passed the test, something I needed to see for myself. I could be an organizer in Newark because I had the gift of listening and making conversation.

Well, at least that was a start. But just for the record: neither Jesus nor anyone else in the Bible said, "The Lord helps them who helps themselves." This was total improvisation. I didn't know at the time and thought I had good Biblical authority. Closest thing is James 2:17, where the Word speaks about that faith without work is dead. And when you think about it, why doesn't God help them who can't help themselves, or won't help themselves—or is that asking too much of God? Oh, well, I meant well at the time.

Back to Vickie

Things were going well for me on all fronts. I was learning about the project, sampling the many things NCUP had to offer. And learning about my new home. Vickie and I got along well, a lot of laughter, no arguments, and I came to like the kids. I grew on them as well. One day Vickie had a party in her apartment. I think it was for me. All the NCUP gang was there, plus some other friends of hers that I hadn't met before. A good time was had by all, but after everybody left, our relationship changed. She took away all the doubts I had about the age, and about the approach, and about propriety. And within a few days, we were an item of discussion on the project. I should say *more* of an item, since there had been a lot of speculation beforehand.

Vickie took care of me. Steve Block, who came to NCUP just a little ahead of me, still talks about my first summer in Newark: "While people at the project house were eating peanut butter and jelly sandwiches, you were eating steak." This is true, but most of the steak was on or near the first of the month. The first was "Mother's Day," when women on welfare got their checks. The blues song makes it clear: *"First Day, Ham and Bacon / Next day, ain't nuthin' shakin'."* I had no salary from NCUP, only the $25 or so my mother sent every week, which helped toward the end of the month.

Vickie gave me confidence, gave me a chance to understand that I was attractive, even to older women. I learned that Vickie was not the only one attracted to me that summer. And I learned that these were women not necessarily in the light-bright syndrome urged upon me from my Virginia middle-class, Jack 'n' Jill pioneering mother, but good-looking women of all persuasions who accepted me for whatever I had to offer. It was a man's world, and in the hood, there was very little pretense and foolishness to put up with. I liked the man they all helped me become.

At Home on the Block

It was from the vantage point and security of Vickie's house that I came to know and appreciate yet another level of Newark. I felt accepted in the community, not just as a "college boy," as Vickie called me, but as a real part of the block. A lot of that had to do with race, a lot with my personality, and a lot with my relationship with Vickie.

One day in the heat of July, I saw Vickie look out the kitchen window of her second-floor apartment. Her mood changed immediately. She told me, "Don't come downstairs," and went to the kitchen table, took off one of the legs, and ran downstairs, her eyes on fire. How did she manage to take that leg off without the table falling down? She had obviously done this before, or was this was a well-trained three-legged-table?

I looked out the window and saw a pretty big guy get out of a Cadillac just in time to watch Vickie tell him in no uncertain terms that he wasn't coming in the house. She cursed him. He fired back, but he couldn't match her will. And he saw the table leg by her side and ready for action. People were on the porches; others came out to see the drama go down. I did as I was told, but something in me said, "You ought to be outside and help her if he comes at her." He was big enough to take the weapon away but not before she got in a good few licks, and then what would he do? He must have figured the same thing, decided to cut his loss of face, got in the car, and drove off. She came upstairs, still fired up, and I asked her what that was all about. She told me, "Don't worry about it," and I let it go. To this day, I don't know who he was, or what that was all about, but I learned to trust her instincts in the matter of reading and taking the temperature of the street. Suppose, for example, I had come out, and stood on the porch as her backup? The guy would have seen me and known who I was. Even if he wanted to pretend I wasn't the man who just came out of her house—the house she wouldn't let him in—other people would have seen me and made it impossible for him to ignore me. She backed him off with words and threats because there wasn't much for him to fight about. With me on the scene, he'd have to vindicate his honor. I'm glad I didn't go downstairs!

But there was another time that I did go downstairs. Next door to Vickie lived Georgia and her teenage brother, Tony. One day there was a commotion in the street in front of their house. Everybody started coming outside. Tony and his block were going to fight the guys from around the street on Peshine Avenue. These were gangs, but not like Bloods or Crips, just groups of friends who stuck together based on where they lived. Before I realized what I was doing, I was in the street with Tony's guys, facing off with some guy about my size a few feet away. "Oh, hell," I thought to myself, but it was too late to go back. The rules helped me. It was up to Tony and one guy from the other block to fight it out over some insult. If they couldn't settle it, we would all fight. So the two of them started to fight, throwing lots of punches, but making little contact. The people on each side were encouraging their particular team on. I had one eye on the boxing match, and another on my adversary, sizing him up. He was about my size, no clear-cut eye for the kill, but looks can be deceiving. I would have to take him. I didn't have a weapon, and I wondered if he had anything in his pocket.

As it turned out, I didn't have to find out. The two who were fighting got tired of it, said a few nasty things to each other, and just like that, it was over. Not like today, when the Uzis would have come out, and some of us would have been dead. Tony's manhood had been preserved, and my stock went up. Folks on the block appreciate loyalty. They knew this wasn't my fight, but I had backed up Tony. The women and the men sang my praises for days to follow, until it got to be stale news and we went on to something else. I had a place on the block on Hunterdon, not as a member of NCUP but as a member of the neighborhood.

And being with Vickie helped me see black Newark beyond the personal intrigue on the block. I got to see a forest more important than this one tree. I didn't realize what I was experiencing, but I was seeing and learning nonetheless. Mathematics is cumulative, and so is Newark.

Seeing Black Newark

As a member of the neighborhood, I was able to put faces on the people listed as statistics in the SDS studies. Typically, black men had the least desirable and therefore the hardest jobs. Women worked in some of the few remaining factories, or did "day's work" in the homes of wealthy whites in Newark or in the nearby suburbs. Newark had its independent entrepreneurs, like hairdressers or tavern owners or people who made money in the entertainment business. And some found regular employment in the underground economy as numbers runners or selling illegal liquor in after-hours clubs. Some women were on welfare. A sampling of all of these lived in my neighborhood, and their common gathering spots were churches and bars.

There were jobs in Newark, but they didn't pay enough. At one time there were good factory jobs for the immigrant Germans, Italians, Irish, Polish, and Jews. These were the people who left Newark in record numbers in the '50s for greener pastures in the suburbs, made possible by FHA mortgages, the G.I. Bill, and taxpayer-built highways. They left blacks and Puerto Ricans to deal with vicious police, rapacious landlords, welfare workers, manipulative politicians, and teachers, who saw the darker children of these groups as less worthy. Racism dealt all parties left in town a different hand than the one given to previous immigrant groups of European persuasion, who only had to deal with being poor.

Many times the rhythms of the project blended with those of Vickie's street, but they were indeed different rhythms. NCUP provided a daily drum beat to awaken the people to resistance.

NCUP, the Organization

NCUP organizers went from house to house to get people to come together to form block associations. NCUP organizers said it was "to get people to overcome their fears and go on eventually to become their own community organizers and leaders." Not the fear of the Ku Klux Klan, but the self-doubt perpetuated by Jim Crow, or distrust of working together, having no experience with doing anything in organization, except in church where the Spirit and a different brand of politics prevailed.

Ray Trent came to Newark from North Carolina, and lived on Peshine near Bigelow. I talked to him about his NCUP experience:

> One day a white guy comes up and asks me was I satisfied or did I want a change. I told him things could be better. The guy asked me, How can things get better?... They had ideas of challenging the system on housing, which was deteriorating.

Ray said his apartment was all right, but he was concerned about the neighborhood. Somebody called the white organizers "communists," but that didn't bother him. "Communists never burned [black people] at the stake," he said. His impression was that "These were really interested students, sacrificing their careers... they could have gotten good jobs." So he joined NCUP.

In this context, being white was sometimes helpful. Despite the mark white supremacy left on black people, when a white person showed up, lots of black people responded, "Maybe I ought to come on out and see what these white folks have to say."

But what helped convince Ray was the fact that he knew Thurman and Bessie Smith and Terry Jefferson, neighbors who had already joined NCUP. Having local black organizers and members muted the damage when somebody called the white students "communists" and "outsiders." Ray pointed out that for some people, it was easier to talk to him or Jesse because they were black. Some people had fear and distrust of white folks. The integrated crew of organizers offered something for everybody: those who responded better to white people, and those who didn't.

What was the conversion process, taking people from fear and self-doubt to believing they could become empowered? Ray Trent again:

> You had to get 'em to a meeting, where Bessie or Tom would take over. People would talk about their problem. In the discussion, people would find out they had a lot of common problems. By coming to the meetings, they were encouraged to talk. How could this help? Ninety percent of the people coming were women, raising their children without a husband. They were willing to do something . . . whatever it takes.

People got mad about the issues such as bad housing, but they oft times thought too little of themselves to help each other overcome. Coming to the meetings helped people overcome their personal fears and distrust of one another.

In NCUP, if the issue was bad housing, somebody had a solution. People were taught how to do a rent strike: Collect the rent, hold it in escrow, and maybe picket the landlord's house. Herein lay the contradiction to the SDS slogan, "Let the people decide." If the people knew what to do, they would have done it, I always thought. The organizer always has to have an ace in the hole: he or she must come to the table with something to offer that people don't already know. Otherwise, the *negativos* prevail. After the necessary period of fretting, moaning, teeth-gnashing, and self-deprivation, somebody has to put an idea on the table. If it comes from the group, that's fine. Leadership will emerge, and the organizer will nurture it. But if the organizer can't tease that out of the people, the organizer has to be ready. Over time I learned to get people past the complaint stage, to disarm the self-doubters, and to anticipate the need to be proactive with a solution people could then discuss. Even today, I'm still learning, trying not to have "the answer" too soon.

Not everybody at NCUP was an organizer. Terry Jefferson was the first staff person recruited from the neighborhood by the students when they came east of Bergen to begin their organization. She became the office manager. She took care of administration of the office, provision of food, monitored who came and went from the office, and was on the Fund-Raising Committee. Nothing went on in NCUP without her quiet or not-so-quiet approval. Terry told me she didn't want to knock on doors and see what was on the other side. To be an organizer, you have to want to see, or at least you have to take the chance that you can cope with whatever you find once the door is open. I have seen things I didn't want to see, had to cope with people I didn't want to tolerate. But once you're inside, you're on your own to figure out how to cultivate a relationship, or figure your way out. I learned to make those judgment calls. I like being an organizer.

Betty Moss, originally from North Carolina, reminded me of a few campaigns that were legendary in NCUP: NCUP picket lines drove a store out of business for selling bad product and charging too much on credit. NCUP people went to see Mayor Addonizio on the issue of police brutality, "and he wouldn't see us." So they sat in and got arrested. And then there was the time "we went to a landlord's home in South Orange. The maid came to the door, opened it, and we turned loose some mice and roaches in his house! Then we ran."

Organizers have to protect their people, and so there was a certain amount of social work all organizers had to do. Depending on the situation, people had to be housed, fed, provided a lawyer, and clothed. There was a regular group of lawyers in Newark who were affiliated with NCUP: Len Weinglass, Mort Stavis, and Irving Solondz come to mind. Len had a house on Bleeker Street in Newark. In the front he did his lawyering, and in the back he had his home. I always thought that was cool. (Many years later, with Len in mind, I combined my home and office in Irvington, New Jersey: living quarters on the first floor, law office in the basement. My dog, Dreyfus, was free to roam in home or at the office, often to escape into the night when a visitor came and I was too slow to grab him.)

NCUP Expansion

I arrived at a time when NCUP was expanding from the South Ward to the Central Ward. I spent a lot of time at the office on 18th Avenue and Lily Street. Tom spearheaded this effort, with Phil Hutchins, the young black man from SNCC, and BJ, a local man of many talents. The people in the neighborhood decided to work on getting a stoplight because of a lot of speeding on 18th Avenue between Belmont and Bergen Streets, down and then up a hill. It was drag racing, the people said.

The office attracted a different crowd than the office on Clinton Avenue. I mostly remember men in the Central Ward, like BJ, Sampson, and his brother. Then there were Phil, Tom, and I and a few others at a demonstration for the stoplight. We blocked traffic, kind of like hit-and-run until the cops came, then back out there, on and on (see the picture on the front cover of the book). The police sergeant who showed up was more exasperated than mad, just sorry it happened on his shift. He stopped traffic and let us do our thing. I don't remember any other NCUP issues over there, just the stoplight, and my first encounter with the Central Ward Negro politicians.

Johnny Barnes came by to talk us out of the demonstration, nice suit and stingy brim hat, matching shoes. I don't know if he was Mayor Addonizio's man, or if he represented Honey Ward. Honey was the Chairman of the Democratic Party in the Central Ward and thought nothing should go on in his ward without his knowledge and approval. We called them Uncle Toms, and they called us communists. In a land where nonviolence was neither preached nor condoned by many, I just can't imagine Johnny calling BJ a communist to his face and expecting to make it back across the street. Johnny was just a homing pigeon: he came out to scout the damage, and flew back to city hall or to the ward boss. Come to think of it, they never called me or Phil "communist," or any of the black folks on the project, to my knowledge. Their antipathy was reserved for the white organizers, Tom in particular.

The guerilla campaign for the stoplight continued without arrests. And the NCUP offices were vandalized at night, either by the police or by the Negroes. The office was like a hangout for the guys, some young, some not so young. There was never a problem with who was in the office. BJ was the most good-natured enforcer I ever met. He "organized" with Phil and Tom, which meant people came to the office a lot because of BJ. BJ was unemployed, but not without means. I didn't ask him how he spent his days, or nights, or how he earned his living. If you want a movie reference for BJ, think about a black Zorba the Greek.

This was entirely different from what was going on at the other NCUP office in the South Ward, which was much more structured and had more women.

Let the People Decide, or Decide for the People?

One problem that faced NCUP throughout: where do we go when certain issues threaten to take the organization beyond protest and the organizers couldn't handle the fallout? Like police violence, which threatened to racialize the protest, since 99.9 percent of the vicious cops were white and their victims were young black males.

Also, neighborhood people who fought every day to survive had to see some victories from time to time. The speed and cost of change spiraled up because of the demands from groups like NCUP and the resistance to these demands by those in power. There was no time to bring the blocks along slowly, though conversely, time was necessary for people's development. How to resolve the seeming contradiction of the need to take time, and yet move quickly and to gain some victories?

NCUP and the War on Poverty

In 1964 the War on Poverty was created out of the momentum generated by the Civil Rights Movement. President Johnson said it would cure the nation's "problem" of poor people through a variety of social programs. The violent rebellions in places like Birmingham and Harlem in 1963 and 1964 put "poverty" on the government's fast track. The federal government looked to head off future unrest with grants for programs coming through the Office of Economic Opportunity (OEO), called the United Community Corporation (UCC) in Newark.

The OEO legislation included a phrase that sent shock waves throughout city halls around the nation: the program had to assure "maximum feasible participation of the poor." An ERAP (SDS) newsletter of November 16–23, 1964, had this to say about the "War on Poverty":

> If government support could be gotten without inviting smear and investigations, without jeopardizing SDS tax status, and without seriously diverting resources and energy to get the grant, [the] money [however dirty] should be taken.

And thus it was, NCUP entered the struggle for control of UCC, and a brand new chapter in organizing emerged in late 1964. "Development" of the people on the blocks meant learning another set of skills, which led to my further education when I arrived in the summer of 1965.

Newark's antipoverty plan adopted the model of decentralized area boards urged by Cyril Tyson, from New York's HARYOU-ACT youth employment program, who became the director of UCC. Under his vision, there would be nine area boards, each with a separate board of directors and a budget for staff and programs. NCUP decided to take over Area Board III on its home base in the South Ward.

Tom told me once that he saw the UCC as "a government for the liberals." He meant that it became the institutional staging ground for a war not so much against poverty, but between insurgents (us) and the city Democratic Party political machine (them). This meant groups like NCUP and CORE and their sometime allies, the wannabe black politicians then in disfavor with Mayor Addonizio, lined up against Addonizio's black and white minions for control of the money. I call the black politicians on our side and Addonizio's side the Black Political Class. Their personal allegiance may have changed, but their affinity for participation in the electoral process as a means to obtain deliverance never wavered.

The UCC Battles as a Training Ground

I thought my first UCC meeting in the summer of 1965 was a three-ring circus. People were jumping up all over the place, objecting to what was said, using Robert's Rules to hammer their opposition into submission. The air reeked of testosterone. Most of the verbal combat was among black men, but a few women were involved as well. The objectives of these shouting matches were very seldom enlightenment, but always about power. UCC meetings were showdowns among as many as a hundred to two hundred people, and were not for the faint of heart. I saw more black folks fighting black folks than I had ever witnessed before—a portent of things to come. When black people fight white people, as under the rule of Jim Crow, the battle lines are clear. But when black people fight each other, the issues become more muddled: ordinary people get confused and back away because the fight is around unexplained but dominant class issues or personalities.

NCUP learned about building coalitions joining other insurgents, which included members of the Black Political Class out of favor with

Mayor Addonizio. This meant that they had helped elect the mayor, but he had failed to deliver as promised, so at that point they were against him. Sides could change from motion to motion in a matter of minutes in the meetings, in a shifting game of interests. Early in the game, NCUP teamed up with other South Ward groups and elected the charismatic NCUP member Bessie Smith as chairwoman of the board in Area Board III. At the next meeting Tom offered a motion that said 51 percent of the board had to be certifiably poor, and "poor" was defined as people who made $4,000 per year or less.

Very seldom did we go into those meetings knowing for sure who would win and win what. It always depended on two things: whether we brought our people, and whether we hooked up with allies who had brought theirs. If you had the votes, I learned that the best way to proceed was to "run it," that is, "move the previous question" as soon as you could, with minimum debate. Of course, this did not sit well with the opposition, who sought to prolong the debate, hoping that some of our people would wear down from the heat or from the energy in the room (there were no air conditioners at these meetings), or that their people would drift in. Sometimes we prolonged or disrupted the meeting, waiting for our people to arrive.

I came to love this new arena. UCC meetings, and all meetings where mostly black people are the players, were like jazz improvisation. There is a theme, but once stated, everything else gets made up along the way. And everybody got a chance to play. All you had to do was raise your hand, or not raise your hand, and start talking. The speeches and the tactical moves were the solo performances of the evening. And though one might predict an ending, when and how we got to the "bridge" was anybody's guess. Some of the most brilliant oratory and stage performances I have ever seen were played out on the floor during those hot summer meetings at the UCC. And you had to be tough on your feet to withstand the verbal barrage that would come out of the blue, starting with the proverbial "Point of Order, Mr. Chairman!"

Thurman Smith was one of the best "floor men" I ever saw in action. When he started out with one of those, "I'm not very well educated, but . . ." kind of speeches, you just held on for a ride. One of Thurman's great gifts was the ability to sow the seeds of confusion and create delay. He would start out with one of his self-deprecating speeches and either divert to another topic or ask questions to which there were no answers. His comments were usually picked up or picked on by somebody who felt the need to appear important or hear himself talk, and thus the seeds were planted for prolonged discussion and resultant confusion. Ego generated most of the commentary, including deliberate personality attacks.

But during my first summer, I was definitely in the background, which was the chorus. I would join in the general din of approval or disapproval, and carry a message to some ally on the other side of the room, but I would never take the floor. I didn't have standing or the heart to jump into those arguments. But I learned my basic meeting-disruption skills, and how to "run the vote" skills from watching Thurman and Harry Wheeler, a bombastic former schoolteacher. I learned how to maneuver at these meetings, watching people play different roles: there were spokesmen, disruptors, messengers, lobbyists, appeasers, and observers. I learned the value of pre-meetings with our folks, the night before, so that everybody would be on the same page and understand his or her role. I learned that everybody couldn't be the leader. But I forgot: We didn't have leaders anyway, did we?

Sometimes victory went to them that knew the rules better than the other side. Sometimes to them that got the best crowd response. Sometimes it was the side that won the most votes. Sometimes the side that kept the vote from taking place at all. Sometimes it was the side that waited for the other team to go home, and then recall the vote. And always using Robert's Rules of Order! Poor Robert. But then again, Robert might have been very proud of the nifty moves made in his name!

The UCC, NCUP, and Black Leadership Development

Let's go back to my earlier point about the need for victory as well as political development. What victory was at stake? Jobs. And NCUP got its share of them for our members. What skills were developed? Insider skills, to buttress the outsider skills learned from the politics of confrontation that NCUP members were already so good at.

But also the UCC was a beauty contest for people who wanted to be future leaders in the city. This was the place to show your oratorical skills, your understanding and use of technical data, your people-producing skills, meeting-manipulation skills, and your willingness and understanding of the need to build coalitions. Bessie Smith became impressive to a broad constituency through positioning at UCC, but died before she realized her maximum potential. Jesse Allen was elected to the position of Central Ward Councilman in 1974. NCUP organizer George Fontaine and UCC member Jim Walker became the chief executives of the Newark Construction Trades Training Program (NCTTC), which trained hundreds of black and Latino men for construction jobs as a part of the Medical School Agreement (see chapter 7), Phil Hutchings became the national Chairman of SNCC. And Junius Williams—well, you have to wait to find out.

How far we had evolved from the mass meetings in the major centers of the South, where the enemy was outside on horseback or hidden under white sheets, chomping stogies, shotguns on hips, representing "the law" and waiting for us to come out. How different the tone of the meetings in the South, where we listened to our leaders who gave us the itinerary for that day's demonstrations, which was followed without debate or even participation in discussions. The War on Poverty was an arena where black people developed their individual voices and didn't have to wait to be led to the Promised Land. In so doing, there was often conflict, but togetherness as well. It was a high-water mark in the growth and development of the politics of the Newark black community, where the issues were about power, control over money, and ego, with the white man in the background directing his favorite Negroes to beat us insurgents to the spot. It was at the UCC that activists began an ever-shifting alliance with members of the Black Political Class to challenge Mayor Addonizio in the streets over the next five years, and ultimately for the election of the first black mayor in 1970.

NCUP's success was not without costs. Spending so much time with UCC caused some of the NCUP staff to worry about our neighborhood standing. Phil Hutchings said that the center of NCUP shifted from the NCUP office to the PAG office (Area Board III). Jesse Allen was no longer in people's houses but at the PAG office. There were new titles, and less of a sense of a neighborhood. Phil concluded that the PAG experience showed that "NCUP was better at protest than it was at administration. We could attack and demonstrate, but we were not ready to administer a federal program."

Juny on the Block

I must have done well in the eyes of whoever made decisions about my work because at some point in the summer, I got my own block assignment. I worked with Corrina Fales, a Goucher College dropout, who came to Newark from the SDS project in Chester, Pennsylvania. We worked well together.

Every day I would drive with Corrina over to the corner of Avon and Badger, in the Central Ward, about four or five blocks from the office and the action at 18th and Lily. We began knocking on doors. "Hello, I'm Junius Williams and this is Corrina Fales, and we're from the Newark Community Union Project. We're talking to people in the neighborhood about getting together to make things better for the children and for the neighborhood. Would you be interested in talking to us?" This was our invitation to join, the opening to a sermon

119

that was short and hopefully interesting enough to encourage some converts. It was a question that invited the answer "what do you have in mind?" or "yeah, things sure are bad." We hoped to talk our way into as many homes as was possible.

There were only two of us, ebony and ivory, and we stood out as strangers on the block. We walked along Avon Avenue, a busy major street with stores and houses on either side, wide enough and busy enough to be considered a boulevard. Many of you older readers know the corner of Avon and Badger. On the cover of *Life* magazine in the last week of July 1967, released at the height of the Newark Rebellion, there was a picture of the body of Joey Bass, age twelve, lying in a pool of his own blood, shot by the New Jersey State Police. This was the intersection of Avon and Badger, where Corrina and I crossed every day for at least half of the summer of '65, exactly where his body lay two years later.

There was an openness about the '60s before the Rebellion, when people were still willing to listen to two strangers coming into their lives, not talking about Jesus, not selling sewing machines. We were not cops or welfare workers, but a black man and a white woman talking about organization and "standing up for yourself." How truly amazing to feel safe enough to wander around in a new neighborhood and expect somebody to say, "Come on in, let me hear what you have to say." It was indeed a blessing to have been there and at work during those times.

People have a lot on their minds. They want somebody to be concerned about the rats and roaches and everything else on a full list of horribles that affected their quality of life. The organizer lets the people talk, but in the end, we ask for a commitment of time, because the soul cannot find heaven here on earth without first coming to a meeting. Power comes from the ability of people to come together and organize. Come to think of it, isn't this the model given us by Jesus with his twelve disciples? Wasn't Jesus always teaching and preaching and healing with the support of his organization? Jesus brought the little people continually to the front—the man at the well, the adulterer, the Roman centurion—always giving them direction on how to empower their lives. "Follow me, and I will make you fishers of men," he told his disciples. It was an invitation to join, an invitation to become more than followers, to become organizers based on Jesus's teachings. Where does the modern-day preacher get off telling the flock only about individual salvation, when Jesus himself was organized and all about organization? Don't get me started.

So a few people said they would meet with us to talk about some of the problems people faced in the neighborhood. It was as if to say, "Just maybe these people may have some answers I don't have." Or maybe they were just curious to see what ebony and ivory had to say? Or both?

After a few meetings, we got an indication of what people wanted to do. Avon Avenue, people said, was like a speedway, with people running their cars from Bergen to Belmont unimpeded by any stoplight for about four blocks. A speeding car hit at least one kid, somebody said. We talked about what people were doing on 18th Avenue, not far away, and one or two of the block folks may have decided to come over and see the demonstrations for a stoplight on 18th Avenue. The people decided that they too would take some direct action to dramatize the need for a stoplight, and that a stop sign would not be enough.

The Five-Hundred-Pound Gorilla: Race

But there was one person on the block that gave Corrina and me a problem, and that person was Billy. Billy was a young man about my age or a little older. I don't remember what he did with his time—maybe he worked, maybe he didn't. He was intelligent, well respected by some of the other people in the neighborhood, especially the ones who hung out on the block. He asked good questions, and didn't like white people. Billy told me he couldn't see working with Corrina: it was time for black people to realize that there were no trustworthy white people, that he liked the idea of fighting for a stoplight, but we were black and Corrina was white, NCUP was white. "Black people have to do it by ourselves," he proclaimed.

Race was the five-hundred-pound gorilla sitting in the living room that NCUP tried not to notice. The students understood there was racism, but their philosophy and approach left them without language to deal with its impact on people like Billy. Some of the black staff too had bought into the idea of an integrated army of the poor, and so any suggestion of separation in the movement by race was untenable.

Billy's was my first confrontation with someone who openly told me white people on the block were unacceptable, although I'm sure many more people felt the same way. Phil and I talked a lot during those days about the contradictions of having white people out on the blocks. We could make a distinction between whites on the NCUP student staff, and whites like Addonizio. But how effective were we in building up black people to fight racism while we were still relying on white organizers?

The white staff was beginning to feel the pressure as well. NCUP couldn't develop a movement on racial terms, nor were they able to corral the energy of black youth around police violence or any other issue where clearly race trumped class in formulating remedies.

I liked Corrina, and I liked NCUP. I was committed to staying with NCUP that summer, committed to playing the integration hand and not Billy's. I thought I could get him to see the value of the organization and to work around his nationalism.

The Stoplight Demonstration

After much discussion by our small group of members meeting regularly in Mrs. Niclow's house, the group decided to demonstrate for a stoplight. On the appointed day, at the appointed hour, we went out in the street with women, children, a few men, including me, and began blocking traffic on one of the busiest streets in the Central Ward.

The effect was predictable: cars backed up in both directions, as far as the eye could see. Avon is a county road and was at that time one of the main ways to get to and from the downtown from the western suburbs, particularly Irvington and beyond.

People came out to see what was happening. The cops came and the negotiations began. "Who's your leader?"

We replied, "We have no leader!" Who did they talk to? Mrs. Nicklow, her sister Mattie Murray, and me. The cops asked why we didn't go see the Mayor; these people in the cars didn't do anything to hurt us. We kept our little line of protestors thrown loosely across the street, enough to keep traffic stalled. Somebody tried to sneak through, easing his car between two folks, almost hitting them. This provoked an angry response from the crowd. "Don't you hit that woman!" somebody warned. A few more people joined, warming up to the cause and the occasion. Demonstrations can get your adrenalin running, even when you didn't come to the meetings.

Then I looked up and saw a man I had seen at the UCC meetings. Honey Ward, Central Ward Chairman of the Democratic Party, came on the scene with his lieutenant, Arthur Love. Just the look he gave us said, "You're causing me trouble in my ward." My first impression of Honey was his hard edge. The second was his self-confidence. He talked easily to the cops; he knew people on the street. Honey and Arthur Love wore those stingy brim hats so popular at the time, looking like real players. They were tougher than you wanna be!

I could see the evidence of Honey's legendary prowess as a boxer in his not-too-distant past. Here was a man not to be taken lightly. To my surprise Honey directed most of his questions and comments to me. He wanted a man to talk to, not a woman, and I was the only one around that seemed to have some authority.

I remember talking but not what I said. Generally, I must have said that the street needed a light at this corner. Too many injuries. His promise of a stop sign was not acceptable. Honey's hard eyes penetrated mine, and I held my ground, looking right back at him. He was searching for weakness, looking for an opening to take me out. Honey Ward was your old fashion Ward Boss, a street-smart politician, a product of the war to seat Irvine Turner as the first black Central Ward Councilman, a war that was won with baseball bats as well as the ability to convince and deliver voters in 1954. A few years later, he pulled another coup and took over the Chairmanship of the Democratic Party in the Central Ward, using the art and science of electing his own district leaders and getting them to the meeting, supported by those same bully boys against the Italian opposition. No, Honey wasn't about to let me, a college student, and a bunch of women embarrass him in his own ward. The only word NCUP had for him was "Uncle Tom," because he was an elected official. "Politician" and "Democrat," yes, but Honey was no Tom. We were violating some unwritten code, and if he could have gotten away with it, he would have taken us around the corner and whipped our collective butts. Stop signs seem to be what they all promised. Whether Honey could have delivered or whether he was just trying to get us off the corner is another question.

The First Black Political Class

Honey was representative of the other black folks who thought about Black Power. There were other men and women I saw that summer at UCC meetings who put Central Ward councilman Irvine Turner in office in 1954. Mrs. Larrie Stalks, Virginia Jones, Tim Still, Lorraine Hayes, and Harry Wheeler. They were smart, tough fighters, literally in some cases. Political power to them came from developing organizations to win elections. The spoils of victory? Low-level jobs in city or county government, putting somebody on welfare, a fixed parking ticket. Lest we condemn too readily, they came of age in the 1950s. In 1962, some of the original Turner organization decided to enter into a coalition with the Italians to elect Hugh Addonizio as Mayor and defeat the Irish incumbent, Mayor Leo Carlin. Others like Honey maintained relations with the Irish who controlled the Essex County government.

But in their success, their vision for power for black people was too narrow and shortsighted. It made sense in 1962 to go with Addonizio when he first ran for mayor, and support Dennis Carey, the County Democratic Chairman. But what was the plan for later on, with all those black folks spreading throughout the city, and not just in the Central Ward, where we were mostly confined when Turner first got elected? Whether they supported the Italians or the Irish, most of this Black Political Class felt threatened by our insurgent civil rights and community organization advocates because we saw a bigger picture. Were a few jobs for the present worth fighting against people like the folks in NCUP or CORE, who envisioned a future for blacks in the city with far more impact than a few jobs at city hall or at the county government?

The question became, with whom would the ordinary people align themselves? Would this vast sea of potential power join the rebels like NCUP and CORE, or the homegrown traditional leadership that came from these same mean streets? Under the vision of this Black Political Class, of which Honey played a leadership role, what role would the poor and working class play? Would they become leaders and organize to determine their own politics on a day-to-day basis, as NCUP urged people to do, or just come out and vote every once in a while, the way the Democratic Party asked them to do?

Honey's eyes showed the threat we posed, that day at the street light demonstration. At some point, he and Arthur Love left, as if to say, "We wash our hands of the matter; let the cops take your a—downtown!"

Tom Hayden

Soon after Honey left, Tom Hayden arrived on the scene and joined the picket line in the middle of Avon Avenue. That was fine. But by that time, the cops had grown tired of us, with cars backed up a mile in both directions because of our little demonstration. They told us to move or be arrested. The game plan was to hit and run: move when the cops said move, come back when they left, even if it meant another day. We discussed it earlier in our planning, and nobody wanted to get arrested.

Most of us slowly and sullenly began to move to the sidewalk. Tom and two or three other people we recognized, but who hadn't come to the meeting, stayed out there in front of the cars with drivers now blowing their horns full blast with the assurance of police intervention. Tom and the other people were handcuffed and put into the patrol car. With the cop directing traffic, things got back to normal. But Corrina, Mrs. Nicklow, Mattie Murray, and I were standing on the corner looking at each other with our mouths open, asking ourselves, "Why did Tom do that?" Or more precisely, the other two looked at Corrina and me with the unspoken question, "He's one of yours; why couldn't you control him?" We had no answer because there was none.

I looked at Billy across the street. He had been watching the whole thing. He looked disgusted, as he had every right to be. We—Tom—had sent two of his buddies to jail, needlessly, in his opinion. But the stare that Billy gave me said so much more: "You're the leader, Williams, so how come *you* didn't go to jail? You let that white boy come in here and take over. I told you they can't be trusted, and now we can't trust you either."

Every time I play that day over in my mind, I see that double accusation in Billy's eyes. I pride myself in never asking people to do something I'm not willing to do myself, and yet we asked people to take a chance with us, and I didn't pay the same price. It's not right, especially when you're looked upon as a leader.

So why didn't I stay and get arrested? It was a little bust, payable by fine. I felt myself moving back toward the middle of the intersection. But a voice inside told me to "listen to the advice you were given."

The Price of Wanting to Become a Lawyer

Earlier in 1965, when I decided to go to law school, somebody in the Southern movement told me I would have to be careful about getting arrested again until I passed the bar and became a lawyer. There is something in the lawyering process called the Character and Fitness Committee, something they don't tell you about in law school. You can spend three years, graduate at the top of the class, pass the bar exam with flying colors, but if this committee decides you are not of good character, you will not get licensed. I had the one arrest already to explain, and made up my mind to stay out jail, unless it was totally out of my control.

When I took the bar and passed it in 1969, I stood before this august committee and heard the chairman tell me I was not of good character because of the one arrest in Montgomery. I had to call Annamay Shepherd, my mentor as a law student at Legal Services. She called a very influential lawyer and politician who then used his influence to get the chairman to change his mind. The intervener convinced the chairman, "It was for a noble cause down South." I wonder what would have happened if I had that second arrest, for a stoplight at the corner of Avon and Badger, because Tom Hayden, and not the people, had a different concept of character and fitness at the moment?

After the demonstration that summer, I think I tried to talk to Billy the next day. There was no trust, no possibility of a friendship, much less a political relation. I let it go. I asked Tom why he did it, but I don't remember really challenging him. Tom was Tom, the Big Man on the Project, the project Guru, the one who brought me to Newark. I let it go, and suppressed the anger. Maybe because it was so close to the end of the summer. I never talked to Billy again. I have forgiven Tom, and we remain friends.

Tom Hayden, despite the disclaimers about "We have no leaders," was the most influential individual on the project. Barry Kalish, who opposed Tom most frequently as they vied for leadership, didn't have the same impact, as would be seen later after I left for law school. Barry and others were opposed to NCUP involvement in the George Richardson campaign for state assembly, even though George ran as the standard-bearer of an independent party, and had NCUP members as running mates for other offices on his party line on the ballot. Tom backed the community people who wanted "in." They enjoyed the idea of flexing their community muscles, believed in the electoral process, and believed they could win. Barry was more ideological in his opposition, feeling that politics, other than grassroots organizing, corrupts absolutely. Tom was more of a pragmatist, a thinker who had a vision that the main event for power in Newark would be the fight to elect a black mayor in the not-too-distant future. So why not let the people get some experience? I liked Tom's pragmatic approach merging grassroots and mainstream politics. That's what persuaded me to come to Newark in the first place—that, and his quiet delivery of his point of view. There was very little to be upset about in his delivery, and he used his way with ideas to get people thinking his way. But I sure didn't like what he did on *our* block on that day. He didn't think through all the repercussions, and Corrina and I got left holding the bag.

For days after that debacle, I felt like the Southwest Airlines commercial where the woman knocks down the medical cabinet in her date's bathroom, and the punch line reads, "Gotta Get Away?" I did indeed need to get away, and for the first time, law school was looking really good. In fact I didn't even go back to the block very much after that, unable to face the people. I felt bad for Corrina. She told me that Billy and his brother managed to take over the block organization from her after I left.

After the demonstration, there was no stoplight and no agreement to get a stop sign. Maybe we should have taken the stop sign and said to the block, "See what we have so far? It's more than you had, and we're waiting and still fighting for the light to come." But that was NCUP, and the year was 1965. It wasn't the way we did things.

What Did It Mean; What Did I Learn?

NCUP was a training ground unlike any school I ever attended. Each day offered a new set of instructions, or an opportunity to reinforce the lesson learned the day before. None of what I described above happened to me in a linear fashion. I may have been in demonstrations during the day, and at the UCC meetings that night. It was more like a continuing, spontaneous lifestyle. Work and play often merged into one, because even in the local bars or socializing on the block, we were always looking for new recruits, watching out for spies, gathering intelligence, or celebrating some conquest. I never had the lead. My most important role was to learn from it all. I became more and more conversant with the politics of confrontation, and its companion forerunner, the art of making the demand.

College gave me confidence to stand up and say what was on my mind. But NCUP gave me a new kind of confidence, as it did for the community people who didn't go to college. Once they took the first step with NCUP, they may have gotten arrested in the mayor's office, or the landlord might have gotten his rent from the judge eventually. But the protests brought respect, and knowledge of possibilities.

The experience with the battles for control of the UCC—the War on Poverty—was like a bonus. It took us in an entirely new direction from traditional protest, created a new role for community advocates like me, and connected us with new people who though they may have organized differently from the way we did, were all interested in the same thing: a citywide movement to get rid of Mayor Hugh Addonizio.

More lay ahead for NCUP, and for me. But in September 1965, it was time to go to law school.

5

BLACK POWER AND YALE LAW SCHOOL

And he looked for Justice, but saw bloodshed;
For righteousness, but heard cries of distress.

—ISAIAH 5:7

That September at Yale, in my first torts class—the law of negligence—the professor told us, "Gentlemen, I know all of you are hotshots from wherever you came, but I want you to look to your left . . . and to your right" (we did). Then he said, with a bit of merriment in his tone as he inspected each face to get a reaction, "Half of you are going to be at the bottom of the class." There was a look of absolute horror on the part of some of America's best and brightest. None of them had ever thought about that before. To get that good job at the end of the rainbow, they had to be in the top percentage of the class. But I knew what I wanted, and the Movement folks in Newark didn't care about my grades. In fact, my goal was to maintain at least a C+ average, and that in fact is what I did. "The law" was a tool for me to enhance my community-based politics. I wanted to be like Marian Wright Edelman, Charles Houston, or Thurgood Marshall. So a "Gentleman's C+" from Yale was fine. Very different from my frantic first year at Amherst.

Yale Law School was but an extension of the process I began at Amherst. I knew by then I could think and write, and so it was just a matter of adjustment. We had to learn to dissect a case: learn the facts and understand how the court applied the law to that given set of facts. This case analysis was different, and the writing style based on legalese vocabulary was a challenge.

There *were* some anxious moments as I tried to adjust to what the professors expected of me. For example, there was Contracts 1, with Professor Kessler, the iconic professor who wrote *the* book on contracts. But I couldn't understand what he was saying most of the time, so thick was his German accent. I sat in the class in a daze oh-so-many times. I read the cases and thought I understood what they meant.

I had another class in property law, taught by a younger luminary of the time, Professor Charles Reich. He taught the class based on his theory of the "new property," which included welfare payments and other federal entitlements. "All that is fine, Professor Reich," I wanted to tell him, "But when they ask me how to cure problems of 'unclear title' on the bar exam, what will I tell them?" I knew from the beginning that Yale didn't teach the law as it was interpreted literally in any one jurisdiction, as students learned in some state law schools. Generally, Yale taught broad legal principals and doctrines, how to do research, examine cases, and legal writing. We, as the "best and the brightest," were supposed to be able to go to our home jurisdictions and learn state laws and practice. I was okay with that. But Professor Reich was a little bit too indefinite for me. I already had my left-wing credentials. I came to law school to be a lawyer. Some of it was interesting, but other than the Rule in Shelley's Case and the Rule against Perpetuities, both of which are standard property-law doctrines, I don't remember what he was talking about.

Ironically, some years later I read Professor Reich's monumental best-seller, *The Greening of America.* I loved it. I wish I hadn't rejected the man off-hand earlier. Professor Reich, I apologize.

A Change of Mind

I began to see at Yale a connection to what I was doing in Newark, and the value of that work. In the summer of 1966, after my first year in law school, I worked at Essex Newark Legal Services (ENLSP). I still maintained my NCUP identity at the beginning of the summer, but I had a job as one of the first four law students hired by ENLSP. I worked out of a street-level War on Poverty community office that was the home of Area Board IV, I believe, almost on the Elizabeth-Newark city line on Frelinghuysen Avenue. My first client was a man named George Napier, a fascinating old man who walked on two canes with a dignified, lilting gait, and lived in the Otto Kretchmer Housing Projects. He was a district leader in the East Ward as well. He hadn't been paid for some work he performed, but there was no written agreement. That was enough for me. I used everything I had learned in my first year of contracts classes: express contract, implied contract, and unjust enrichment. In my first complaint, I had all three counts, plus a plea for punitive damages, in a matter worth at best a few hundred dollars. So don't tell me I wasn't a lawyer, or that I hadn't listened to Herr Kessler.

That same summer I spent time in Newark Municipal Court in support of NCUP people who were arrested and charged with something or another. I had by that time taken a semester each of criminal law and criminal procedure, and I was amazed at how laxly the cases were handled by the Municipal Court judge. Sitting there for hours, waiting for our case to be called, I saw all kinds of situations and fact patterns go by. I found myself cross-examining the witnesses in my head. One case still sticks in my mind: A man I didn't know was accused of disorderly conduct, resisting arrest, and assault on a police officer. Those are the big three charges that police use whenever they need to hide their own misconduct. Judge Narol presided that morning, at times barely awake. I could tell his mind was already made up for the prosecutor. In fact, most people were guilty before their case was called. All the defendants were black, all the lawyers and most of the court officials were white. It was Newark, 1966.

After the prosecutor finished his case on behalf of the state, the lawyer for the defense called his key witness, the defendant himself. The cop earlier had told this story about the defendant failing to stop, turning around, and taking a swing at the officer. He neglected to mention that the cop was off duty, and that the cop had shot the defendant in the head, and with a weapon other than his service revolver. Judge Narol sat straight up, and his eyes got big. Clearly something was unusual, but Judge Narol found the defendant guilty anyway, and the cop not guilty on the countercharge. I wasn't impressed with the way the lawyer handled the case. I knew already that I was a better lawyer than that, and that I wanted to be the lawyer this poor man needed to have. In my second year at Yale, I gravitated toward criminal law, civil rights, and constitutional law courses.

At some point I realized I had to take the bar exam, and I hadn't taken some of the really hard technical courses. So in my third and last year at Yale, when others in my class were chilling, I took Federal Income Tax with Boris Bittker in one semester and the Law of Bankruptcy with J. Willie Moore in the other. I mention these two gentlemen by name because they were the reigning experts who wrote the recognized books in the field, which we of course used in class.

I think I had the ability to have become a great legal scholar, but my head just wasn't there. It's not as though I was playing Frisbee or drinking with the guys or looking at TV; I just had other priorities beyond law school and purely academic pursuits. I was using the talents of analysis, speaking, and writing almost every day, but not to get good grades.

I found a new way of looking at the world, new skills that enabled me to break things down to their least common denominator—a new vocabulary for concepts I could use to explain to my friends on the block back in Newark or anywhere else. Yale offered skills worthwhile to me and my future clients, like George Napier and the unknown defendant in the Newark Court from the summer of 1966. I was glad I was at the law school, and balanced my responsibilities as a student with those in Newark, in the community in New Haven on the "Hill," as an advisor to the black undergraduates, and as writer and campus commentator in a periodical I coedited called *Harambee.* I could write with confidence as a lawyer, and as a journalist, a critic, and an advocate. I enjoyed my fluency in each language, and the interchangeability of styles.

The Hill

In my first semester at Yale, I became involved in the community with a local group in the Hill section of New Haven called the Hill Neighborhood Association, I believe, led by a man named Fred Harris. It was a group very much like NCUP in Newark, except that the leadership and membership were black. I spent two or three days a week at the office, going to meetings, and staying away from confrontations with the police as much as possible.

Most of the people were black folks, with Southern roots, as in Newark. Then there were a few Yalies like me, and one or two SNCC folks who had come up for rest and relaxation and didn't return to the South, at least for a while, like Eddie Brown, a SNCC veteran from Albany, Georgia.

The Hill Neighborhood Association eventually became the New Haven Black Panther Party. Johnny Huggins, a good friend I met there on the Hill while I was in law school, was later killed in a much publicized conflict between the Black Panther Party, and "US," Ron Karenga's cultural nationalist organization in Los Angeles. Things got uglier and uglier in New Haven, in Newark, everywhere.

I took refuge on the Hill. It soothed me to be around ordinary black people. Here was the contrast and the conflict of interest that was with me at all times: Yale Law School, and my place reserved among all that privilege, against the Hill Neighborhood Association, where black people were struggling to survive and change their world, as in Newark. The five-hundred-pound gorilla called race (and racism) preoccupied my mind more and more. Culturally, spiritually, politically, I belonged in another place, so what the hell was I doing at the Yale? I had to remind myself occasionally: take what Yale has to offer, and move on.

I didn't have time to go back and forth to Newark in my first two years, so I kept in touch by telephone. I missed Newark, especially when I heard about the third party campaign of George Richardson for state Assembly. NCUP had decided to support him after much debate. George lost the race but forced the Democratic Party to reconsider him as their candidate in future elections.

Reality at Yale

One of my friends at Yale, a black man named JR who was one or two years ahead of me, worked in the dining hall serving food and busing tables to earn his way through law school. He's now a successful lawyer in Connecticut. One day a white law student approached him after the dining hall had closed for breakfast. The guy insisted on being served—something about, "I'm only a few minutes late."

JR said, "I'm sorry, but the dining hall is closed," whereupon Jerko (not his real name, but he was a jerk) hit JR in the mouth, breaking his front tooth. Jerko didn't get expelled—probably suspended. But I do remember that he was a well-heeled young man who wore a preppy sports jacket and brown loafers without socks. I also remember staring him down in the law school, hoping he would say something so that I could get in his face. All the black guys did that, but he always looked away. I also remember that JR sued him and got a lot of money.

Then there were the Vietnam War confrontations around the television, also in the dining hall. Those of us against the war (black and white) against those for the war (mostly white). Lots of tension at the tube when the news came on—people took their war positions seriously. One day, somebody on "their" side got mad at something one of us said. He jumped out of his seat, and threw a big heavy armchair into the television set in the lounge area just off the dining hall. I guess this was his definition of due process.

When I first arrived, I was one of four black first-year students, who included Chuck Lawrence, Stan Sanders, and me. Did the admissions office at these New England exclusive schools all call each other and say, "Four blacks, please?" The next year we were joined by D'Army Bailey and Jeroyd Greene in my class. Greene (now Sa'ad El-Amin) was thrown out of Howard for protesting the Army's Vietnam recruitment effort. I don't remember why D'Army left his previous law school for Yale.

And then there was Joan Anderssen. Joan was white, and from an "Old Left" family in Los Angeles. In my dealings with SDS and other phases of the Movement, I met people with connections to various left-wing traditions connected to old-line socialism or the Communist Party. People with Old Left backgrounds were stereotypically very intense, full of themselves about their political correctness, and generally plain, with a worn-down, disheveled look. Joan was none of the above. She came to Yale with a California tan, wore short dresses, and she was fine. I couldn't help but notice. However, I was not interested in dating white women, and so we became friends.

Life for me at the law school was not pleasant socially, because most of my schoolmates, white males, all at the top of their academic games, were against or lukewarm to everything I had come to believe about politics, civil rights, life values, priorities, organizing, protests, direct action, and on and on. "Direct action" for them was asking somebody out on a date and "scoring" the first night. I didn't have very many friends. As at Amherst, I led a pretty lonely existence. I spent a lot of time on the Hill for that reason, just hanging out with the people. And I went to Newark on some holidays.

But all that changed almost overnight thanks to a debate I had with Stan Sanders, one of the black men in my class, in the hall in the law school. Stan was a graduate of Pepperdine College in Los Angeles, a Rhodes Scholar, and had an offer to try out for the Chicago Bears football team. He chose Yale Law School instead. He had been featured in *Ebony* or *Life* magazine that fall talking about the Watts riot of 1965. Stan is a great guy, but his politics were conservative compared to mine. And so we were debating whether Richmond Flowers, the attorney general of Alabama under the racist governor George Wallace, should have been invited to speak at Yale in the next week or so. Flowers was allegedly a "liberal" and he had a "right to speak," said Stan. "Besides, he might have something we need to hear, a new voice of the South," he argued.

I responded, "If he was so great, why didn't he convince white people in Alabama to let black people have the right to vote?" I'm sure I reminded him of my earlier stay in Kilby State Prison in Alabama, and the jailings, beatings, and killings endured by black and white advocates in Alabama throughout the decade, all on Flowers's watch as attorney general. "He didn't speak up until the passage of the Voting Rights Act," I reminded Stan. "He's a politician and wants all those new black voters in Alabama on his side when he runs for office." To me Flowers was a phony, and I didn't see giving the enemy a forum. "Where was he when the [stuff] hit the fan?" I demanded.

Stan and I were really going at it. It wasn't unusual to have topical debates in the hall, but very unusual seeing two black lawyers squaring off and raising their voices at each other. And so a crowd gathered, and still others came over to see what was attracting so much attention, until the hall was full of people. In the law school tradition, other people joined in the argument. They all took Stan's side. I was battling back and forth, until I realized I wasn't alone—Joan was on my side! We stood there like two gladiators, side by side, shooting them down one by one.

No one wins or loses that kind of debate, and Flowers did speak, giving us platitudes and sidestepping race as much as he could. However, he looked good to the liberals, got some headlines, and went home. But I had won something else in the process: a new respect for Joan, a new friend who shared my views, an ally, and pretty soon after, we were an item in the law school.

Joan and I were together for almost a year. We saw each other through a dry spell that was Yale Law School, mutually supportive in a school hostile to the ideas that made us who we were. Joan was invited to join the *Law Journal,* and I wasn't, with my C+ average ("What did you expect, JW?"). This tested my chauvinistic attitude, but I reconciled my relatively sparse grades against her A's by looking at the goals we both shared. And she helped me. When I didn't go to class because of my other commitments, she was generous with her notes, and gladly explained what happened in class. For some reason, the same notes she used got her A's and the highest they ever got me was a B. I wanted to say, "It's racial, man, it's racial," but then she did go to class, and kept up with the class reading on a timely basis. Again, I had to focus on my objective: discipline over emotion.

The Black Undergraduates

Discipline kept me away from black undergraduate student conflicts with the administration on campus. There was always an issue, and I spent a lot of time talking to and counseling the undergraduates. I had to pick my battles. My attitude was that if Yale left me alone to do my work on the Hill or increasingly in Newark, I would leave Yale alone. There were all kinds of sit-ins and demonstrations, especially among the younger students at the undergraduate campus. As a result of the

Civil Rights Movement demands for affirmative action, there were lots of black undergraduates at Yale College, compared to when I went to Amherst. I met with them often, went to some of their confrontations, but stayed in the background. I couldn't afford another front added to my studies and my work in the community. I wrote a campus news-letter, which addressed some of the issues on the campus. *Harambee* was originally coedited by Dick Talbot, another graduate student at Yale, until he got mad with me about something. I think we published about six editions.

The Five-Hundred-Pound Gorilla Catches Up to Me

My relation with Joan was difficult because I couldn't stand the way people looked at us and judged us—especially white men and black women. I was always ready for some insult from the men, but the look of "brother, how can you be with her" from the sisters elsewhere on campus was painful. It didn't seem to bother Joan. We didn't do much politics together on the Hill. It was assumed that was what I did, but not with her. At the law school, we were the subject of much discussion, and since she had more friends than I had, she got more information about "us."

But then national events did something to redefine our relation-ship, and my relationship with Yale, and white people in general. There was a voice that was pulling me away from everything white, everything that Amherst and Yale stood for, except the academic tools I had come to possess. It grew louder and more persistent in the year 1965, coming to a head in 1966, as the debate over race and racism grew more prominent in the national and international discourse. The call was one I already recognized. But "Black Power" would prescribe a whole new set of rules.

"Black Power"

Willie Ricks coined the phrase, but Stokely Carmichael made it famous. When James Meredith was shot by the Klan on a march in Mississippi in summer 1966, Stokely said that black people needed Black Power. At that moment, Meredith was no longer the primary subject of attention of his own march for justice. The whole country focused on a dramatic expression that had been the operational basis for some of us for a long time: "We need power for black people!"

And just like that, all things changed. "Black Power" were the two most significant words put together in the late 1960s, the most influential phrase since "Freedom Now!" In the twinkle of a sound bite on national TV, a new relationship with America was forged. For other ethnic groups, who rose to power within the American system of democracy through city hall and the two-party system, power was as American as apple pie. There was no panic, no tearing of hair, gnashing of teeth, frothing at the mouth. Those who were out were now in, and those who were in never got pushed completely out. That's how the game was played. But when black people demanded power, defining ourselves by how much power we needed, and pledged to get it on our own, all hell broke loose.

Some white people understood. Joan understood. When we came back to Yale after the summer of 1966, both of us knew our relationship was doomed. We hadn't talked that much over the summer, me in Newark and she in Los Angeles. So that September was a reunion, but by then our relationship was colored by national events. What could we do in a country so polarized by race? Neither of us wanted to hide or be hidden by the other, and so our relationship ended. We are friends today because of that decision.

Newark and National Repercussions

Tom Hayden also understood the need for black folks to do our own thing. In the Port Huron Statement in 1963 or 1964, calling for "an interracial movement of the poor," he had warned about separating the black poor from white poor and thus diluting the natural relationship they had toward each other around common economic issues. But by 1965 and certainly by 1966, he saw that white racism in the country had driven an ever-widening gulf between the two groups, making an alliance less and less likely. To his credit, he went with the flow. When Phil Hutchings asked to use the NCUP Central Ward office as the headquarters for Newark SNCC, he agreed. In essence there were two organizations operating out of the 18th Avenue office with competing ideologies but with the same people working harmoniously with each other.

In the summer of 1966, the summer of Black Power, I came back to Newark from Yale to live in an apartment on Hunterdon Avenue in the middle of NCUP-land. My friends were still my friends, black and white, students and community. The big news on the block was that a black man named Ken Gibson, an engineer who got his degree from the Newark College of Engineering had run for mayor and received 15,000 votes in May 1966, forcing a runoff between former Mayor Carlin and Mayor Addonizio. Addonizio won the runoff, but who was this man called Gibson? The inside story was that he was the surrogate for George Richardson, who planned on taking the Central Ward Council seat from Irvine Turner and then run for mayor in 1970. But George lost to Irvine Turner, even though by this time, Irvine Turner was very sick with dementia.

That summer I took a job at the Essex Newark Legal Services as a law student, and I chose to identify more with Phil and his SNCC operation on the other side of town than with NCUP. Black people had to do it ourselves.

From that time on in SNCC across the country, issues became less important than organizing around being black. Phil and BJ and Bob Fullilove (back in his hometown from his work in the South with SNCC) and a few others spent their time in the community teaching young black people that it was okay to be in resistance to "the Man, because we're black and we need to do what's necessary to get the Man off our backs." But in organizing this way, there were few definitions of issues to be resolved, and even fewer boundaries set on the kinds of resistance that could be undertaken. The most popular embodiment came from the saying by Malcolm X: "By any means necessary."

Black Power, to most white people, and some blacks, was an affirmation of violence. In actuality, self-determination and direct action were the essence of Black Power. But neither SNCC nor anybody else organizing in the ghettos was preaching nonviolence at the time. Malcolm was more on people's minds than Martin. All over the country, local Black Power groups who adapted this new form of swagger replaced the large national organizations. Even Dr. King recognized he was losing his hold on the people, asking them to suffer too much in the face of the violence that was continually perpetrated by the forces of white supremacy all over America at that time.

What was the role of white people of good will? I found a place in my own head where I could separate between white racist institutions, the white supremacists who ran them, and individual white people who believed in justice.

But what about Billy, the guy on the block at NCUP before I was ready to embrace Black Power? In Newark, for the class from which Billy came—young black males on the economic margins—racism was an everyday encounter with vicious white cops, white racist judges and other white people in power who didn't care. Hence, unlike Malcolm, who made distinctions among white people by the time of his death in February 1965, the Billys of Newark saw nothing but pain and exploitation coming from white folks of all stripes.

Ironically, it was this racism NCUP sought to eradicate by building an interracial alliance of the poor, configured to give itself a place in such a movement by focusing on the class or economic ramifications of white privilege. Race would take care of itself, the argument went, when white people and black people get together and address their common economic issues. But there was no interracial movement of the poor that amounted to anything. SDS brought enlightened black and white poor people together from time to time at conferences, but not at all in Newark, so there was no evidence to show the nationalists, no model for another kind of resolution. By 1966 in Newark, a man named Anthony Imperiale had his own version of the North Ward neighborhood association where blacks were not welcome, certainly not as equals. Whites were included in the UCC, but the advocacy shared there was with white middle-class liberals like Dean Heckel from Rutgers Law School, or the radical white students from SDS, certainly not anybody poor. And Carl Whitman, one of the original SDS students to come to Newark, who left allegedly because of a conflict over leadership with Tom, reported that organizing poor whites in nearby Hoboken was not working. Whites in positions of power and authority, like Mayor Hugh Addonizio, allowed white cops to viciously attack and kill black people, and the Newark Housing Authority moved thousands of black people through urban renewal projects.

With this kind of political landscape, who could really tell the Black Power advocates that it was morally wrong to want to pursue remedies designed by and for black people? Keeping all this in mind, something was just around the corner that prescribed the course of relations between whites and blacks in the Movement, changed my course of work at Yale the next semester, and impacted all walks of life in Newark for some time to come.

What Did It Mean; What Did I Learn?

Yale Law School was one of the hardest law schools to get into, and I am grateful the admissions office saw my potential as a lawyer. What kind of lawyer? At the time, the admissions people must have seen my interests in civil rights, and yet saw a place for me at the table. In fact, they encouraged them, by allowing me to choose the courses and my course of direction. Yale encouraged a combination of interests at that time.

But my heart belonged somewhere else. I learned skills to make me a far more useful component to the movement in Newark, or any movement anywhere. Yale (and Amherst) gave me tools to talk to my peers who would eventually run the country from private or public-sector positions of power. I learned how to talk to these practitioners of power, and others like them, and challenge them on their own terms. Law is a powerful tool to represent the people in the streets, in their inevitable conflict with the people in the suites, as most of my law school companions were destined to become. Ironically, the argument between Stan Sanders and I was a high point in my education at Yale: two black men, each taking a position in opposition to each other, both armed with the ability to digest the issues, think quickly on our feet, and attract a crowd of followers—that's what advocacy is all about. It was this combination of skills and passionate delivery I took forward with me and will use for the rest of my life. But in the context of my narrative, let us focus on the timing that brought me with this combination of ingredients to Newark in the summer of 1967.

6

THE NEWARK REBELLION

Calling out around the world
Are you ready for a brand new beat?
Summer's here and the time is right
For dancing in the street.

—MARTHA AND THE VANDELLAS,
"DANCING IN THE STREET"

Two big protests set the tone for the summer of 1967. One was called the Parker-Callahan fight. In early 1967, Addonizio urged the appointment of Councilman James T. Callahan as the secretary (business administrator) to the Board of Education. Callahan only had a high school degree. On the other hand, the NAACP, under new leadership of Sally Carroll, as well as Fred Means, the president of the Negro Educators of Newark, and the vast majority of black organizations and individuals supported Wilbur Parker, the first black certified public accountant in the state of New Jersey, and the city budget director, for the job. Even Ray Charles could see who was more qualified. But the mayor pushed ahead, and a big fight ensued.

Many community advocates signed up and spoke at the Board of Education meeting, while hundreds of us cheered them on at a meeting that lasted until 3 a.m. Black people love soulful speakers like Elaine Brodie, a large, pretty black woman who embodied the black preacher tradition whenever she spoke. I sat in the audience, a part of the "Amen" section. I was but a soldier in the army of the Lord. My time to speak was yet to come.

Because of the uproar, Addonizio backed down, and his appointed board decided to keep Arnold Hess, the man already in the job. But the damage had been done; tensions were at a fever pitch. And there was unity from across the full spectrum of the black community, so much so that the House Negroes shut up and in some cases defected to us.

And then there was the Medical School Fight, which came to an initial climax at the June 1967 "blight hearings," which, under New Jersey law, were needed to take private land through urban renewal on behalf of the New Jersey College of Medicine and Dentistry (Now the University of Medicine and Dentistry, UMDNJ). Addonizio initially offered the school two hundred acres of land in the Central Ward, which would have displaced 22,000 mostly black people. Black folks and our supporters said "Hell *no*," and flocked to a series of meetings at city hall before the Planning Board. Like Parker-Callaghan, the local leadership lined up and spoke in the City Council chamber, led by George Richardson; Jimmy Hooper, chairman of CORE; Louise Epperson; and Harry Wheeler of the Committee Against Negro and Puerto Rican Removal. Someone named Colonel Hassan from the Black Man's Liberation Army, originally from Washington, DC, provided the magic moment: one of his lieutenants snatched the record of the proceedings. There was near bedlam at the meeting. That meeting was turned out, but more meetings were scheduled to carry out the process. More and more people started coming out to see what was going to happen next, and to see if anyone could top it.

The Newark Rebellion

This was the climate and the actions that preceded July 12, 1967, when two white cops arrested cab driver John Smith within eyesight of the Fourth Precinct. Ordinarily just another night in Newark. Smith was dragged down the street in front of hundreds of people out on the street on a hot July night in front of the Hayes Homes high-rise apartments, and dragged inside the police station, where he was further beaten by seven or eight cops so badly he had to be taken to the hospital. Somebody said he was dead; others thought he was barely alive. This time, the angry crowd didn't go away. People from various organizations (CORE, UCC, NCUP, and others) tried to corral the anger of the crowd and to direct it into a march downtown for a demonstration at City Hall. Others set up a small picket line at the Fourth Precinct to capitalize on the moment to push for a police review board. But somebody made a firebomb—an empty bottle, gasoline added, a match-lit cloth wick—and threw it up against the police station.

The people had learned new concepts from the marches, demonstrations, and demands made of the power structure. "Self-determination"; "Justice." But this time they didn't listen to the leaders who urged nonviolence, and decided to settle things Old Testament style.

A Personal Account

Nineteen sixty-seven was my third summer in Newark, and I was the director of a Law Students Vista program attached to Legal Services. I was at a Black Power conference of some type in Philadelphia, driving some people back on the evening of July 12. I was switching stations, trying to get some good music to keep me awake on the New Jersey Turnpike, when a news flash held my attention, loud and clear. "There was a confrontation between police and a large number of people in the city of Newark . . . police have declared a curfew . . . police were out in force . . . caused by the beating of a black cab driver." I didn't need music anymore to keep me alert. We just had to get home. If you know the back streets as I did, the curfew didn't matter. I made it into Newark with no problem.

On the following night, I remember having three guys in the car, two of whom I barely knew, from the Central Ward near the SDS/SNCC office on 18th Avenue. We were out after curfew.

I drove up the hill on Court Street, going west toward Scudder Homes. In the background I could hear sirens. Our windows were down; it was a hot night in July. To this day I prefer my car windows down, always listening for sirens and other warning sounds in the city—you never know, do ya?

We were on a tour, checking out what the people were doing and the police response. We were almost to the corner of High Street (now Martin Luther King Boulevard) when I picked up the whirling lights of a Newark police car in my rearview mirror and the noise of a siren growing closer. They were gaining fast, clearly coming for us. There was nobody else but us on the road. Somebody in the car said, "[expletive deleted] cops!" I pulled over toward the grassy street divider in the middle of the street. The police car sped forward and angled itself in front of my car, preventing my "escape." Four cops jumped out with guns drawn, and ordered us out of my car with our hands up. We complied. Then it was, "Up against the car, mother-you-know-whats." We were alongside St. James AME Church, the street was otherwise deserted, and we knew we were in big trouble. It was the first time I looked down the wrong end of an automatic shotgun, and I felt it looking back at me as I turned and assumed the position, hands on the roof of my car, legs spread apart. Even though the pat down produced no weapons, there was something about these guys, the cops, that was very scary. It didn't look good for life ever after.

One cop ordered me to open the trunk of my car, which I did without hesitation. A popular belief among law enforcement and politicians was that the riot, when it came, would be waged by outside agitators, who would supply guns and ammunition. As if black people in Newark could do nothing for themselves! My car had Virginia license plates, since I was living between Newark, New Haven, Connecticut, and Richmond, Virginia. There was no contraband and no guns, so they should have just let us go. But there was a lot of anger in these cops, and there were no witnesses other than us. I could just feel the calculation of the moment: they were waiting for us to make a sudden move, any little thing, and were edging us on. One in particular was very nervous, pointing his gun in short vicious stabs and giving a lot of orders. Maybe moves they had used before; make the urban deer break from cover and shoot him down? Me and my guys were cool. No outbursts, expressionless faces, no eye contact with the hunter. And fortunately for us, there was a sergeant who was older and calmer. He must have seen where this was going. In the trunk of my car was a box of law books that I hadn't taken out for the summer. Maybe he was trying to stop the others, maybe he knew it would be harder to explain killing a law student, but he told them, "He's got law books in the back of the car. They're law students. Let 'em go." He had to say it more than once. He had the rank, but was he really in charge? We stayed put, silent, hands on car, weight forward, just as they had ordered. Gun-pointer made up his mind, holstered his weapon, and shotgun man followed suit. Just as quickly as these predators descended on us, they were back in the car and turning right on High Street, their lights whirling with the siren off.

I have played and replayed that story in my mind during the intervening years. What if I were a real lawyer and not a student? Then there would have been no books. Or if I had taken the books out by then, what would the sergeant have done? Was he on our side, or just smarter than they were? The sergeant valued life, I would like to believe. Actually he lied to keep us alive, telling his men all of us were law students. My companions? Hardly fit the bill, but then again, neither did I. The books gave him a prop to use. At least one of the other cops wanted a kill, and the others would have backed his play. Did they get it later that night, or later during the killing season when the federation of state and local cops rioted for real on Friday? I will never know, but always be thankful for that sergeant.

Law Student in Charge

I was out each day of the first three days of the riot, night and day. As stories of police-inflicted injuries and property damage began to flood in through the community grapevine, I marshaled my team of Vista law students, who were up to that time focused on urban renewal, as well as a team of regular Vista volunteers. As law students, we interviewed witnesses and prepared sworn affidavits for Oliver Lofton and Annamay Shepherd, the Director and Deputy Director of the Essex Newark Legal Services Project, for possible legal action against the police.

I preferred this role to that of "peacekeeper." The UCC called together several people who were active in the community to go out and calm things down. For some reason, somebody got the cops to give us billy clubs. To me, that made us cops. I never went out on those patrols. I heard there was a mixed bag of reactions. Some people threw bottles at them, at respected men like Tim Still, the president of the UCC, and George Branch, a boxer turned community caregiver. I saved my billy club, kept it nearby in case somebody broke into my house. I have it to this day. And since during the Rebellion I lived in a basement apartment shared by a SNCC man, Phil Hutchings, and since I knew the cops knew where we lived, I didn't know who might be breaking in our house. In case this sounds like puffery, an overstatement of my importance, several friends pulled my coat to how much attention I did receive. In 1968 the House Un-American Activities Committee, the same HUAC that branded so many people with the scarlet letter of "communist" back in the 1950s, convened a series of hearings to find somebody to blame for the rebellion of 1967 other than the police and the white power structure. To my initial surprise, I was on the list, guilty by association with NCUP, Tom Hayden, and Phil Hutchings. In the transcript of the hearing, Newark Police Captain Kinney gave my address as "642 High Street." Actually, the address was "624 High Street," an error in intelligence perhaps, or a typographic error that may have prevented Phil and me from getting some unexpected visitors? We mostly slept in our bedrooms on the floor, because the windows were right at ground level, vulnerable to flying glass or bullets. And we decided at some point to sleep somewhere else.

I was in the streets not to plunder but to understand and to document. Two weeks after the last shots were fired by the police, I said in my reflections:

> Violence such as was exhibited in Newark two weeks ago was purely an emotional expression. It was release; it was fun; it was in answer to a dare posed by both the city and one's comrades. Indeed, it became the thing to do.
>
> Little boys became men in the eyes of themselves and adults. The manner by which this was attained? Every mother's child had to go into a store and bring out something. I saw one youth, about six years old, enter a store which was just about empty except for paper bags. So he took the bags.... Teenagers were the main movers. Their bricks usually hit windows first; their garbage cans went usually through the windows of passing automobiles....
>
> But because people were joyful, was there no control (of emotions and actions); was there no purpose except for reckless abandon?... An old lady walked up 17th Avenue with a fishing rod in her hand; she and her spouse were returning from a full day of fishing somewhere. A child ran by, his arms full of food, dropping a loaf of bread as he passed them both. As he returned to pick up the booty, I thought she would scold him for stealing. Instead she said, "Hurry up son; get all you can get." He looked up, smiled and kept running home. They both understood that the time was ripe for taking and that there was nothing "the Man" could do

about it. [To the people involved] it was indeed a joyous occasion; one that may never occur again, so it should be taken advantage of to the fullest extent....

My reportage of a carnival-like atmosphere may be hard to accept in contemporary circumstances by those who read this book. How dare I be so glib? But I tell you, reader, only what I saw and only what I perceived. Think of me as Newark's Alexis de Tocqueville. You didn't get mad with him as he matter-of-factly described American colonialism and imperialism back in the nineteenth century, did you?

But I realize now I was wrong in some of my analysis of what I was witnessing. There was more than just emotional release. Aside from displays of bravado and release of testosterone, there was a kind of frontier justice on display that I didn't recognize at that time. The instructions from the old people to the young—get what you can while you can because things will be back to normal tomorrow. My middle-class values had no place in the mind of the older lady as she was living her revenge through that little boy. This was frontier justice. This was Old Testament justice: now was the time for an eye for that eye that had been lost long ago. Cops, merchants, all the representatives of the institutions middle-class people take for granted as good, were not seen that way by many people in the ghetto. People felt this was a time when they could strike back at those who had held them hostage and bled them dry for many years. Indeed, from their standpoint, this was justice, but destructive of the very infrastructure they needed for the lifestyle people wanted to have. Violence, destruction, is always so shortsighted.

I also remember standing on a corner across from Morton Street School with Central Ward Democratic Leader Eulis "Honey" Ward watching people run into furniture stores on Springfield Avenue and returning with sofas, chairs, lamps, and whatever, running up the steps (thirteen flights in the building) and bringing down their worn out dilapidated furniture to put it out for garbage collection the next morning. What we didn't see was the deliberate removal of credit records in just about all the stores from the file cabinets so that they would be destroyed or burned in the ensuing fires. And not all white merchants were targeted. If they had the reputation of being fair, they were spared. The problem was how to convey the message to those who only saw "white," thus making all whites fair game, to those out of the informational loop. I saw one black guy back down several black passersby in protection of his white friend who had helped him loot Sears Roebuck on Elizabeth Avenue. The few black merchants on the various commercial streets and avenues wrote "Soul Brother" on the windows or doors hoping to avoid the riotous invasion and torching. A local Chinese vendor discovered his windows had been so labeled as such on South Orange Avenue by the people from the neighborhood who were trying to protect him. How did he discover it? He heard shots and saw some police force members shooting at something. The next morning he discovered bullet holes in his shop, and the words "Soul Brother" written on his building. The combined police forces singled out stores that they concluded were black-owned for their own brand of retaliation and lawlessness. Everybody had his or her own definition of fundamental fairness.

Let's go back to my notes from 1967:

This spirit [carnival atmosphere] was there until Friday morning (the third day of the riot/Rebellion, when the National Guard and especially the state police came into town).

[Once the state police went on a rampage, and the violence seemed to have run its course after Day 5]. In essence I think people in the ghetto are scared. [Lots of people] participated in rebellion, when it was free. But on Friday the arrangement... became much more costly. Using the only means it knows anything about, force, the power structure dealt a severe blow to the spirit [of rebellion] existing prior to this time. Being in the streets was an open invitation to death; houses offered little sanctuary to high-powered bullets.

In short, people have been whipped and whipped hard. The analogy is with the child who steals a cookie and gets away with it. Feeling his oats he gives the neighborhood more goodies from the cookie jar. [Once discovered,] the wrath of the parent convinces the child for quite some time not to do it again.

[At some point,] there was a rumor that another riot was going to happen. Most people stayed inside... most people didn't want anything to do with it.

Newark is a whipped community. Force has been used effectively.

There were many stories of police excesses. The grapevine got us names and contact phone numbers of witnesses to the police crimes, and so we set up interviews with the witnesses, most of whom had never been contacted by law enforcement. And even though the rioting had stopped, we were in great danger from the cops if they found out what we were doing. Our work was painstaking, and it was hard to keep from crying at the stories we heard. Each of the twenty-six people killed had been shot by policemen from Newark, the state police, or the National Guard—a fact confirmed subsequently by the Governor's Select Committee on Civil Disorder.

Through my sources, I found and interviewed the only witness to the execution of James Rutledge by the state police inside Jo-Rae's Tavern at the corner of Bergen and Custer avenues. Two young men were in the bar looking for something that may have been overlooked in the original looting. They were surprised by the state police, and couldn't get out of the bar. They both initially hid, but Rutledge stood up, his hands in the air while the witness stayed hidden behind the broken and smashed bar. The witness recounted hearing the conversation among the state police. "Well, look what we have here... a nigga caught in the act!" Rutledge died a horrible death, shot thirty-nine times, including in the top of his head after he had fallen to the floor. Had the witness stood up, he too would have been killed, but the police were satisfied and searched no further. I converted my notes into an affidavit, as I had been taught to do by Annamay Shepherd, and gave the signed document to Oliver Lofton. Baraka found out about the slaying, and went to the funeral home and had pictures taken of the corpse. In the days that followed, pictures of the mutilated body were mimeographed on a flier and passed out in the community. Eventually I was called before the Essex County Grand Jury and asked by the assistant prosecutor, "Don't you think it was inflammatory to put pictures on a flier?"

"First of all," I told him, "I wasn't responsible for the fliers." And then I asked him, "Don't you think it was inflammatory that James Rutledge was shot thirty-nine times?" We must have eyeballed each other, but then the prosecutor let me go. Blame always rested upon us in the community, and not on the police who were allowed to riot and kill with impunity. Even with the scathing condemnation of police violence in the Riot Commission Report, no police officers or National Guard were ever prosecuted.

At the fortieth year commemoration of the Newark Rebellion in 2007, at a panel convened for commentary by Rutgers professor of history Clem Price, I heard former governor Brendan Byrne, who was the Essex County prosecutor in 1967, tell the audience of more than a hundred people gathered at the Newark Museum that he was especially bothered by the death of Jimmy Rutledge. I sat in the back of the room, and listened intently as he said, "I thought the circumstances of his death were suspicious, but we had no witnesses." I had to bolt from my seat and run out the door to keep myself from standing up and challenging that statement. Clem Price is my friend, and I didn't want to ruin his program. But there was at least one witness, *my* witness, and he was never contacted by the prosecutor or any other arm of law enforcement. And I know the authorities had all the affidavits since they were given to the Governor's Commission by Oliver Lofton, who sat on the committee. There is no statute of limitations on murder, Brendan; do you want to reopen the investigation now?

Fear

But my observations in my journal two weeks after the rebellion were off for another reason. I said Newark was suffering from the "whipped butt" syndrome, but over the weeks that followed, something else became clear. As we raised our heads after the shooting was over and the smoke from a thousand fires cleared, we realized white folks in power were afraid of us. Louise Epperson put it best, in an interview for a video documentary called *City of Promise*, a 1995 PBS production about Newark: "Before the riot, I couldn't get anybody to talk to me [about the Medical School taking all this land]. But after the riot," she said with a sly smile on her face, "Everybody wanted to talk."

Louise's experience is just one example of how things changed. This period of random violence changed everybody's life, and everybody's perspective on power in Newark. In fact, there were winners and there were losers among a cast of central players on the stage of power politics in Newark. Take a look at my ranking thus far, with a little bit of a forecast, in case you're falling asleep on my story:

Winners

LeRoi Jones/Amiri Baraka: Baraka had a national and international reputation because of his literary achievements. He was heralded as one of the fathers of the Black Arts Movement in Harlem before his return home to Newark at the end of 1965. He and his wife, Amina, organized youth and adults in the neighborhood around Shipman Street using his art as a playwright and poet. During the Rebellion, he was badly beaten by the police, falsely accused of crimes by his assailants, represented in court by one of the best criminal lawyers in the country, Ray Brown Sr., and eventually acquitted. Baraka's celebrity increased after this encounter with the police, and he made a brilliant speech at a Black Power conference in Newark just after the Rebellion. Soon thereafter, he called together the leadership of black Newark to form the United Brothers in 1968. This organization morphed into the Committee for a Unified Newark (CFUN), the primary vehicle for the election of Ken Gibson as the first black Mayor of Newark, and of a major city in the Northeast.

Anthony Imperiale: Newark's most notable white vigilante. He and his men endeared themselves to the white ethnic communities most notably in the North and West wards, the last strongholds of the remaining Italian and Irish populations, by "standing guard" at the perimeters of white neighborhoods during the Rebellion. He vowed, "If the Black Panther comes, the White Hunter will be waiting." On the strength of this challenge, in 1968 he bullied himself into a position as a vice chairman of the then new Model Cities Neighborhood Council, parlayed this into a seat on the city council, and organized his racist constituency into a successful run for the state senate as an independent. He tried to become mayor on more than one occasion, but the voting numbers were no longer there in Newark for his style of Jim Crow politics.

Ken Gibson: Gibson ran unsuccessfully for Mayor in 1966, some say as a stalking horse for then-Assemblyman George Richardson. But Ken saw the 15,000 votes he garnered in 1966 as a sign that he should run again in 1970. When the United Brothers looked for a candidate, he let it be known that he was running whether we picked him or not. Ken became our candidate, and on the momentum of the Rebellion, the Medical School Fight, and the resources put together by the leadership of the black community under CFUN, the rest is history.

Steve Adubato: with the rise of Imperiale and the fall from grace and office of Addonizio, both because of the Rebellion, there was a need for a more "moderate" Italian to fill the power vacuum in the North Ward and in the city. Adubato became the enemy of Imperiale in the years following the Rebellion, and at a tension-filled meeting at a church in the North Ward in 1970 he garnered enough votes of the predominantly Italian district leaders to become the chairman on the Democratic Party in the North Ward. He has wielded disproportionate power in the politics of Newark and Essex County ever since. A vocal foe of Black Power, he has benefited from blacks in political office far more than most black people through his well-organized North Ward Center, located in a castle in the North Ward. His politics, combined with the gullibility of black elected officials, has earned him a Lifetime Achievement, Master of the New Plantation Award from this author.

Losers

Hugh J. Addonizio: Mayor Addonizio was indicted and eventually convicted of charges related to graft and corruption. Word had it that he planned to run for governor of the state of New Jersey, but then came the Rebellion. Instead of a promotion, he was convicted, lost his election for mayor in 1970, and was sent to jail.

Larrie West Stalks and her brother Calvin West: as Director of Health and Welfare, Larrie was the highest-ranking black person in the Addonizio administration, and a most effective politician. In 1962 she was one of the architects of the coalition between blacks, Jews, and Italians to unseat the Irish candidate, Mayor Leo Carlin. And she helped engineer the election of her brother Calvin as the first black Councilman at Large in the City of Newark. But because of the Rebellion, Hugh Addonizio did not become governor and could not pass the baton to Larrie or her brother to become the first black mayor, in the style of ethnic succession. The original Black Political Class who supported Hughie was rendered temporarily moot with Addonizio's defeat, despite their awesome voter turnout skills. In the 1970s, she was elected to the countywide office of Register of Mortgages and Deeds.

Willie Wright: Willie was actually a winner and a loser. After the Rebellion the media was searching for "black leaders," and they found Willie. He told them that his organization, the United Afro-American Association, had a thousand members, and the reporters believed him. So he won access to the media from that point forward. Willie never had more than a dozen loyal followers, but was able to take over Area Board II of the UCC. When we rejected Willie as a member of the Medical School Negotiating Team, he went out of his way to sabotage everything we did from that point forward. That rates him the big L for "loser" on his forehead. He eventually became the titular head of the New Community Corporation, which successfully developed housing for low- and middle-income people in Newark for many years under the leadership of Monsignor Linder.

As you can see from my summary, the Rebellion set in motion some relationships and results with long-term consequences. And in fact, I can add one more name to the column of winners:

Junius Williams: when the *New York Times* and the *Newark Star Ledger* attended a press conference in the little one-room office of the NAPA on South Orange Avenue and Bruce Street to mark the rejuvenated commencement of the Medical School Fight with a lawsuit and an alternate plan later in 1967, I was recognized for the first time as a leader, and eventually as the architect of the winning strategy. Along with Harry Wheeler, I cochaired the Medical School Negotiating Team and eventually assumed responsibility for the implementation of half of the provisions won at the negotiating table, notably housing construction and the Model Cities citizen representation initiative. Had it not been for the Rebellion, it is doubtful the chain of events would have taken place so fluidly for me.

In the next chapter we shall begin to see how the Rebellion led to the victory in the Medical School Fight, and how coming out of the Medical School Fight there was an organizational high point for black people and our supporters, which created new opportunities to create solutions for housing and employment and helped propel us toward electoral victory with the election of Gibson in 1970. Check it out, and from this point on, the pace quickens. So pay close attention.

7

NAPA AND THE MEDICAL SCHOOL FIGHT

We build it up, and build it up, and build it up
And now it's Solid,
Solid as a rock.
That's what this love is,
That's what we got!

—ASHFORD AND SIMPSON, "SOLID"

The Rebellion and the Medical School Fight are to Black Power in Newark what Muddy Waters is to blues and Louis Armstrong is to jazz: together they are the "wheel within the wheel." They combine into one story about how the violence that no one wanted became useful in changing the power relations and led to the election of the first black mayor of a major Northeastern city—namely, Newark.

The Beginnings of NAPA

For months after the Rebellion there was a power vacuum as the stunned city, state, and federal administrations tried to figure out what to do next. And before the power structure recovered, my roommate, Phil Hutchings, and I realized there was a chance to fill that vacuum with our own vision for the community. Some of the older advocates like those in the UCC demanded more federal dollars, which was okay, but we were young, black, and wanted more than just additional antipoverty dollars.

As the heat lingered, and the afterglow of the flames still smoldered throughout the city, Phil and I planned a new organization that would organize the people who were what New York University law professor Derrick Bell called "the faces at the bottom of the well." These were the people who scared the white folks in charge. The question became, "Organize around what issues?" We chose to focus on the Medical School.

Reviving the Medical School Fight

After the Planning Board hearings in June of 1967, there was no effective organized resistance to the plan for a medical school, which would take away 150 acres of the Central Ward from the black community that was established there. The raucous protests before the Planning Board did not alter the plan. Nor did the lawsuit that focused upon insufficiencies and improprieties in the blight hearings. The final land sale was imminent. So what if there was more pushing and shoving at the final sale date? What would it have achieved?

Why was the Medical School so key? Black folks had long since spilled out of the Central Ward, living mainly in the South, West, and a portion of the North wards, mostly living in privately owned slum properties. There was a black majority in Newark, and it was no secret that all these black folks needed was organization to elect a black mayor and city council in Newark. So in the minds of the white power brokers, urban renewal should be used to clear away the slums, package cheap land for big developers, but also keep the mostly black population on the run. Since there were few places for the masses of black folks to live, they would move to another slum dwelling, which would eventually be knocked down for another urban renewal project. Landless, rootless people are no help to anybody interested in organizing for power, and so the status quo could be preserved.

What we needed was a vehicle to stop the dislocation and pull the black community together at the same time. An organization that would stop the power structure in its tracks, and save the "people's land" for neighborhoods with mixed-use development based on our needs.

Developing the Strategy

It was at this point that some of the threads of my summer legal work started coming together into a working plan of action.

I had a group of about three or four law students under the umbrella of Law Student Vistas, assigned to find ways to derail the urban removal that impacted people's lives so negatively. There were people in Newark at that time who had moved two or three times within a year because of forced dislocation.

"How do we prove that urban renewal was out of control in Newark?" we asked each other. The U.S. Supreme Court had already determined urban renewal was constitutional, so we had to show that the program as administered in Newark was outside the statutory or regulatory boundaries as prescribed in law and policy. Specifically, we examined every aspect of the way Lou Danzig had run his shop, from notice, to governmental hearings, to property acquisition, to relocation. And that's when we found the Achilles' heel of urban renewal in Newark. There was no place to put displaced people. I asked Ellsworth Morgan, the regional director of OEO (the War on Poverty), for some help. He assigned Molly Bundy, a young white woman, to document the misexperiences of people who had been displaced for Urban Renewal and highway construction.

I also read Rutgers professor George Sternlieb's books, researched by Mildred Barry Garvin, later a state assemblywoman from East Orange and a dear friend and supporter. They concluded that only 1 percent of Newark's code-conforming units were actually available to be rented on any given day, given the number of ongoing urban renewal clearance projects in 1967. The remainder, if vacant, were below the standard acceptable by the U.S. Department of Housing and Urban Development (HUD).

It was also my theory, having spoken with Professor Pat Goeters of the Yale School of Architecture and Planning during the preceding school year, that the school envisioned could be planned on far fewer than the 150 acres demanded by the Medical School officialdom at that time. We planned to make "an alternate plan" a prominent part of our organizing strategy, based on a smaller footprint for the proposed school. In a two-part call to action, I shared my thinking:

> There are three basic reasons for doing an alternate plan for the 150 acres of land:
>
> (1) The completion of an alternate plan will put the community in a much enhanced bargaining position concerning construction in the 150-acre site and in Newark in general. This is because of the additional factor of knowledge. Too many times we react to what is being done out of blindness and ignorance. It is harder to keep an informed person down. Even if the idea of total or large-scale community involvement fails, there will certainly be at least ten or twenty people who can now sit down with Danzig (NHA Director), or people from HUD or other officialdom and appraise their statements critically....
>
> An alternate plan will provide us with an opportunity to talk to people about concepts of community. Involving them in the future planning of their neighborhoods must begin by convincing people that their land is worth fighting for. Houses need replacement or rehabilitation; it is up to them to stand and fight for this housing. ("Argument for an Alternate Plan," August 15, 1967)

We are what we believe. In addition to stopping city hall, we wanted this planning process to engage people in a way that would establish a connection between people, land, and community. I wanted to go beyond protest and instill an ethic that was constructive of some concept of neighborhood. Back to the document:

> At this point, it is necessary to form a group that will best put the [legal] information amassed and make the most mileage out of it. This mileage can only be attained by recognition of the true nature of the fight: it is essentially a political struggle, and not a legal one.

We were not the first to think about the political aspect of the work. My dear friend, Louise Epperson, did the initial organizing from her house on 12th Avenue. Louise is now deceased.

In 1966 urban renewal had already taken the land or was about to do so on the north side of 12th Avenue, and she lived on the south side. She thought the bulldozer had stopped, but there they were, poised not only to take her land and the property of her neighbors, but they were planning to go all the way over to Springfield Avenue, a distance of several more blocks. She got on the phone, called a mass meeting at her house, and included "people who rented rooms" as well as the homeowners. She said the place was packed, so much so that they had to seek larger places to hold meetings. She brought in Harry Wheeler as the "coordinator," and was joined by Honey Ward and Russell Binga, one of Honey's lieutenants who had a colorful history of his own outside of politics. Louise told me how, because of her advocacy, Addonizio's people put sugar in the gasoline tank of her car, blocked her from meeting at union halls and other places, and called her into the office to try to get her to take more money for her house. "But I told him, 'what about the other people?'" She fought on, joining with George Richardson, CORE, and others who had designed and implemented the June protests just before the Rebellion in July 1967.

On My Own

In August 1967, Phil Hutchings was making ready for his transition to a national stage, to follow Rap Brown as national chairman of SNCC. So the work of creating the organization envisioned and to pull the legal and planning components together in a working strategy fell largely on me.

The name of the group became the Newark Area Planning Association, Phil's idea. We called it "NAPA" for short. We envisioned NAPA as the people's organization to take on urban renewal citywide, starting with the Medical School. We would do more than holler at demonstrations with our Black Power fists pumping the air. I was tired of demonstration after demonstration with no follow-up beyond the immediate outlet of hearing ourselves shout. We had to appeal to a larger audience with a new approach. I learned through the years in Newark that effective political organizing is always a matter of reinventing oneself as often as necessary. Here was such an opportunity: a new organization, to be housed in the community that was slated for demolition; a new set of objectives, based on the law of relocation, and an alternate plan—something around which to galvanize the community, showing the school really didn't need that much space.

The Alternate Plan

In my September 6, 1967, "Memorandum about Contemplated Strategies (MED SCHOOL)," I said, "Mike Davidson of the NAACP Legal Defense Fund is very much interested in the case from the courtroom litigation aspect. We are awaiting a decision from Jack Greenberg, his director, as to whether the Inc. Fund will get involved in a suit on our behalf."

The "Inc. Fund" was originally a part of, and the legal arm of, the NAACP, headed by Thurgood Marshall, famous for the series of cases known under the heading *Brown v. Board of Education* of Topeka, Kansas, which ultimately led to the legal undoing of Jim Crow segregation in the United States. Jack Greenberg took Marshall's place when Marshall was selected to become Solicitor General of the United States under President Johnson, on his way to become the first black man to sit on the United States Supreme Court. I met Jack Greenberg and was happy when he decided to make this the first Northern and urban non–civil rights case they would take.

When I returned to Yale in September 1967, I teamed up with Professor Pat Goeters and his classes of planning and architectural students at the Yale University School of Architecture to do the alternate plan. I told him that whatever they did, it had to be done fast, and it had to be very visual: plans, maps, and models, with lots of references to the American Medical Association standards for medical schools and teaching hospitals.

Between the Yalies and the Inc. Fund, we now had the two technical aspects of our new approach on track before we had the first meeting of NAPA in the community.

But there was a problem with my Yale connection: How was I going to do all this and still complete my last year at law school? It was September 1967. Was I going to quit law school after I had put so much time into it? I was actually enjoying the thought of becoming a lawyer. I had used the skills I learned at Yale to put forward the legal attack on the lack of replacement housing. And I used my contacts at Yale to come up with the idea and the workers for the alternate plan. I was so close to the end, almost finished with school, probably for the rest of my life. What about my parents, who had invested their hopes and money in me? I wasn't about to leave Yale.

But I wasn't about to turn away from this project. This moment was not going to wait for me to go back to school and come back next summer. This thing, which had grown to occupy so much of my time and energy, was an opportunity that had my name written all over it—and this Medical School land-grab had to be stopped. So I did the only logical thing that I could do: I decided to do both. I would stay in school, and in fact take two of the hardest courses I hadn't taken in the first two years (Bankruptcy and Federal Income Tax), and organize NAPA to fight the Medical School at the same time. Sounds logical, doesn't it?

So, first, I organized my school life to meet my needs. Fortunately I could fit all my courses in a schedule that would see me in New Haven, Connecticut, on Monday and Tuesday of each week, which would leave the rest of the week for me in Newark. Usually I left New Haven on Tuesday afternoon and made the two-hour drive back to Newark in time for "the meeting." I would study nights in Newark, which meant way into the wee hours of the morning, or I just wouldn't study at all. By then I had learned how to cram my reading, review, and test prep into the last possible moments. I still use that skill. It's like an unconscious or semiconscious clock that says, "You better get started now, 'cause this is all the time you have left!"

I usually went back to New Haven on Sunday night, Sunday being a slow day for organizing and people generally didn't call meetings. But on some Sundays, something came up in Newark, or I had to be in town on a Monday. So I juggled, arriving in New Haven in time to go to my Monday morning class. Or, I just missed class that day—and since it was no point going on Tuesday, was it, I just missed the week. I was skating on thin ice as well as juggling that whole year. I integrated my legal research and issue organizing as much as I could into my scholarship at Yale. I was on borrowed time, but I did it anyway. Sometimes you just have to do what the spirit says do. And just work to make it come out all right. I had five days a week to organize the community, rehearse the strategy with our allies, and make it happen. Simple, right?

Organizing NAPA

Before Phil left, we rounded up the first set of suspects for NAPA: college students, college dropouts, people from other organizations. Some people were waiting for the next act, hoping it was one notch above an ordinary picket line or demonstration.

I don't remember how or when we first assembled—we just came together to make NAPA a reality. I do remember riding around the area designated for the Medical School looking for office space on a main artery, and finding an abandoned storefront on the corner of South Orange Avenue and Bruce Street. It was in the heart of the area vandalized by rioters, a few blocks from the Nation of Islam Mosque and retail stores, and across the street from some stores and bars that were not destroyed during the burning season. I found the landlord and saw how bad the place was, once inside: no heat, no hot water—it was a former candy store that was just dark, cold, clammy, but located just where we needed to be. And it was cheap!

Abdullah and Jamil took over the task of fixing the place. Ab and Jamil had been in the Black Man Liberation Army briefly under the leadership of Colonel Hassan, who had disappeared just as quickly as he came to Newark. Ab was handy with hammer and saw, and fixed the heating supply and lights. It would do. But when the full force of the winter was upon us, the place was cold in the morning from when the heat went off the night before. So the only way to get warm when I first came to the office was to do like Ab and Jamil: drink some wine. The wine hit the spot, but it was cheap, sweet, and syrupy, and I wondered how long I could keep doing that before I became a hard drinker like them. Every morning I was "hittin' the bottle." Eventually they began sleeping in the back of the building and kept the heat going. I always wondered how we didn't all get killed from an explosion, but God is good. And I stopped drinking my morning breakfast and heat supply.

There was Joe Brown, Fran Henry, and Julie Saunders. Joe was a student at Rutgers. Julie Saunders was raised in Newark, and a freshman at Mount Holyoke when I was senior at Amherst. Then there was Big Hakim (Fran's little brother) and Little Hakim (smaller than Big Hakim). One day Mai Cox showed up. Add to the mix another college graduate and visual artist named Marsha Clark, now married to my friend Bob Pickett.

They didn't all arrive on the scene at the same time, and there were others who came and went: Mississippi Jackie, Anasa, Tommy, and some of the Vista students. Eventually we attracted a younger set like Roger Newman and his brother Atno, then high school students, and Arthur "Bebop" Diggs, a young man with quite a following of young men. He became my little brother, and I a member of his family.

Nobody got paid when we started, including me. My mother was still sending me little checks after the summer job was over while I was technically in law school. I don't know how I maintained two apartments, in New Haven and in Newark. Rent was cheap in both places, and I had a scholarship and loan from Yale. Maybe I saved enough from the Legal Services job. Sometimes I ate with friends in Newark. Otherwise it was lima beans and chicken wings from the little store across the street on South Orange Avenue. It was a fascinating period in my life, when I didn't even worry about money. Sometimes less is best, because the rest just comes to you.

From Amherst to Montgomery to Harlem to Newark: the politics of confrontation brought out skills I never knew I had. I realized that all of these skills were cumulative, so there I was in Newark with my own organization, with responsibility for a major undertaking with people looking to me for leadership. But I couldn't do it all by myself, and so each one of us in "the office," as we came to call NAPA headquarters, had a role to play. We were all important, each in his or her way. Without each other, there would have been no NAPA. What a wonderful experience to share, but it can't be replicated unless you go out and do it yourself.

Into the Neighborhood

In the August 15 call to action, I set forth some beliefs about the character and mission of our new organization:

> The nucleus group must be the base of a new and growing political base. The newness is meant to express and emphasize the need to include new people from the site area in the struggle. There has been no sizeable involvement or concerted effort by the residents. Legitimacy will depend upon success in involving them.
>
> The purpose of the nucleus group and the political movement that will grow up around it will be twofold: (a) it must counter the appealing image of the Medical School as put forward by state and local officialdom; (b) it must serve as a symbol of unified resistance to a Medical School on 150 acres of land. There has been opposition but the powers-that-be have seen no evidence of the community's ability to sustain a long-term effort against the Medical School.

In 1967, the NAPA area was tough to organize. This was the Central Ward, and the people were poorer than anywhere else in Newark. Unlike the homeowners and working-class tenants Louise Epperson organized on the north side of South Orange Avenue, most of the people we met on the other side hadn't heard about the Medical School and didn't care about moving because they were living day-to-day. Therefore the Medical School Fight meant nothing to them.

On the other hand, we met some people in our neighborhood whose lives were a little more stable. They didn't want to join us, but they understood the message. We became a yellow sticky as we passed through the neighborhood day to day. Organizing is building trust, and trust takes time to build. They made no commitment to us, but they kept an open mind.

Knocking on doors wasn't working. We had to try something else. Remember the kids whose natural curiosity brought them into our little office on the corner? We set up a Freedom School that was fashioned after the SNCC Freedom Schools in Mississippi and other places. Marsha taught art and tied it to African awareness. The kids came in after school from a one or two block radius, and we became known as "the group on the corner that helps the kids." It was our reason-for-being for many of the neighbors. It was our way to connect with the neighborhood and build trust. Gradually, our work with kids became the icebreaker for some of the adults. They came first out of curiosity, then to talk, to hang out, and eventually to support us in some manner. In addition, we did what other folks did in the neighborhood—we went to the local bars.

Bars and Churches

Newark in the '60s had a culture dominated by two institutions: churches and bars. I was accustomed to lots of churches, having gone to school in a section of Richmond called Church Hill. In Church Hill, there were churches on just about every other block. Newark had a similar array. There were big churches, and little storefronts. There were Methodists, Baptists, AME, COGIC, Pentecostal, and Catholic Churches, just to name a few.

But the number of bars staggered me when I first came to Newark. There were bars everywhere, and each one had its own personality. Hoops was the bar where the teachers hung out. The Owl Club was for the black politicians associated with Addonizio. Knobby's was another neighborhood bar in the Central Ward that sponsored a baseball team and served as a hangout for black politicians like George Richardson and Honey Ward, and the Bridge Club was owned by our friend Carl, who catered to the city hall wannabes and insurgents like the NAPAs. In the Clinton Hill area the SDS "students" and neighborhood staff at NCUP often hung out at the PON, on the corner of Clinton and Bergen. But usually people who went to bars had more than one in their rotation. I met Earlene Provit in a bar called the Pink Palace where she worked as part time barmaid. (Or was it the Tippin' Inn?) Earlene Provit was a community legend in the area. I heard a story about Earlene fighting five cops, and winning! Hard to believe she was still alive, but Earlene never confirmed or denied the story. Legends don't always want you to know the whole truth. I remember the first time I went into the Pink Palace. Earlene was wearing a cape made out of window draperies. Each bar had its set of groupies who revolved around a few grand personalities like Earlene. After a few moments, I knew I wanted Earlene in NAPA.

Then there was Jerry O'Neal. I remember being in the office and hearing somebody shouting, "Fire!" So whoever was in the office at that time ran with me around the corner and sure enough, there was a house ablaze. Somebody said, "There's a little boy still on the third floor!" From among the crowd of onlookers, a tall muscular guy ran into the building, up to the third floor, and then came back down to the street. Fortunately, it was just a rumor. All the people had gotten out in time, and Jerry made it back unharmed.

I knew in an instant that I had to have Jerry in NAPA. I just went up to Jerry right there, when he was talking to the people after the fire, and began to talk to him about what we were doing on the corner.

Jerry and Earlene both joined NAPA. Jerry loved the Black Panthers and Martin Luther King, and Earlene cared about the people in the neighborhood. Jerry had a string of bars that included Little Joe's Tavern, and others that overlapped Earlene's hangouts. But they needed a place and people like us to broaden and deepen that other calling in both of them, and so they immediately began coming to the office regularly. They loved the fact that we were there in the neighborhood with them every day, and that we "took care of the kids." We began to hang out with them, especially in their favorite bars, learning bar etiquette as we went along.

We learned to trust Jerry and Earlene about who to meet and who to get involved with in the neighborhood. Some people we met on our own, like John and his wife, and Lawrence and Jean Tarbeart. They both lived in separate apartments in a three-family walk-up two doors down from us on Bruce Street. They too introduced us to people who had some life and spunk. We stopped knocking on doors and hung out with Jerry and Earlene, or went over to the apartment building with Lawrence, Jean, or John. We let these introductions bring the neighborhood to us. And parties at Lawrence and Jean's were always interesting.

The Alternate Plan and the "Lawsuit"

A lot of what organizers do has to be psychological, just to get people to believe they can do it themselves, but we didn't have a lot of time to hatch that egg properly. Back to the September 1967 document:

> All too often, we who advocate change for poor black people become too content to stay on the defensive.... It will be to our advantage to be able to assert independently what we want for the community. Real legitimacy is based on concrete proposals grounded in affirmative action. An alternate plan will certainly enable the people in the neighborhood to say what should or should not be.

As it turned out, we didn't have the luxury of engagement of the neighborhood people in the making of the alternate plan.

The power brokers were gradually coming back to fill the vacuum created by the Rebellion, planning to move to the land acquisition stage for the Medical School construction by the end of 1967. I asked

Professor Pat Goeters at Yale to speed up the design. His students responded and within weeks there was an alternate plan for the College of Medicine and Dentistry designed for seventeen acres, complete with visual full-color plans, charts, and a desk model. The students had used the airspace and reduced the footprint of the buildings, all within AMA standards. It was then that we talked to the neighborhood people and citywide community advocates about the options. And we told them the reduced site size would mean more space for badly needed new housing for low-income working people, since the NHA had long since bulldozed the buildings on the land for Phase I.

The citywide constituency flocked to the alternate plan, with important elements from the earlier struggle that ended in June in chaos at the Planning Board Hearings. So in December 1967, the Committee Against Negro and Puerto Rican Removal and NAPA jointly convened a press conference at the NAPA office. Joining us was Jack Greenberg from the NAACP Legal Defense Fund, our lawyer. The *New York Times* and the *Newark Star Ledger* covered the announcement extensively, and that's all we needed to get the word out: The Medical School Fight was revitalized and headed in a new direction (see the press article in the insert). Walter Waggoner of the *New York Times* reported what I said:

> Mr. Williams also insisted that his organization was not opposed to the medical college, but only to its size and the failure to meet the needs of the community....
>
> He proposed a seventeen-acre alternative, designed, he said, by Yale architectural and planning students, which can provide all the buildings they want without moving more than one story above what they have planned....
>
> The youthful head of Newark planning group also proposed that the medical college double its capacity from the proposed 272 beds to about 500 beds and enlarge its facilities for outpatients....

"Anything coming into the black community must serve the black community," he declared. (*New York Times,* December 21,1967)

Did I sound militant in that last sentence? Was I "black enough for ya?"

NAACP Legal Defense Fund ("Inc. Fund") attorney Mike Davidson filed an administrative complaint with HUD and the Department of Health, Education, and Welfare (HEW), the two federal agencies with sign-off and funding authority for the Medical School. Mike worked tirelessly with us, providing us the additional catalyst we needed to reorganize, redirect, and rejuvenate the fight. The object was not to go to court and fight it out before judges of one kind or another. Our goal with the complaint and the alternate plan was to energize and galvanize the people, using new cards to play in an age-old struggle for control over these crucial tracts of land.

Listen to the ultimate observation in my August 15, 1967 manifesto:

Newark is known now as one of the famous riot cities. We should capitalize on this. The rebellion was caused in part by the Medical School controversy, and no one wants a return of violence.

Let no one think that just because we had an alternate plan and a good legal argument that we would have prevailed against the white power structure based on cleverness and novelty alone. We got everybody's attention because of the Rebellion, still fresh in the minds of the people who made decisions all the way up to Washington, DC. The alternate plan and the Legal Defense Fund were necessary to make use of the upheaval because otherwise we would have been isolated and marginalized for crying wolf: "There's going to be another riot if you guys don't stop." It sounded good to some people, but what happens when the next wave of violence fails to materialize, or does in fact happen and we get blamed for inciting a riot? The alternate plan and the legal suit were ways to translate the power of the moment in ways the power structure understood and had to address due to the publicity the whole thing attracted. The plan done by students at a prestigious school of architecture and planning, and a lawsuit by a noted group of lawyers, was attractive to Newark organizations like the NAACP, the Urban League, some ministers who were not clinging to the bosom of Mayor Addonizio for earthly sustenance, and organizations like the UCC, CORE, SNCC—you name 'em and we had 'em. But remember, they were not the scary ones in the coalition. It was NAPA that embodied the element the federal and state power structure feared. If the local politicians ignored us, they risked more bad publicity and possibly another insurrection. We had 'em by the you-know-what—and they had to talk.

Negotiations

First was an invitation from Governor Hughes to come talk. Hughes knew all the other players from the Committee Against Negro and Puerto Rican Removal, having dealt with them through the Democratic Party in New Jersey. I was invited to the table as the wild card, literally, in their minds. NAPA had put together a new combination of voices, combining elements of the suites (lawyers, planners, architects, professionals) with the people in the streets (Jerry, Earlene, Ab, Jamil, Phil, et al.). And the powers that be, like the governor, had never seen this before.

In any organization of which I have played a leadership role, our trump card has never been great numbers but the way we worked with neighborhood people in conjunction with professionals in suits and ties. I want the Obama generation to try to understand this concept, and use it as a real yardstick for their ability to make change. My life personifies the straddling of two cultures: the world of Amherst and Yale and the world of Newark, New Jersey. As you will see, it is the power of the streets combined with the power of the suites that is the most effective mix for making things happen. Anybody who comes to you and says "we want change," without addressing the intersection of these two powerful forces in combination, is just whistling status quo.

Splitting the Power Structure

The Feds, from an order by the Secretary of HUD, Robert Weaver himself, I was told, and his equivalent in HEW ordered their people on the ground to settle this impasse. Because of our groundwork, this thing was potentially embarrassing to then-President Johnson, and quite possibly still inflammatory. The Wood-Cohen Letter, addressed to Gov. Hughes and signed by Undersecretary Robert S. Wood of HUD and Undersecretary Wilbur J. Cohen of HEW said, among other things:

> (c) representatives of the Medical School and the City Demonstration Agency (Model Cities) should meet with neighborhood representatives to discuss neighborhood concerns and to resolve all differences. (Wood-Cohen Letter, January 10, 1968, 3)

It was that last clause that no one on our team had ever seen before coming from the Feds: *"and resolve all differences."* Guaranteeing "participation" in the War on Poverty is one thing, but telling the state to make sure they meet with us until all differences are resolved was a strong, strong mandate.

The letter went on to frame the issues to be resolved: the size of the site-to-be in accordance with consideration of a quality school but also considering the "social impact of the amount of acres removed from residential use"; that construction and operation of the Medical School bring about "an increase in scope and quality of medical services . . . offered the neighborhood"; that a relocation plan be developed that "meets the needs of the residents involved"; that "suitable plans for employment of neighborhood residents be made in construction and operation of the center"; that "opportunities for training of neighborhood residents in health fields... and a health careers program be provided"; that further "long range planning for additional educational and health care facilities" be carried out under the umbrella of the Model Cities Program.

Somebody high up the food chain read our demands and gave all the subordinates a checklist they were required to fill in with numbers and due dates. This was an incredible beginning.

The governor also wanted this Medical School matter over and behind him. He told Paul Ylivisaker, Commissioner of the Department of Community Affairs, and Ralph Dungan, Commissioner of Higher Education, to "make the city sit down with these people." And the mayor? He was on the hot seat. We heard through the grapevine that he was blamed for letting the city get out of hand: the Rebellion, the police misconduct, the taint of corruption. He was told to sit down with these people (us) and listen to what they wanted. Addonizio did so through Donald Melafronte, his Director of Community development and the man who really ran the city from behind the scenes, Lou Danzig, the head of Redevelopment at NHA, and sometimes Norm Schiff, the Newark Corporation Counsel. HUD and HEW officials were at these hearings offering "technical and other assistance," and Manny Caraballo represented Ylivisaker once we established the rhythm of the meetings.

In essence we had split the power structure. The state and federal government were willing to isolate the city government for the only time I can remember, to write them off as unclean and unworthy, and make them respect the community. Why? Because the mayor violated the rules of the game: "You can be greedy, you can even be racist. But Hughie, when black folks are in open rebellion, that means you let it get out of hand."

But Addonizio didn't roll over. Nor did the feds and the state people consider the mandate to be more than just the convening of meetings where black folks would get up, holler, complain, clap, cheer, and generally get off on Addonizio and Danzig. In the end, they would throw us a bone (less acreage, a few houses, a promise of jobs), and the Negroes would go home happy. They were in for a surprise.

The Medical School Negotiations

The first meeting was called at 1100 Raymond Boulevard, the state office building, early in January 1968. We came prepared to spell out our demands in detail, backed up by the Wood-Cohen Letter, and with data and expert testimony. We formed a nine-person negotiating team, composed of three members each from NAPA (me, Joe Brown, and Jamil) and the Committee (Louise, Harry, and I don't remember the third person), and one each from UCC (Duke Moore), Legal Services (Oliver Lofton), and the United Freedom Party, George Richardson's independent party, represented by Reverend Horace Sharper, pastor of the Abyssinian Baptist Church in Newark.

Ralph Dungan and Paul Ylivisaker immediately asked, "How do we know you people represent the community?" White people in power always want to play the "who-do-you-represent game," And of course there were all kinds of vocal, articulate people in the audience who wanted to speak and agreed with the implications of the question. Many of them were sent by the mayor to spread confusion and create doubt. Those of us on the Negotiating Committee knew these tactics. And so at our first meeting, we had to silence the opposition from within the black community by putting them in their place.

Black ministers sent by Addonizio stood up to have their say. Willie Wright demanded to be heard. Al Brown, then a law school graduate and employee at the Newark Housing Authority, asked why he couldn't speak. And every time one of them poked their heads up, Harry Wheeler or I shut them down, backed up by the two hundred or more supporters we had in the audience. We questioned their community credentials; we talked about 'em bad. "Where were you,

Mr. Johnny-Come-Lately, when the struggle first began? Where were you when the work needed to be done to research and develop these demands?" We told others that their feelings were precious and they were entitled to their opinions. But if we came there just to become engaged in a speak-out session, we would lose the opportunity to hammer home an agreement that would really benefit the community. And we would not let that happen.

We learned well from the UCC battles: never leave home without your people. Collectively, we shouted down anybody who dared challenge our authority or legitimacy to be seated at the front of the room as the Negotiating Team for the community. One by one our detractors shut up and sat down, realizing they were outnumbered and outgunned. Slowly but surely Ylivisaker and Dungan realized who they had to talk to. They smiled, genuinely impressed, and relented because they had no choice. This was a show of unity and discipline they had never seen before. We were the team to be reckoned with, exclusively.

More than Just Having Our Say

We did our homework for each negotiating session, with the help of the professionals or students either in the law student Vista program, the lawyers at the Inc. Fund, or the architecture and planning students from Yale. Over a three-month period, meeting periodically, we hammered out our demands. I visited the HUD regional office in Philadelphia and further studied their requirements for relocation, the Model Cities Program, and other aspects of urban renewal. Gus Heningburg of the Inc. Fund was well versed on employment affirmative action programs just then beginning to take root across the country. Other people looked at the issue of health care and the HEW guidelines. The Inc. Fund Administrative Complaint filed on our behalf was like a backdrop to the event, along with the Wood-Cohen letter. And we had the image of that nameless and faceless brother with a brick standing behind us at each session. We were on a roll.

In addition to the Medical School project, there were fourteen urban renewal projects underway, a code enforcement program, and an extensive highway system (routes 280 and 78 under construction, and the proposed Route 75). So we demanded fifty-four acres of vacant urban renewal land designated for the community to be used for subsidized affordable housing. We told them the state and federal government had to pay for it, but it was to be developed by local nonprofits, with a high percentage of the apartments with four and five bedrooms. And we knew where all the vacant land was in the city.

With respect to employment on the construction site, we knew this was going to be a union job, and we knew there were few and in some cases no blacks or Hispanics in some of the construction locals. The laborers had their own black local, but the skilled crafts unions like the steelworkers had none at all. So the contractors chosen for the job would say, "We can't find any qualified minorities, and we have to use the men in the various locals." We therefore demanded that there be a state-sponsored skills training program that would prepare apprentices for the job, and that the skilled minority journeymen have access to the jobs with the reward of a union book once they reached the union standards for experience on the job. And we demanded that there be a Review Council democratically inclusive of all the stakeholders (unions, med school officials, and state, community, and contractors representatives) to iron out problems and monitor progress of placement on the job. We had done our homework, with the help of Gus Heningburg, then of the Inc. Fund, and Mike Davidson. We knew about the Philadelphia Plan and all the other attempts to desegregate the workforce around the country. The Philadelphia Plan called for use of minority workers on publicly financed construction jobs, and it was the result of demonstrations in that city, led by the NAACP and other groups. In short, we were prepared and determined that ours would be structured to succeed, unlike all the predecessors.

The status of health care was another issue. The black community believed that the school was coming to practice only experimental medicine. Martland Hospital (the city hospital where all the poor people were sent) had a dismal track record. The plan for the Medical School would have little impact to upgrade the health of the general community. We insisted that the new Medical School assume the duty of dispensing health care for the people of Newark. We projected a Health Council to be formed to monitor success in treatment, and in training for jobs once the facility was in operation.

Harry Wheeler and I did most of the talking. Most of it was statement of demand, response from the state or city, reply from us, the Negotiating Team with our support group, which may have included additional technical or professional witnesses. Then by mutual agreement, we temporarily adjourned, and allowed time for deliberation. At the next meeting, which may have taken a week or more to reconvene, there was another offer made by the state, further discussion, and then some decision by the powers that be, oft times to say, "We'll come back to that one." We conferred in between meetings as well, worked with our experts, and came back with a new demand or acceptance of what they offered.

I learned a lot from Harry, but I was on top of the technical side right from the beginning, and so he had to run to catch up. Every morning before one of our negotiating sessions, at about 7 a.m., he would call me to find out what we were going to put on the table that day. Harry was a quick study, but why study at all if you had Junius to tell you what to do at 7 a.m.? Harry then would be the first out of the box with our demand and the color commentary to follow, all of which I had supplied for him. And, of course, the press ate it all up, especially since Harry knew how to feed it to them in bite sizes they thoroughly enjoyed.

For a while, Harry was getting front page and I was getting page seventeen in the two daily papers. But "My momma and daddy didn't raise no fool," I thought to myself. Sometimes those morning calls from Harry didn't get answered, or when they did, I saved enough for me—and sometimes I spoke first. And I learned to talk in short, succinct statements, instead of long rambling sentences. Oh, yes, I learned a helluva lot during those three months of negotiation, lessons I still use today.

The community people who came, regularly or only sometimes, were impressed. We had the information, and we handled it well. It was like a big court case, and the sides seemed equally prepared. The community mostly sat quietly and enjoyed what they saw: a group of nine black people, eight men and one woman, working together, led by two black men, but with ample opportunity for all on the Negotiating Team to say what was planned for the evening. And they enjoyed the way we hit Melafronte and Danzig because it had never been done like that before. And we punched hard, to the delight of our constituents. Tempers flared early and often, but there was plenty of room for humor as well, though oft times it was sarcastic and cutting. Lou Danzig, the director of the Housing Authority, was my favorite target. Taken from the transcript of the hearing, I said:

> For those of you new in the session, you are getting indoctrinated in the whole process. Number one, you can't talk because Mr. Danzig talks. Number two, he has been successful in making something that is very simple into a confused mirage. [We say] fifty-four acres of land is necessary to house the people that are going to be dislocated, and somebody is going to have to find that land. It is just like that. Until that happens, there shall be no Medical School.

The state reps were getting a lesson they didn't expect to receive, and Lou Danzig and Don Melafronte were always on the defensive.

Because we had done the homework, we all enjoyed popping Danzig and Melafronte upside their bald heads (figuratively, of course).

Then there was Dr. Cadmus, the president of the College of Medicine and Dentistry. He wanted a medical school of golf-course proportions, and a teaching hospital used "primarily for research." He envisioned his physicians doing heart replacement surgery, not lancing boils on somebody's black behind. Our coup de grâce with him was in arguing about the standards for space allocation: he had been the chairman of the American Medical Association committee that promulgated the construction standards for new hospitals that we used for the alternate plan. "How ya gonna argue against your own standards, my man," I laughingly told him on one occasion off the record.

The Medical School Agreements

On or about March 15, 1968, we reached the substantial agreement that:

- The Medical School acreage was reduced from 150 to 57.9 acres.
- The community was entitled to sixty-three acres of specific tracts of vacant urban renewal land around the city for development of low-income housing featuring medium-rise housing for small families and low-rise apartments (four and five bedrooms) for large families to be subsidized by HUD under one of its programs. A Housing Council would be set up to determine which community-based sponsors would receive parcels of land, and the Newark Housing Authority agreed to convey land to these groups.
- The workforce of the Medical School would include one-third of the journeymen and one-half of the apprentices as black and Puerto Ricans. There would be two groups established: a training group to train individuals in skilled construction trades, and a Review Council to insure compliance with this agreement on the site, composed of unions, contractors, and state, city and community representatives.

- The Medical School would upgrade the health services available to the community by taking responsibility of "Martland Meat Market," as local residents knew the city hospital. In fact Martland was to go out of business, and all medicine would be practiced from the new facility. Community medicine was to be a priority.

- The community would be the majority stakeholders in a Health Review Council to monitor the quality of health care and an affirmative action job training program for blacks and Latinos in the allied health professions.

- Addonizio was ordered to disband the Model Cities Citizen Advisory Board, which included handpicked supporters of the Addonizio administration, to be replaced by a body in an election conducted essentially by the community. Also, the new Model Neighborhood Council would have joint veto power with the City of Newark over any Model Cities proposal that was to be sent to HUD for funding. (I know of no other such arrangement in the country.)

- The state would assure that demolition and construction on the main forty-six-acre site would not proceed until there were adequate replacement dwellings found for the families that still had to be moved. Tenants would be given rent supplements. A Relocation Review Board would be set up to review progress and offer residents a place to make complaints.

Everybody cheered! Well, almost everybody. Addonizio was mad; Lou Danzig had been publicly spanked, and he didn't like that. Cadmus saw his dream go up in smoke (no pun intended). And some of the folks in my organization, NAPA, like Jamil and Abdullah, were not happy. I had been very careful to bring everybody at NAPA up to date on what we were doing. Jamil was on the Negotiating Team, as were Joe Brown and I, from NAPA. Our little band was in attendance at just about all the sessions, and generally they had been briefed on what the Negotiating Team would try to accomplish on any given night.

But to some, 57.9 acres was too much land to concede, even balanced against the commitment of 63 vacant acres for construction of housing.

But the Medical School Agreements were the talk of the town. Those who were there sang the praises of the Negotiating Team: "Y'all stuck it to the Man," we heard quite frequently at the Bridge Club. Most people who demonstrated or picketed on one issue or another in Newark during the 1960s never got a chance to see the city fathers on the defensive, as we accomplished during these negotiations.

But having the agreements on paper was one thing. Making them actually happen is a part of the rest of my story. We had the skills and the knowhow to form an organized body of resistance to create the documents that became known as the Medical School Agreements. But without the memory of the destructiveness of the Rebellion, we would not have had the strength to get as much as we did. I didn't know it at the time of celebration, but I was in for many more battles that shaped my perceptions of people for years to come, and helped refine what Black Power was to be about, for me and for the community of Newark. In retrospect, it was my introduction to a combination I have used successfully for a long time: "Those who control the streets, but know how to use the technical information usually available only to those who occupy the suites, win!"

The author's parents and siblings.
From left: sister, Connie; the author; brother, Maurice Cameron;
brother, John; father, Maurice; mother, Bernyce Williams (1946)

Armstrong High School boys' tennis team: Thurman Gordon,
John Lewis, the author, John Williams (1960)

Name: WILLIAMS, JUNIUS, C/M
DOB 12-23-43, 6', 168 lbs., brown eyes,
black hair.
Address: 2713 Barton Avenue, Richmond,
Virginia.
Occ.: Student, Amherst College, Amherst,
Massachusetts.
Arrest: 3-18-65, Failure to obey lawful
police order. Montgomery Police No. 125327
Organization:
Associates:

Montgomery, Alabama, police photo taken at the author's arrest
during SNCC's "Battle of Montgomery" for voter rights (1965)

Newark Medical College Is Protested

By WALTER H. WAGGONER
Special to The New York Times

NEWARK, Dec. 20 — The N.A.A.C.P. Legal Defense and Educational Fund protested today to the Federal Department of Housing and Urban Development against the location of a 150-acre State Medical College in a largely Negro area of Newark.

The New York-based fund, which is independent of the National Association for the Advancement of Colored People, entered the long-standing dispute on behalf of some Negro residents and two organizations formed to combat a medical college of that size in the blighted Central Ward.

The administrative complaint, directed to Robert Weaver, Secretary of Housing and Urban Development, did not oppose the location of a medical college in the area. It argued, however, that it should be "reasonably sized," designed to meet the health needs of the city and planned together with "a positive program to build housing for those it will displace."

Jack Greenberg, director-counsel of the fund, told a news conference that the complaint, designed to exhaust efforts for "administrative relief," would be the last step before court action would be taken.

Harry L. Wheeler, a Negro schoolteacher and director of the Committee Against Negro and Puerto Rican Removal, one of the protesting organizations, also told the news conference:

"For once in this city, the black people are going to stop the power structure from enforcing its will on the black community."

Junius Williams, a Yale law student who heads the recently formed Newark Area Planning Association, another protesting group, said that the effort to get 150 acres in the Negro community was "a land grab" comparable to what happened to the Indians when they were deprived of the land and their one source of wealth.

"The black people cannot slide out of their control that which they can have just by sitting on," he said. "If we are shuffled around, we are rootless and then we are controlled."

Mr. Williams also insisted that his organization was not opposed to the medical college, but only to its size and the failure to meet the needs of the community.

He proposed a 17-acre alternative, designed, he said, by Yale architectural and planning students, which "can provide all the buildings they want without going more than one story above what they have planned."

The youthful head of the Newark planning group also proposed that the medical college double its capacity from the proposed 272 beds to about 500 beds and enlarge its facilities for outpatients.

"Anything coming into the black community must serve the black community," he declared.

NEW YORK, N.Y.
TIMES

D. 767,239   S. 1,473,981
NEW YORK CITY METROPOLITAN AREA

DEC 21 1967

(l. to r.) Junius Williams, Jack Greenberg, Harry L. Wheeler

Reprinted compliments of

News article and photograph of the launch of the second round fight against the Newark College of Medicine and Dentistry by NAPA and the Committee Against Negro and Puerto Rican Removal. Seated from left: the author, Director of NAPA; Atty. Jack Greenberg, Director and General Counsel of the NAACP Legal Defense Fund; Harry Wheeler, spokesman for the Committee (1967)

Flier used by the author's community organization,
Newark Area Planning Association (NAPA),
to gain support for the campaign against Route 75
in Newark (1968)

The author as Director of NAPA, Newark (1968)

The author and Tom Hayden of the Students for a Democratic Society (SDS) and
the Newark Community Union Project (NCUP) at a street demonstration (1965)

The author
as a young Newark
attorney (1972)

The author as President of the National Bar Association at the annual convention
in Los Angeles (1979)

The author as Model Cities Director explaining a planning document
to Mayor Kenneth Gibson in the Mayor's office (1971)

The author with U.N. Ambassador Andrew Young at the NBA Convention,
Dallas, Texas (1980)

COMMUNITY RALLIES TO SUPPORT JUNIUS WILLIAMS

Supporters of Junius Williams rally for justice.

Community members, senior citizens, church groups, Newark parents and city workers, including NTU, are rallying to support Attorney Junius Williams.

Mr. Williams was recently ousted as Director of the Essex-Newark Legal Services (ENLS) project. He has charged that political interference by Mayor Kenneth A. Gibson is behind his removal.

Further, Atttorney Williams charges that his ouster as Legal Services Director was promoted by the Gibson administration because of his involvement in the recent school board election controversy.

Mr. Williams brought suit on behalf of Newark voters to overturn Supt. Columbus Salley's refusal to seat two elected Board Members, Rev. Oliver Brown and Mr. Edgar Brown. This suit was successful.

Newark community members praise Junius Williams' dedicated work on behalf of the city's poor and needy citizens.

"We are all in bad shape when poor people lose a defender like Junius Williams!" they state.

"When they attack Junius Williams, they attack us all!"

Rally to support the author after a tie vote of the Legal Services Board denied him a contract extension (1984)

Photo by Risasi Dais

The author with Khalilah Ali, former wife of Muhammad Ali, and Amiri Baraka at a Baraka house party in the late 1980s.

THE BLACK BUSINESS
ASSOCIATION OF
AMHERST COLLEGE
PRESENTS
JUNIUS WILLIAMS, ESQ.
LECTURE ON
ECONOMIC
SELF-DETERMINATION

BE   THERE

CHARLES DREW HOUSE
TUESDAY, 7:30 PM

Poster announcing the author's speech at his alma mater,
Amherst College, in the early 1980s

Opposite: The author's supporters prematurely
celebrate his contract extension
as Legal Services Director (1984)

Vote spurs controversy on chief of Essex-Newark Legal Services

By JASON JETT

In a contested action that remains to be certified, the Essex-Newark Legal Services board last night voted 13-12 to approve a one-year contract renewal for its executive director.

Immediately after the tally, however, an absent trustee cast a vote by phone that tied the result and placed the contract renewal in jeopardy.

The prearranged conference phone call, supervised by board of trustees president Jacquelyn Rucker, came at the conclusion of a disorderly, highly charged four-hour meeting in the ENSL headquarters in Newark.

The propriety of the phone vote was quickly challenged by Executive Director Junius Williams and numerous members of community groups that supported his contract renewal.

"As far as I am concerned, the vote is 13-12 and I have a contract," Williams maintained prior to adjournment of the raucous session. "As far as I am concerned, the vote stands and will stand up in court."

Several trustees and numerous supporters of Williams charged that if the board accepts the conference call vote, cast by board member Susan Green who was absent in observance of the Jewish New Year, then all absent board members should be allowed to vote. Twenty-five of the board's 30 members attended the meeting.

Defending the vote by phone, board president Rucker asserted that arrangements for it had been announced and accepted by trustees prior to the meeting.

In addition to citing the tie vote, which in effect would be a rejection of Williams' contract renewal, dissenting trustees charged that both the motion on the contract and the vote violated board rules of procedure.

Lucas Phillips, a member of the board's personnel committee, asserted that the motion to renew Williams' contract was improperly introduced. Following the meeting, he said the mover of the motion, board secretary Gerald Jarrett, "did not vote on the presiding side on the issue in the board's previous meeting" in August as required by board by-laws.

In that Aug. 2 vote, the board rejected the renewal of Williams' contract in a 12-12 vote.

Phillips said the introduction of the motion by Jarrett and the vote on the contract both were "illegal." He said the board will schedule a special meeting for next week to discuss "contract procedures for the board's next executive director."

Politicking for the contract renewal vote dominated last night's meeting, and the intense, lengthy discussions and debates on the issue made it apparent the matter has been prominent among board trustees for some time.

The meeting began with the unopposed seating of Edith Garcia as a trustee representing the Hispanic Community Coalition, one of 10 community groups represented on the 30-member board. She voted for renewing Williams' contract.

Division among trustees arose when three community group directors attempted to switch trustees for the vote in an effort to ensure that their representatives would vote for Williams.

A motion to seat new representatives of the Newark chapter of the National Association for the Advancement of Colored People, the Newark Coalition for Neighborhoods and the United Community Corporation, failed 14-10.

The meeting ended in disorder and confusion, with Williams and his supporters maintaining the 13-12 contract renewal vote was final. They said legal action would be taken if the call-in vote that tied the result is honored or if other efforts are made to deny renewal of the contract.

Meanwhile, Phillips and other dissenting trustees contended the contract renewal had been rejected and that a new executive director will be sought.

Williams, a 1982 Newark mayoral candidate, was named executive director of the ENSL last October. His contract is due to expire Oct. 1.

According to Phillips, Williams' contract renewal is being opposed because of administrative shortcomings in running the project.

Phillips cited a list of "problems," including unchecked attorney attrition, lax financial recordkeeping and poor staff morale.

He charged that Williams has a lack of communication with and respect for trustees and staffers and charged that Williams' involvement on behalf of Newark school board members Edgar Brown and Rev. Oliver Brown in their suit to be seated on the Board of Education after the April election victories jeopardized the agency's federal funding.

He charged that Williams acted improperly and without board authorization in the case by becoming involved before eligible clients were found and in representing a municipal employe.

Several public officials and residents spoke on the contract renewal issue prior to the vote.

Jacquelyn Rucker, president of the board of trustees of the Essex-Newark Legal Services Inc., speaks at the meeting as Junius Williams, left, executive director, listens

Photo by Mark Abraham

The author with his daughters and mother at an NBA
Convention. Seated: Camille and Bernyce Williams.
Standing: the author and Junea (1988)

The author playing his blues harmonica with Bo Diddley, Jr.,
at the first Bika's Blues Festival in Newark (1989)

"Return To The Source," the author's singing group.
Back row: Arnie Parker, Karen Ferdinand, Anthony Jackson, Jackie Jones, the author. Kneeling: Joe Scott, Janet Van Kline (1990)

Junius Williams and his brother, John B. Williams
in San Francisco (2003)

The author with his wife Antoinette Ellis-Williams and two sons,
Junius and Che (2000)

THE magazine for the guy who's good at being a dad!

FATHER OF THE YEAR

SPECIAL DAD'S DAY EDITION!

Date of issue: June 17, 2007

Junius W. W...
#1 Dad in the...
We Love You D...

EVERYTHING YOU EVER WANTED TO KNOW ABOUT BEING A FATHER BUT WERE AFRAID TO ASK

Top ten reasons my family thinks I'M THE BEST!

The author surrounded by his children on a mock magazine cover,
presented on Father's Day.
Camille, the author, Che (behind), Junius, Junea (2002)

The author on the steps of City Hall, Newark (2011)

Photo by Tobias Truvillion

8

NAPA AND THE GROWTH OF COMMUNITY POWER

Uh! Your bad self!
Say it loud! I'm black and I'm proud!

—JAMES BROWN, "SAY IT LOUD"

Much of the growth of NAPA took place after the Medical School Agreements. We grew because of reputation. How many people get to shout down familiar figures from city hall, as we did in the Medical School negotiations? How many people win an agreement that provides the promise of land and jobs? Our reputation took hold and spread through the community grapevine beyond our little office stronghold on the corner of South Orange Avenue and Bruce Street. And reputation carries a lot of weight in Newark.

In our neighborhood, the primary institution for carrying the word about NAPA, meeting new people and planting seeds of acceptance, was the local bars. In addition to the four bars I already named, within a two- or three-block radius of the office there were at least three other bars. But the Jive Shack became our point of mutual departure, given Jerry's and Earlene's preferences. There was an etiquette I learned from traveling the circuit among Tippin' Inn, Lil Joe's, the Pink Panther, and the Jive Shack.

Bar etiquette says that if someone who knows you offers to buy you a drink, you have to accept it. Often it was somebody who liked what we were doing. Sometimes a big spender would order a round for all of us, usually trying to impress some of the women on our staff or some of the other women attracted to us because we were good company. Women appreciated that we weren't always hitting on them, generally respected them, and sometimes respected what they had to say. We attracted some fine women, staff, and those who were curious, and in bar culture, the conversation between a man and a woman is usually opened with a drink. Our ladies learned that if you accepted a drink, you were obliged at least to have a conversation, and since we were organizing, they had to accept the drink. That's why a lot of the middle-class student types didn't hang with us, but the neighborhood women could hang tough. We had to get our women out of some tight spots on occasion. Somebody went too far, and it had to be done with tact and respect. We didn't want anybody mad with us because one of our ladies was called a "teaser."

And the music: I look back now in amazement at what we took for granted. In the neighborhood bars there were jukeboxes filled with the latest R&B hits of the day, two songs for a quarter. James Brown, Gladys Knight, The Temptations, Marvin Gaye, Ike and Tina Turner, the Dells, the Dramatics. And the songs often went back to some oldies but goodies like Shep and the Limelighters and Mary Wells from the late '50s and early '60s. We were surrounded by this music at all times, and took it for granted. Riding in the car, in the office, at somebody's house, or in my apartment, supplemented by jazz when I wanted a change. This was the source of American music, much copied, recreated, and forgotten the next month as another Top 10 list would ease its way into the public consciousness, never straying far from its bluesy, soulful, and funky roots. I listen now to what has been homogenized and pasteurized by the record industry, dumbed-down, symbolized by the most popular show on television, *American Idol*, and I'm so glad I got to experience good music. The roots of black music run deep, but now you have to search hard to find it. Not so in the days of bar culture throughout Newark, New Jersey, and everywhere else in the '60s and '70s. Black music at its peak of universal appeal. Music to sooth and satisfy. Music that advanced the narrative.

Skill Acquisition

I learned to watch people in different situations, to see what they're all about, to read not what they do or say but the inside of their heads. My people-watching started back with NCUP and was brought to a science with NAPA in those social settings. I studied strengths and weaknesses, awareness and self-confidence levels; self-control and anger management. I wanted you mad at conditions but able to control it so that it could be channeled in the right direction. I watched for hang-ups, bad habits, truthfulness, how people handled pressure. Eventually, I watched for dependability, patience to blend in and be apart, willingness to play the role that needed to be played at a given time. All this provided an index for growth potential, and the person's potential role in organization.

As NAPA grew, we offered people a chance to grow by discovering who they were based on their potential. Jerry and Earlene took on more and more responsibility. They went with me to meetings, and Jerry became my personal security. In the office, Earlene was the disciplinarian with the kids, helping Marsha, who couldn't have done it alone. Marsha was a talented art teacher, not an organizer, and was content to work with the kids. Mai Cox had an interesting name with an interesting derivation, which she told me about but I forgot. She knew how to cook, with simple implements and ingredients, and she loved to fix us food. In fact, where did you cook for us, Mai? Julie, Joe Brown, and the other ex-college types were always ready for the front line. Julie had great office-management skills. Joe Brown started out as "cute little Joe Brown," but with the confidence he gained through NAPA, he became my deputy director and eventually became the president of the Black Organization of Students (BOS). Abdullah fixed things, and Jamil hung out with Ab most of the time. "Ab," as he liked to be called, was a jack-of-all-trades when it came to fixing things, self-taught from the school of hard knocks. My last memory of him was over at the lake in Weequahic Park, coming out of his beat-up car with a fishing pole and a bucket. Earlene's mother, Florence Jackson, who I affectionately call "Ma," didn't come to the meetings, but her family was on call when needed. Earlene had four brothers and one sister. Didn't "nobody mess with the Jacksons."

Alliances

NAPA also grew because we helped other organizations. In 1968 we formed an alliance with the recently formed Welfare Rights Organization, the Newark base in a national network created by George Wiley. In Newark, NAPA went with them on their welfare office "raids." If a woman didn't get the response she needed from the welfare office, we accompanied "the Welfare Mamas" to the office, occasionally taking it over until a mother got her check.

Through Joe Brown, we had a pipeline into the Black Student Movement at Rutgers Newark, and helped guard their flank when they took over Conklin Hall in 1969 to force Rutgers to admit more black students and hire more black faculty. We slept overnight in Ackerson Hall, across the street from Conklin Hall.

After negotiations, Rutgers created an affirmative action plan that was one of the best in the nation, with a goal of 25 percent black and Latino students in each entering freshman class. Rutgers Law School by the 1970s produced the third-largest number of black law school graduates, next to Howard and Texas Southern, traditionally black law schools.

In return, the Welfare Rights members, BOS, and other various and sundry folks would accompany NAPA to fashion new solutions to enforce the Medical School agreements and constantly challenged

Lou Danzig at the Housing Authority. Sometimes we had to take over NHA in protest against their relocation policies in other urban renewal and highway projects, in similar manner as we dealt with the bureaucrats at the welfare offices. I got to know Lou Danzig very well and, I think, hastened him into a timely retirement. Of all the adversaries I had, Lou was one of the most gracious, and deadly.

Lou sent one of his Negro minions, T.T., over to see me one day. He told me, "Lou Danzig wants to know if you would like to have your office refurnished?" I looked at this guy and smiled, because T.T. was a well-known but likable "Tom," because we were located in a cold-water storefront former candy store, and so what the hell did we need with an "office makeover," and smiled because Danzig was trying to buy me off at bargain-store prices. I just told him, "No, not interested," and after a while, T.T. left. No more offers from Lou Danzig or the rest of them.

NAPA Soul Sessions

In addition to the bars in Napaland, every Thursday evening we would gather our friends and supporters from all over Newark and places like East Orange, organizational members from BOS, the Welfare Rights Organization, the folks from the Medical School Fight team (like Gus Heningburg and members of his new staff in something called the Greater Newark Urban Coalition), our bar buddies and individuals in the neighborhood who had their children in our Freedom School, and anybody else people chose to bring. I remember Donald Tucker and his folks brought up African drums and other people brought in other instruments. It was time for the weekly "NAPA Soul Session," brought to you free of charge by the Militants of Newark!

We laughed, talked about our accomplishments, sang freedom songs and the latest R&B hits, danced, made plans for coming events—all made possible in one swirling seamless string of events, lubricated by a drink called "MF" (yes, folks, it's the word you think it is—and we liked using the full name!).

MF was made in a metal garbage can we kept assiduously clean and ready for next Thursday's incantation. MF had a Kool-Aid base, into which was added scotch, rum, bourbon, beer, gin—anything anybody was able to get their hands on. It was thoroughly mixed, and ice was added. How did it get its name, you reasonably inquire? Because after several glasses, people came back with their cup in their hand and a smile on their face, ready for more, perhaps fooled by the sweetness and subtle pace at which our brew tugged at their senses and dulled their central nervous systems. They boldly proclaimed, "That drink sure was a m— f—." Hence the name MF. Lots of people came to the NAPA Soul Sessions.

Visitors

One day I remember being in the back of the office, maybe on the phone. All of a sudden the women stopped talking. My head came up automatically, and I looked up front. I thought the cops had come in, which is something we always anticipated. But instead it was Larrie Stalks and her longtime friend, Ann Crumidy. Larrie was the director of the Newark Department of Health and Welfare and was our enemy by virtue of her position with Addonizio. I had heard many stories, seen her from a distance, heard the power in her voice at meetings. Here was the lady that helped mastermind the election of Hugh J. Addonizio through developing a coalition between blacks and Italians in 1962; here was the lady who also participated and helped maintain Mayor Addonizio's takeover of the NAACP; here was the lady who was the head of the city's Department of Health, but mainly known as Addonizio's chief black operative—and now she was standing in my office, smiling. She looked around at the pictures we had on the walls, pictures of Africans, pictures of

African Americans with naturals and African garb. Her eyes took in everything. Ann stood nearby, smiling pleasantly as always. I came forward, not knowing what she wanted but quite sure she wasn't welcome. "I was passing by and saw your office," she said in a pleasant, friendly voice. No horns protruding, no police waiting to pounce. "I thought I'd come in to say hello. I'm Larrie Stalks." Big politician grin, hand extended for shaking. She knew damn well I knew who she was, and her coming here told me she knew who I was. But her straightforwardness and friendly manner was disarming. "Why shouldn't I come in to see what you were all about?" she seemed to say. I shook her hand and introduced myself as well. We talked for a while about what we were doing with the kids in the Freedom School in the back of the office, probably some arts and crafts project Marsha had going at the time. We didn't talk about politics. She knew what I was about, and I knew where her loyalties lay. So here we were, sworn enemies, coming to like and respect each other. I learned a lot from her that day: you don't have to be disagreeable when you disagree. You don't have to be at war all the time. She and Ann got back into her city car driven by someone who had parked by the curb and kept the motor running. We would be open to each other, at least, if we weren't yet friends.

Ruth and Napa, the Big Red Dog

Then there was the time I met Napa. We were standing out in front of the office on a warm day, when I saw this big red Irish setter walking determinedly west on South Orange Avenue. I said, "Wow, what a beautiful dog.... What's he doing out there by himself?" At about that time he tried to cross the street and almost got hit by a car. I ran out and called him. The car driver looked defiantly at me, as though it was my fault he almost hit "my dog." Did I say that already? As soon as I laid eyes on him, I wanted him. I love dogs and hadn't had one in years. And here on South Orange Avenue came a beautiful animal that needed my help. I called him and he came. He wagged his tail; I patted his big red head. It was love at first sight. We took him in the office. Mai Cox found a pan and gave him some water. He drank as if he hadn't had any for a long time. We fed him something, and he lay down and went to sleep. I checked—there were no tags or identification. He must have broken out from somewhere and started his trip, as setters are prone to do. Who did he once belong to? No way to tell, so he was mine! We named him "Napa." I took him over to Ruth's house, because I knew my landlord wouldn't let me have him on South 9th Street.

Ruth and I weren't married, but were going together at that time. Ruth and I met in the doctor's office where she worked as a nurse. I asked her for a date the first day we met, and she said yes. By this time, I wanted a girlfriend who was not a part of my work: I didn't want to talk shop, discuss strategy and tactics, compare notes, hear about who was good or bad on the issue. And Ruth fit the bill. Of course she had to be pretty and clever, and all the other qualifications I had grown to need and expect from a woman. Ruth was from Opelousas, Louisiana, about as different from Newark as any combination imaginable. Opelousas is the home of Creoles, those of black, Native American, and French descent. Ruth was the last of nine children. Her parents spoke Creole, but as was the tendency of so many bilingual parents living in the United States, they thought it best not to speak it to their children. Ruth heard it growing up, but it was the older folks who tended to keep it for conversations among themselves. And don't ever confuse Creole with Cajun. Cajun's are the whiter version of the same combination of people, although few of them will claim their black roots, hidden somewhere in the deep recesses of the bayous surrounding their homes. Eventually, after we were married, I went to visit Opelousas and fell in love with the people and the country. Especially Uncle Temille!

That day I found Napa, I told her there was a surprise when she got home. And there he was. I ended up buying him. The owner saw him one day when I went over to my apartment. Napa jumped out of the car, trained by that time not to go in the street. When we were going back to Ruth's house, somebody saw me, flagged down a cop, and both of them followed me to Ruth's apartment in East Orange. The owner tried to have me arrested. I explained to the cop I didn't steal the dog but saved him from a sure death out there on South Orange Avenue. The cop understood. By then I had had Napa for more than three or four months. He was my dog, by his choice as well as mine. We had bonded. The cop saw that and didn't know what to do. I offered to buy the dog. There was a child involved, and I felt bad for a minute, but the child in me needed that dog just as much as the kid standing there. In conversation, much less full of tension now, the parent admitted they couldn't care for the dog the way he needed to be handled. He was a large, athletic dog and needed to run. I walked him two times a day, never with a leash; Ruth walked him a third time. And I was hoping the owner needed the money. The cop left the dog with us while the owner "thought about it." Ruth and I worried for two days. We took Napa up to Bear Mountain in New York for "our last day" together, whereupon he jumped in the lake without thinking about how he was going to get out. There was no shore, just a stone wall too high for him to crawl out. I had to pull him out; almost fell in myself. How was I going to get out? Didn't think about it at the time. He was happy, we were happy, with a big red wet dog, at least for one more day.

The day of decision came: the owner decided to sell me the dog. I got his papers (a thoroughbred!) but more importantly, I got Napa. He was a fixture with Ruth and me for the next twelve years, until I had to put him to sleep.

Perils at the Office

Life was not always so peaceful and rewarding at NAPA (the office). Sometime during 1968, I came back to the office and found the plate glass window shattered. I asked Ab what happened, and he strangely knew nothing. Neither did Jamil, although those two were hanging around all the time. Either Mai Cox or Mississippi Jackie told me, "Clint did it."

Clint was a wiry black man who had spent some time in law school somewhere, and some time with SNCC somewhere else. His most recent claim to fame was his association with Colonel Hassan, whose number-two man knocked the books out of Joe Bradley's hands at the Medical School Planning Board hearings at city hall back in June of 1967. So here was Clint. I guess he was in town for good? I didn't know, but he decided to break our window, and put the word out he was looking for me. Why?

So I got ready. I put a hammer inside a brown paper bag, and went off to lunch at the little black-owned restaurant across the street on South Orange Avenue. I sat at the counter and ordered my usual chicken wings and lima beans. Clint was like a ghost. Even though I was looking for him, he caught me by surprise and slid into the seat on my right at the counter. My lima beans came, and I left them untouched. He was alone. Too bad I didn't have Jerry or Earlene with me. "Damn," I thought. "I should have waited for one of them." No way was he going up against me with Jerry and Earlene around. Clint probably watched me when I came out to cross the street and chose this time to make his move. So there we were, looking at each other, seat-to-seat, man-to-man. My move: "Why did you break the window, Clint?" He gave no real acknowledgment of his sin, just a rambling tale of jealously and envy: he said I got all the credit for the Medical School victory, and he got none. His words were unclear. I realized he was high on something. And my beans were getting cold. I was a little scared because he had his right hand in his pocket. He was gesturing during his soliloquy with his left hand, close to my face, but I was concerned about his right. I made up my mind: whether it was a knife (he looked more like a knife man) or a gun, I was going to hit him with the hammer if he pulled the hand out of his pocket. Finally, the hand came out. I grabbed my bag on the counter, which he had not suspected contained the key to his undoing. His hand came out empty, just full of blood. He had cut his hand when he broke the window. Probably put his fist through the plate glass. Me with the hammer, and him with nothing—what a refreshing turn of events, eh? I started to just beat him down with the hammer, but I'm not an assassin—and though I was mad, I felt kind of sorry for him. We each sold some more wolf tickets, and he slipped out the same way he came in, looking more like a junky looking for his next fix. I sat down, ate my lima beans and chicken wings, and went back to the office. I paid $50 to get the window replaced, and never trusted Abdullah and Jamil again. They knew what Clint had done; may have even been in on it. He was more of a friend to them than I was, and they didn't want any medical school at all. But they needed the NAPA office. It was a place for them to live. I needed them to keep the heat and lights working. We had an ugly stalemate, a crude but telling state of mutual interdependence. Life went on. Word went around to look for Clint and whip his ass, just so. I didn't care. I never saw him again.

Then there was the time I went to Europe for the first time. I went away for two weeks in 1968, all expenses paid to integrate (my observation) a "new towns" tour in five countries in Northern Europe: England, France, Finland, Sweden, and the USSR (Moscow and Leningrad). I forget the sponsor of the trip, but it was meant to introduce housing advocates such as me to the latest in factory-constructed housing technology, delivered to the site in parts or totally constructed, called "systems housing production." The trip was fantastic, and opened my eyes to so many possibilities. It influenced my decision to use prefabricated construction when I became a developer, years later.

I was in a restaurant in Paris, an old-style "automat"—the closest thing to fast food in the late '60s. I looked up and saw a vision of loveliness headed my way, tray and food in hand, and I said to myself, "That French woman su-u-ure is fine"—and familiar too. She looks just like . . ." She wasn't a French lookalike but actually someone I knew, the woman we called "Boston Jackie," to distinguish her from "Mississippi Jackie," who was fine too, but in a different way. Both had worked in the Movement, and in Newark. Mississippi Jackie worked at NAPA for a while. But Boston Jackie had moved on from Newark very quickly—and here she was, in Paris.

"What a coincidence," we shouted, as we hugged and carried on in the middle of the restaurant. We had lunch together. People from my group were looking, the Parisians were looking, 'cause we were making such a happy fuss over each other, and being with Jackie made a man's stock go way up.

I don't know how she got to Newark, but her Movement credentials were based on certain people she knew. With them, she moved around quite easily. In Paris, she and I agreed to see each other later, which we did, and took a walk on the left bank of the Seine River, in the springtime. "It don't get no better than that!" I said to myself. But all the while, she was asking me questions about what I was doing, and I told her about the new towns tour. But my sight was on more than city planning, and my hopes were rising with each step we took. But after thirty minutes or so, she ended the questioning and started walking faster, ahead of me. Whenever I caught up to her incessant quickstep, she walked a little faster. I asked her, "What is the problem?" By this time, my male ego was enraged. She was supposed to be walking with me, not making me run after her. I stopped trying to keep up, figured out she was in a hurry to go somewhere else, and without another word, she just walked on out of my life, forever.

Many years later, I got beyond my bruised ego and figured this may not have been coincidence. Perhaps the government was interested in knowing what I was doing, and had assigned Jackie to find out? I had my eyes so much on the prize that I didn't see this other possibility for a long time—and it is still just a possibility. I hope I'm wrong.

Later in 1968, when I came back from seeing my sister Connie in Los Angeles, my suitcase came down the checked-baggage ramp at American Airlines at Newark Airport half open. The clothing was definitely not in the place, the way I had carefully packed it. I thought something was strange, but put it out of my mind. A couple of days later, Jimmy Hooper of Newark CORE called me and said the FBI asked him what I was doing in Los Angeles, and so I put two and two together around that suitcase happenstance.

I was on the police and FBI radar screen by 1968. By any means necessary, our government tracked and trailed people like me around the globe. I should be flattered, and relieved: flattered because I was in such good company as a target of their inquiry, relieved because I didn't get hurt, as so many people did.

And when I got back from Paris, I returned to find NAPA in an uproar. I had left Joe Brown in charge, but under the influence of one of the NAPA family, Joe got involved in a demonstration with the Welfare Mamas, and he and some people went to jail. I took it up at the next staff meeting, or should I say a member took it to me. He said I was irresponsible for being out of town so long, and should have been there with the troops when they went to jail. He was questioning my authority, and for the first time, some of the NAPAs were listening. But he made his move too soon—or better still, he convinced the wrong people to be more militant and go to jail. Some of the college types were backing his play, but not the folks from the neighborhood, specifically Jerry and Earlene. Jerry and Earlene had no intention of going to jail because they had been there, done that. No matter how militant this young man said he was and we needed to be, they were still on my side. He backed down. He thought he could whip my butt, but he knew damn well it was nothing he could do with Jerry and Earlene. And he needed that faction for legitimacy. He was trying to destroy the organization. Was this based on black male testosterone ego, or was he also an agent of one police force or another, sent to infiltrate and destroy? Or was it a little of both?

"When I Was Twenty-Three . . . It Was a Very Good Year"

All in all, this was the best period of my life. Each chapter brought more and more adventure, more and more challenges. I met each with all of the energy and enthusiasm I had inside me, for we (me, the NAPA family, black people in general) were seemingly on a roll, and there was more to look forward to with far greater implications than mere takeovers, lessons in friendship, and vengeful egos. More even than that big red dog. We really thought this would last forever, backing off the Man, stopping him from doing his thing from our perch right there on South Orange Avenue. But in reality, how long could it last?

Black Power

By 1968, during the post-Rebellion period, Newark had produced a world with many groups organized around a form of Black Nationalism. It was an excitement generated by the positive association with identifying with all things black, and the recognition of the fear most white people had of black consciousness. Yes, we got great joy and delight in watching white people's faces when somebody shouted "Black Pow-er," scaring whitey at the most elemental and basic level. But we were just having fun (well, sometimes we were).

Not all black people were comfortable with being called "black," much less with "Black Power." Some Negro leaders from the Black Political Class had to run to catch up with this new positive, unashamedly bold consciousness of being "black," or they just lay low. They were at least curious. Many sought to preserve their little privileges with Addonizio but saw a new day coming when there might be a black mayor. So some played both sides: "I'll give you information, but just remember where you got it from and don't tell nobody." Just in case you actually get some power.

Black Power showed up in different ways, depending on the goals of the group. There were some aspects of the burgeoning Black Nationalism that NAPA and some of the other organizations avoided. We were pro–Black Power, but not anti-white. Some promoters hated white people instead of hating what white racism had done. There was self-righteous anger about the lies and half-truths white America used to justify racial supremacy, and everybody who believes in white supremacy benefits in the suppression of the truth about African Americans and Africa. But anger against institutionalized racism, which is a process set up to perpetuate white supremacy, is different from being mad at all white people. Such blind anger against all individuals of a particular color negates the power of discovery made possible by knowledge of the new African identity: afro hairdos, afro music from all over the world, travel to Africa, expansion of consciousness to develop "an African perspective," awareness of African contributions to history and culture all over the world, especially right here in the USA. NAPA projected this new awareness through our after school program for the kids, and in our in-your-face politics through the adults. We had a black agenda, but I never felt like we couldn't work with white people. To be exclusively black was to deny the possibility of all collaboration and coalitions, and that didn't make sense to me. For example, take the Medical School Fight or the case of Route 75.

Route 75

By 1969 there was one more urban clearance impediment in the way of realizing the goal of electoral black power in Newark. Route 75 was an eight-lane highway planned to run north to south directly across the middle of Newark, connecting routes 280 and 78, which had already ripped the heart out of the North and South Wards, respectively. Route 75 would cut the Central Ward in half and displace thousands more black and brown people. After the Medical School victory, some people went to sleep, but we didn't.

I felt like we had to go to Trenton, to challenge the highway on the enemy's turf. I made a call to the Department of Transportation, and to my surprise got to speak to the Commissioner, David Goldberg. He had obviously heard about me in the context of the Medical School Fight, and he heard we were beating the drum, which grew steadily in volume and tempo to stop the highway. He didn't say so, but he was scared this thing might tip off another riot. So we agreed to meet. I told him I would bring a few people to Trenton at the agreed-upon date and time.

And I did bring a few people. I got one of our white minister friends from the Ecumenical Ministry to rent us a bus. On it were black and white ministers, members of the NAACP, Welfare Rights mamas, and the hard corps of the NAPA family. And we invited the Black Panthers for good measure.

There was no real chapter of the Black Panthers in Newark, although Newark men and women were in the Jersey City Chapter. I talked to Captain Carl and he sent some of his guys, with their black outfits and black tams, looking very much the way I wanted them to look. This was my first time (and it would turn out to be my only time) working with the Panthers. I'm glad it was on this occasion.

Our bus drove up at the Man's office, and we were shown to the conference room. Somebody said, "we weren't expecting quite this many," an apprehensive little smile on a cute white face. I said, "the people wanted to be heard, and so here we are." The conference room available was one that could seat us all. In came the Commissioner, we shook hands and began the conversation. But there were quite a few voices asking the questions, telling him what we thought, telling him what would happen if they brought that highway through our neighborhood. "If you think 1967 was bad, you ain't seen nothing yet," was the general scope of the message. At some point, somebody locked the door, and so you might say this was a "closed-door high-level meeting." I remember seeing Earlene and some of the Panthers standing on the conference room table. Most of the people were on their feet the entire time, cheering on the more aggressive. I just shut up and let them talk to the man. Some of those people scared *me,* so I know Goldberg was scared. To this day, I don't know why he didn't call the state police, who I know would have waded through that crowd like General Sherman rode through Georgia. But the Commissioner and his staff were stunned and eventually just sat there in a daze. And I knew we had to stop it because it was on the way to getting out of hand. So I stood up, thanked the Commissioner, urged him to reconsider Route 75, and we all left—some people slower than others, still selling wolf tickets going out the door. Somebody had called the state police after all. They were outside, but both sides were cool. We got on the bus and celebrated our presumed victory all the way home.

Within one or two weeks, someone called on behalf of the Commissioner. He said, "We really don't need that highway after all." There was joy in Napaland! Can you imagine knocking off a highway with only one show of strength? We never filed a suit—didn't get to the legal piece at all. We became one of the few groups in the United States at that time to be able to claim a victory over a highway, wiping if off the books. And we did it in coalition style.

Listen to the news analysis of what we did and what it meant as portrayed in a full page spread in the *Newark Evening News* written by reporter Doug Eldridge:

The Planners concede Route 75 is now a hot potato, thanks largely to Williams's strategy of shaking up certain officials—he took a busload of 60 persons, half of them Black Panthers, to see Goldberg . . . enlisting allies from churches and colleges. (*Newark Evening News*, February 23, 1969)

Between 1968 and 1969, there was no better organization at the politics of confrontation than NAPA. The ingredients? We were small, mobile, and committed to each other. We won major victories because of our ability to develop and direct a united front composed of other groups and individuals, including white people on occasion. NAPA wasn't just about confrontation, as we shall see, because to implement the Medical School Agreements, we had to learn the Politics of Implementation, which required more—well, turn to the next chapter and experience what we learned.

Baraka and the United Brothers

But during that same period, there was a new drumbeat in Newark, heralding the advent of another chapter of Black Power. LeRoi Jones (now Amiri Baraka) came home to Newark in 1965.

He and his wife, Amina (then Sylvia Wilson), set up a cultural organization called the Spirit House Movers, using their gifts of poetry, drama, and dance to involve neighborhood children and adults around issues they thought were critical to black people. He was beaten by the police on July 13, 1967, during the Rebellion, just because he was LeRoi Jones, the internationally acclaimed but controversial writer.

The picture of him sitting in the wheelchair with a bandage on the right side of his head went all over the world. Timing is everything, and the assault burned his image into the consciousness of black Newarkers and people who stood up against injustice throughout the country.

But there was a more perfect bit of timing that projected his future. Baraka was a part of the planning of the Black Power Conference chaired by Nathan Wright, scheduled for Newark in the summer of 1967 before the Rebellion hit. The Black Power Conference Committee was composed of nationally recognized black leaders of all stripes, and Nathan Wright was selected to coordinate this three-day event at an Episcopal Church property in downtown Newark. The local power brokers said, "call it off!" but the planners said, "No way!" And so the conference convened, fresh on the heels of the embers of the fires that had consumed Newark for days; and there sat Baraka, once again with that bandage, not too long out of jail and the hospital, one of the main speakers among a cast of characters that was a veritable who's who in black politics: Jesse Jackson; Ron Karenga; Floyd McKissick of CORE, Rap Brown, the new chairman of SNCC; Charles 27X Kenyatta, whose organization they called the "Harlem Mau Maus"; representatives from the civil rights organizations like the NAACP and the Urban League; and Malcolm X's organization, the Organization for Afro-American Unity. Baraka quickly attracted a local following and became the center of attention. He bypassed and outshone a lot of other people who toiled unrecognized in the vineyard of social change but who didn't have the spotlight Baraka now commanded. What role would Baraka play in the new table set for the next move in our quest for power in Newark?

In November 1967, I got a letter signed by two friends of Baraka's, John Bugg and Harold Wilson, inviting a small group of "black leaders" to meet at the Abyssinian Baptist Church in Newark on December 8. Twelve men and one woman were asked to be a part of the development of a "Black United Front," to move forward to taking power in the election of 1970. I was proud to be asked, proud of my new status of "leader," earned because of my work in reviving the Medical School Fight. For Baraka, his role was clear, and my future was becoming much brighter as well. Like I said, timing is everything.

What I Learned, What I Wanted

In the beginning of 1968, through protest and in coalition with other groups, NAPA learned how to stop the local power structure on any number of fronts, like highways and the Medical School as it was planned originally. But how long can movements last by just stopping things through action in the streets?

People had to eat. Raise a family. Look at TV. How long can you keep going to the well of people power before the well runs dry? Power based on bringing folks into the street is an awesome thing to behold, but how do we sustain other aspects of people's lives?

And what about other kinds of skills? "In your face" confrontations relied upon one aspect of advocacy. Wasn't there something else to what we now called "Black Liberation" besides bravado and the camaraderie of the hunt?

What about creating community? This required an entirely different skill set, starting with envisioning what we wanted instead of just fighting against what we didn't want. It was the kind of process I learned in feeling our way through the development of the alternate plan to fight the Medical School. We learned how to envision a different neighborhood, fought for the resources to make it happen, and in March 1968, through the Medical School Agreements, had been given the green light to proceed. All we had to do was make it happen— and ascend to a new level of power in the community. Pay attention, Occupy Wall Street. Though I'm walking through my memories in the context of operational Black Power, this one's for you!

9

REAL POWER

The Parallel Approaches to Power
The United Brothers and the Road to Cultural Nationalism

But that's what makes the world go 'round
the up and down, the carousel. . . .
People make the world go round.

—THE STYLISTICS, "PEOPLE MAKE THE WORLD GO ROUND"

In 1968, Baraka was also in a solid leadership position, paramount to my own. He was more well-known than the rest of us, able to pick up and make calls to people all over the country that we only read about in the paper—Movement people, musicians, writers, politicians. He had done more thinking about this thing called a "Black United Front" as a means to take control of city hall. Even though many members of the United Brothers had just organized ourselves as a united front in the Medical School Fight, we conceded leadership to him in building the United Brothers. He was The Man.

The United Brothers met on Sunday mornings and talked, sometimes for hours. I enjoyed the meetings at first, because it seemed like we were on our way to something bigger and better. Also because it put me at the table as an equal with people I had worked with for a short period of time, now as a leader in my own right.

I had worked with Donald Tucker from CORE and his East Ward group; Earl Harris, former elected official as an Essex County

Freeholder; Honey Ward, the Central Ward Democratic Chairman; Harry Wheeler and Louise Epperson, leaders with me in the Medical School Fight. Ken Gibson was not a radical or a militant, but he had been involved with the Business Industrial Community Council (BICC) and the UCC, the War on Poverty federally funded organization in Newark. Plus he ran for Mayor in 1966 and got 15,000 votes, so he had credentials. I knew Ted Pinckney from the UCC, and I knew that Russell Binga was Honey's man.

But then there were more names I had never heard of before. Who was I to judge? There was so much going on in Newark in 1968 I couldn't possibly know everyone who was relevant. And we could always use new people. I suspected some of that unfamiliar group was there because they were friends of Baraka. Most of them turned out to be valuable players.

But I couldn't help but notice Baraka's security force. They weren't there to secure me or Harry or Earl or whoever else. They were there to secure Baraka. But why did he need so much security, I thought, especially at these meetings?

His first security guy was a man named Kamiel Wadud, a Sunni Muslim affiliated with a man named Hajj Heshaam Jaaber, an associate of Malcolm X. Baraka said in his autobiography that it was Heshaam who changed his name. So one day we came to the meeting and were told LeRoi Jones was no longer LeRoi Jones, but Ameer Barakat.

But soon thereafter another group was presented as security. Black Community Defense and Development (BCD) was headed by a quick-witted brother with Pan-African experience named Balozi Zayd Muhammed, and a karate expert called Mfundishi Maasi, both from East Orange. They began attending our meetings.

Baraka admired Ron Karenga, a cultural nationalist in California with an organization called "US." Subsequently, it was Karenga who changed his name from Ameer Barakat to Amiri Baraka.

Karenga's style was based on discipline and tight control by the leader at the top. Under the tutelage of Karenga, Baraka began to build that kind of organization in Newark, with the help of the BCD. Baraka envisioned the Committee for a Unified Newark, a "larger united front" composed of Baraka's Spirit House Movers and Players, the BCD, and the United Brothers.

So what was I a part of? Over about a several-month period, more and more elements of Karenga's "cultural revolution" were added to the organization. There was an African identity assumed by those who were Baraka's most loyal followers, which required African garb and the regular use of Swahili, the trade language among Africans in East Africa. Discipline was a part of the culture. The women, also in African garb, were taught to support the men, and they too were expected to serve in disciplined fashion. Some of the members in CFUN were named by Baraka or Karenga, and Baraka also married people and named babies.

The building at 502 High Street became the offices for CFUN. The Housing Authority gave use of the building to Baraka, because one day he went over there and scared Joe Sivolella, the director who took Lou Danzig's place. I thought this was a good move, but I must admit I wish we had thought of it before Baraka did. After all, NAPA and our allies, in protest mode, had softened up NHA, with demonstrations and regular takeovers to get housing for people improperly removed from houses during urban renewal or highway clearance. You got to know when to play your cards, and Baraka did so very well.

It was a beautiful building acquired by the Housing Authority through urban renewal, next to the St. Benedict's High School on High School near the corner of Springfield Avenue.

There were "Soul Sessions" at CFUN headquarters, also called the "Hecalu." But these Soul Sessions were tame compared to our Thursday-night soirees, and very much tailored to make the African connection. The brothers and sisters wore African garb and danced to African music. Baraka and Karenga, when he was in town, gave spirited speeches focusing on cultural identity and politics. They were held on Sunday afternoons, into the early evenings.

NAPA people didn't like the Hecalu. Ordinary black folks from the hood didn't feel comfortable. There was a lot of judgment about who was "really black" based on the clothes people wore and the food people ate. And there was always somebody telling you what to do, or running around having been told what to do. CFUN became an organization for people who appreciated structure and appreciated externally applied discipline, and most of my people, including me, didn't like that kind of atmosphere. I remember one time breaking some rule and feeling the intense presence of somebody over my shoulder telling me that was disallowed. What had I done? Probably went to the men's room without a hall pass.

Then there was the time I was sitting in the hallway, waiting for some meeting to start, with one foot on a table. Karenga came up the steps with his main enforcer. Before I could say "Hello," he said, "Junius Williams, you better take your foot off that table." He had to put me in my place; I was a child. Who did I think I was, looking comfortable and feeling secure about who I was? It was clear what he was doing, but I had to make a choice: take my foot down, or have his enforcer punch me out. I was no match for him. "You gotta know when to hold 'em, know when to fold 'em." I folded, put my foot down, got up and left the building without going to the meeting. I never talked to Baraka about this incident.

So I stayed far away from CFUN most of the time, and didn't wear anything African for many years, in protest. But I worked with Baraka and CFUN because despite my problems with the foolishness surrounding cultural nationalism, CFUN was what we had. I try to get my children to see that liking something is not always the most important thing. We gain power over our individual lives when we walk into something we don't like, but do so on our own terms. I had something to offer, and I needed to be a part of that team.

NAPA and the Creation of Institutional Community Power

The Medical School Negotiating Team created a roadmap to get land, created the mechanism to monitor relocation activities by NHA from outside the agency, forced our way into the Model Cities Program with a joint veto on all planning activities, created an affirmative action program for construction and operational jobs, and carved out a way to monitor job-site compliance and the quality of health care coming from the Medical School. Throughout most of 1968 and 1969, NAPA took the lead in organizing community coalitions in three areas: the development of the Model Cities Neighborhood Council, the Newark Housing Council, and the Relocation Review Board. We helped George Fontaine, formerly of NCUP; Jim Walker of the UCC; and Gus Heningburg, formerly of the NAACP Legal Defense Fund, with the construction job training called the Newark Construction Trades Training Council (NCTTC) and the site-monitoring device called the Relocation Review Board. And we watched while the Health Council limped off to a fitful start in its efforts to become the mechanism for health care quality accountability and job training once the school was built. So all the while we were taking over welfare offices, raiding Danzig's office at the Housing Authority, stopping Route 75, having NAPA Soul Sessions, and watching the growth of 502 High Street, Baraka's home base, it was concurrent with the development of community-run institutions that would make the agreements bear fruit.

The Model Cities Neighborhood Council

Model Cities was a grant to cities with a mandate to plan grand integrated designs for the "Model Neighborhood." It was the next big thing after the War on Poverty, President Johnson's signature piece of the "Great Society."

Don Melafronte, Mayor Addonizio's right-hand-man, put together the application for the grant from the U.S. Department of Housing and Urban Development (HUD), and Newark received $5.6 million in the first year. To do this, every city selected needed a plan, and every plan had to have neighborhood participation through the Model Neighborhood Council. The problem was that it was full of people handpicked by City Hall sometime in 1966 or early 1967. The Medical School Agreements earned us the right to throw out this council and start all over with a community election.

NAPA convened the Ad Hoc Model Cities Committee. We quickly got five hundred people together in a church in Newark, and voted in a new Model Neighborhood Council. But Melafronte cried foul: not enough notice. HUD agreed. Score one for Melafronte.

Melafronte had no intention of allowing this new community coalition to have its way because the Negotiating Team had been smart enough to secure a power no other Model Cities program had in the country, which was called the "joint veto." As Director of Model Cities, Melafronte couldn't submit a plan for approval to HUD without the approval of this Model Neighborhood Council, nor could the Council make any plans without the approval of Melafronte.

We (Melafronte and the Ad Hoc Committee) jointly agreed to hold another election. But before we even get to second election, you need to know that Melafronte devised a plan to derail whatever we put in motion.

The HOPERS

Before the Rebellion, one of the functions of the Black Political Class allied with Addonizio was to create diversions and disruption in community meetings. With black people from different sides of the room screaming at each other or otherwise maneuvering for the power of the moment, lots of people who just wanted to see something good come to the community and go to work the next morning just didn't have the heart for all that controversy. They got up and went home. Remember the UCC meetings?

After the Rebellion, a lot of the mayor's Negro minions became useless. They were scared, too old to confront this new crowd of militants. So Addonizio, through Melafronte, had to recruit a new army of disruptors and counterinsurgents.

Melafronte created a group called the HOPERS, which was an acronym about Helping People do something. It belied the fact that these were tough guys meant to jam anything the Ad Hoc Committee and NAPA put forward. At the meetings, some of them had their eyes on me at all times.

Once I noticed their presence, I put the word out: "Who are these guys called the HOPERS?" I found out through Jerry O'Neal. Jerry and Spooky, one of the leaders of the group, had been in jail together, and they liked each other. I mean really good friends. And Juliet Grant, from the Welfare Rights Group and one of my closest friends to this date, had been married to Frank Grant, the overall leader of the HOPERS at one time. Earlene and her brothers also knew a lot of the HOPERS. Jerry explained to Spooky that we were the group on the corner that was working with the kids, and that's all it took. I remember going into their bar hangout on Bedford Street, where it was always dimly lit, with some of the hardest guys I ever saw together, bent over shooting pool and drinking beer. I met Spooky and every one of them; some of them smiled, some of them didn't. But because I was all right with Jerry and Earlene, and now with Spooky, I was all right with them. I never again worried about the HOPERS. When I left, Spooky gave me a big hug, and the friendship was sealed. Later when I became a lawyer, Spooky became my client.

Melafronte enjoyed winning. So did I. As often as I can, I remind him of the time I took his guys away from him. Score one for Junius.

The Second Model Cities Election

The HOPERS were completely turned around, not just silenced. A second election was called, announced by HUD but with the city in control of the voting apparatus. More than five thousand people participated in this election, held in August 1968. While I should have been studying for the bar exam, I was getting ready for this election. In the election for the Model Neighborhood Council, there was no need to be a registered voter, as stipulated in our agreement. It was a question of who could pull the most people out in our area and from around the Model Neighborhood area, in an election that generated a surprising amount of interest. Of the fifty-two councilmembers elected, six were white, six were Puerto Rican, and the remainder were black. Jerry and I ran from NAPA. The NAPA family and all our allies were out in the community we knew, pulling people from their houses, from the bars, including the HOPERS and anybody we saw on the street. All they had to do was show proof of residence in the area and be eighteen years of age or older. We had a slate of people typed on a mimeographed flier, indicating who we wanted to win within the Model Neighborhood Area.

We worked all day long, and at the end, Jerry O'Neal and I won. We took three of the four representatives from our district of the Model Neighborhood Area. My first election victory! Much to celebrate—but much to question. Area-wide, we didn't recognize most of the people who had won. Many were district leaders in the three wards affected, and had their own little personal allegiances to draw upon. Some were our people, like Louise Epperson from the Committee Against Black and Puerto Rican Removal. Some were the mayor's people, like Jenkins Holman, a likable guy who had a record store on Springfield Avenue. Most of them were in between, like Terry Richardson, a Republican district leader from the West Ward, who saw change coming but wasn't with us. He would watch to see what happened.

And then there was Anthony Imperiale, the North Ward white vigilante, there to protect his own narrow interests.

The Rise of Anthony Imperiale

Terry Richardson approached me with an olive branch. He saw which way the wind was blowing, and was not in Addonizio's pocket because he was a black Republican. He was old enough to have been in the circle with Irvine Turner, the first black Central Ward Councilman, but he was still ambitious. He wanted to be chairman of the council, and had friends from the West Ward who had gotten elected, but he thought I had more than he had. We talked and decided to have cochairmen instead of one chairman. This seemed to satisfy a lot of people, but infuriated Melafronte, who was more comfortable with Terry than me. Score another one for Junius.

So the elections for officers proceeded on this, the second meeting of the Model Neighborhood Council (MNC). Somebody nominated Anthony Imperiale as second or third vice president. Was this a joke? I couldn't believe any self-respecting black man could be so ignorant! Imperiale was a man who called Marin Luther King "Martin Luther Koon"—here was a man who "patrolled" the North Ward, attacking and beating black men at will. But when the vote was called, the dumb Negroes let it happen. I learned that some of them (especially the city hall-backed Negroes) wanted to see a white officer among the forty blacks and six Latinos. I left the meeting wondering if I was on some plantation down in South Carolina or somewhere, watching Imperiale strut around the room on the way home to gloat. I never wanted to kick these weak Negroes in their you-know-whats more than I did that night—but I was cool, until I got somewhere where I could holler and curse!

The next morning, the newspapers carried Imperiale's triumph.

And that night, I joined in plotting his overthrow among the United Brothers in our regular meeting at 502 High Street.

Baraka and all the rest were mad about Imperiale, but there was an accusatorial air about the way I handled the meeting. It was as if I had let it happen. I explained the circumstances, and the tone evened out. But we decided that what goes up must come down. We had to talk to the people on the council and let them see what their moment of weakness potentially cost us: we knew from our sources that Imperiale was bragging he had the "Niggas wrapped around his little finger." I personally called the majority of the people on the Council, and explained we had to take back the invitation to serve as a vice president on the council. Some of them said, "Yeah, you're right, we shouldn't have allowed that to happen." I also got some tepid okays. I got a couple of, "You ought to leave that alone; it's done now." So I knew where I stood, and by my count we had enough to overturn the vote for Imperiale.

At the next council meeting it was my turn to chair the meeting. This was good because Terry was one who thought we ought to let it go. "We messed up, that's all," was the counsel of the older man to the younger militant. In fact, we called a special meeting just for the purpose of "A Motion to Review the Selection of Vice President," so everybody had notice, including Imperiale. Two people, whose names shall not be used, agreed to make and second the motion to overturn the election results, and then to nominate someone else. As chair, I would entertain discussion, and then we would vote it up or down.

The United Brothers had decided I needed more security. I had people who would protect me, but there was a different kind of army assembled there that night, on the order of Baraka and the United Brothers. Baraka's BCD arrived first, under the cover of darkness, and arranged themselves on rooftops and in alleys, and in hiding all around the building. We knew Imperiale would drive up with his carloads like they were the mafia, all doors open, clustered in the middle, waiting for the signal from their boss. Sure enough, he arrived. The meeting was downtown, off Broad Street on Branford Place, and he had no reason to suspect anything was up. Any cops assigned would be on his side, and he was not going to back down from this fight.

The council agreed that only members of the council could attend this special meeting, which left Imperiale's guys out front, but brought Jerry in as a member of the body. Jerry sat next to me, between the doorway and my chair at the head of the table. Imperiale came in, confidant smile on his face, looking at me all the time as if to say, "I dare you to do it!"

It was time to bring the meeting to order. There was a quorum; in fact far more than I thought would show up. "We had to do this thing," I said to myself. Terry distanced himself from me—we usually sat next to each other as cochairs, but not that night. I didn't care. I looked for the mover of the motion, and the person who had agreed to second. "If only the mover and seconder of the motion would show up," I thought. I stalled as long as I could. This was a special meeting, so there was no other business. I made a statement, trying to filibuster, but then it became clear that those two were not going to come. I was left out on a limb, by myself except for Jerry and maybe a few others. Somebody raised his hand. I was duty bound to recognize him: "Mr. Chairman, I move we table the matter before us." Somebody else seconded it. This motion allows no debate; you either move it up or down. "All in favor?" I queried, knowing the answer before it was given. There was a resounding "Aye," and just like that the meeting was over. Imperiale never stopped grinning, ear to ear. He said something and I said something back at him—but he had beaten us again. Jerry was now standing; his eyes became those of a predator when he was in one of these moods. Jerry was a knife man, and had a long blade hidden in his waistband. Imperiale came by Jerry and me on the way out the door with nothing but that grin. Maybe he knew better than to say anything else. But what more did he really need to say?

By this time people on the council were moving out as fast as they could, cutting pleasant chitchat to a minimum. In the street there was another kind of tension, as Imperiale's folks began to notice they were not really in control of the perimeter as they usually were. One of the BCD commanders looked in at me, as if to say, "Should we do it?" and I shook my head, "No." The standoff was off.

I got two calls with excuses for why my mover and seconder hadn't shown up. Somebody's car broke down coming from somewhere and somebody else had some other similar excuse. I said, "yeah, yeah." They were scared, and didn't have the guts to even tell me they changed their minds. Instead they left me out there holding the bag, with no other recourse than to pull the trigger to start a race war in downtown Newark. I'm glad I had the discipline to take the hit and let it go. There were those in the next United Brothers meeting who once again blamed me.

Accusation: "Why didn't *you* make the motion?" Answer: "I was chairing the meeting, remember?"

Accusation: "Why didn't you turn the BCD loose?" Answer: "They were there to protect, not to attack. Let's face it," I argued, "We lost the political objective, and I wasn't about to unleash World War III in Newark just because two people got scared."

I backed the hound dogs off my trail. But elsewhere Imperiale was still laughing. That year he parlayed this victory into a seat for himself on the city council in a special election. There were ten thousand voters who always carried his torch, enough for council, and enough later for a seat in the New Jersey Senate as an independent. Eventually, as his Italian and Irish base left town for the suburbs of the Jersey shore, Imperiale became less and less of an icon. When he died in 1999, he said he was sorry he had been such a racist. He claimed he had a vision of the Madonna, and she was black! I'm sorry too. But I'll always wonder if he knew how close he came to being wiped out in 1968, and that the power was in my hands?

Working with the Council

The Model Neighborhood Council then met regularly, looking at the plans promulgated by Melafronte's staff. Imperiale only came to one more meeting. I learned a lot about Terry, who proved helpful and became a friend. I ended up with a lot more new friends, like Wiley Crawford and Retha Perry, both active neighborhood leaders in the West Ward, who, though skeptical at first of my reputation as a militant, came to see me as someone they could like and trust. I also learned about my skills as a chairman of a bunch of people who would never come together except for such an occasion. And I learned a lot about Model Cities, how it worked, and most importantly, how Melafronte had it structured and oiled for operation. Melafronte was a smart man. I took it all in. I knew what I wanted to do in my next rebirth in 1970, and the experiences on the Model Neighborhood Council prepared me for that move.

The Newark Housing Council

Another mandate from the Medical School Agreements was that an entity be formed to pick qualified nonprofit community developers, such as churches, and "coordinate" the development of sixty-three acres of vacant urban renewal land: The Newark Housing Council, the nonprofit corporation we ultimately formed, would not actually own the land or build anything else, but would set forth standards for construction, raise the seed money to get started, help arrange permanent financing, and monitor the progress by the community developers we selected. Does it sound straightforward and simple? The biggest problem was that everybody wanted to get the land.

Before we called the first meeting to begin the process of setting standards and selecting developers, I got a visit from Harry Wheeler, probably at my house. He wanted one church, Abyssinian Baptist

Church, to receive all of the land closest to the Medical School, vacant and ready for construction, about twenty-two acres in total. I was shocked, because we had envisioned four sponsors for that area. In fact, some of the ministers and community groups that supported us in the Medical School Fight had already made known the fact that they too wanted some of the land. "How can we turn around, Harry, and give it all to your group?" Reverend Horace Sharper was powerful in the community, and one of the only old-line ministers to stand up to Addonizio, but I wasn't about to let Horace and Harry get all the land. That is where Harry and I parted as friends, forever.

So when we began having community meetings to get people to buy into a housing sponsor selection process, Harry was not at my side. There were about four such meetings between May and October 1968. All the meetings erupted in controversy. In one meeting at West Kinney Junior High School, now Newark Vocational School, a crowd of about four hundred people gathered one night to hear the plan of the "temporary" Housing Council. This meeting was dominated by people who wanted to become sponsors, and by other Negroes who had been sent from city hall to see that nothing took place. Once again I was secured by the BCD, sent by Baraka to assure that we held off the interlopers. The BCD was to watch for my signal; if I needed help, I would ask for it. There were police on duty, but mostly outside. Jack Hicks, one of Addonizio's minions, and well known for his prowess with a baseball bat in yesteryear, complained loudly that we were taking too long to come up with something, a sentiment echoed by dozens in the audience. I knew we were in for it. I had NAPA out in force (no Jerry, for some reason) but most of our supporters were from Reverend Thomas's New Hope Baptist Church, and not used to hand-to-hand combat among black folk. (Well, maybe in the deacon and trustee meetings, but most of the rank and file never saw *those* clashes of wills.) So I was handling Jack, and really thinking of my next step to force them off guard, when Baraka's security jumped up and ran Jack Hicks out of the auditorium. Back in the day, Jack would have had his guys and wouldn't run like a rabbit, but he was clearly still nimble enough to get out the side door. Pandemonium broke out in the auditorium. I expected the BCD to return to help me keep order. But I found out later that Hicks's sudden exit was part of a trick: the cops wouldn't let the BCD back in the building. And here we were, outnumbered and now without a security force, so the Philistines thought they had us beaten.

Willie Wright, one of those angry because he was not included on the Medical School Negotiating Team, picked up where Jack Hicks left off. I shot back at him and told him he was out of order. The crowd was still buzzing. Clearly a confrontation was about to go down, and it came from Willie. "You guys have had your chance; I'm coming up there to take over." I was prepared to fight him for the microphone. He was joined by Joe Cheneyfield, about 250 pounds of once-hard West Indian muscle, a man with a mean streak. The crowd noise got louder as people picked sides. Willie moved up the aisle with Cheneyfield, telling everybody, "I'm taking over the meeting." When he was ready to move up on the bottom step to come up to the stage, out stepped NAPA family member Earlene Provit from a front-row seat. "I'll be goddamn' if you're going on that stage. If you do, you gotta go over me first!" She was joined by another one of the NAPAs, a short, rotund young lady named Rose Crump, who said, "You got to go over me, too!" These two women stopped those big bad men in their tracks. By now the crowd was on our side because two women had chumped off Willie and his boy. There was laughter and a few "uh-oh-h-hs," which, translated, meant, "Whatcha gonna do now, Willie?" Willie didn't do a damn thing; he and Cheneyfield just stood there while Earlene told them to "C'mon, mutha-you-know-whats." Nothing like a good woman when you need one. And the place was in an uproar. Some of the good citizens from the church started leaving.

So Earlene and Rose saved the night, and we survived another evening. Score one more for Junius and NAPA. The problem with this kind of meeting is that everyone with an ax to grind or with an eye toward a land grab could bring their people. There was no membership roster, nor a requirement that people know what happened already. And there was no need to know anything about housing development. It was just one faction against another, and perhaps another, all trying to shout and bully their way to a plot of land.

Little did these idiots realize that there were larger forces waiting in the background to pick up the pieces after we knocked each other off. The Housing Authority was directing any and everybody who wanted some land to "go see the Housing Council," knowing that we weren't ready to take applications, and that most of the people would never qualify. It's as if Danzig and his staff were saying, "After the Niggas kill each other [maybe even literally], we'll declare the Medical School Agreements unenforceable, and go back to business as usual."

At some point in the next meeting, we realized we would need an election to select the Housing Council. We made sure that at least half of the people nominated for the proposed twenty-five-person Newark Housing Council were supporters of what we considered true community interests. More than six hundred people voted in this election, held in October 1968 in locations all around town. Requirements for voting were the same as in the Model Cities election: proof of residency in Newark, and eighteen years of age or over. NAPA mobilized the same forces we brought out in the earlier election: tenants, college students, community activists, and their constituencies. Some ministers turned out their congregations on our behalf. And then there were our friends and supporters in Napaland who were still in the same bars and apartments (You see why it was so important to hang out?) We gave them a longer mimeographed list this time, stating the "Community Choice" ticket.

The opposition tried everything to beat us, especially me, including spelling my name wrong on the ballot. With the help of security, Bob Robinson (Cali) from the BCD, I got that straightened out in what we shall call "an out-of-court settlement."

But I won anyway. Of the twenty-five elected, ten were either from NAPA or from our allies. The remaining fifteen positions were divided among factions, which up until this point were only held together by the lies and half-truths of people or groups who wanted the land. Their instructions were to "Stop Junius Williams," but they failed. NAPA had the only organized power block on the council. But how to get the remaining votes we needed to get the job to the next stage?

We elected Charlie Bell, a member of the East Ward Social and Civic Association, the chairman. I was already cochairman of the Model Neighborhood Council and didn't want to appear greedy. Bell was a strong and steady hand as chairman, which left me the time and space to maneuver for the votes we needed at any meeting. Our biggest adversary was Willie Wright, who had three people (including himself) on the Housing Council. There was someone from the UCC, the NAACP, and other groups, including Negroes affiliated with city hall. Organizing a working majority proved harder that we thought because we couldn't get a quorum. But one day in December, twelve people showed up, eight from our coalition. So we changed the quorum to eight. You gotta do what you gotta do—this was war, one faction against many others who wanted control of the land. We also made sure that the chairman appointed all committee members and chairpersons of the committees, and gave the chairman the almost exclusive right to call special meetings. We were using our street smarts to come inside the suites to enforce the Agreements.

When they saw their error, eventually "Willie and the Detractors" stopped coming. We got down to the business of picking sponsors, setting guidelines for construction on the land, and monitoring compliance with our edicts.

Paul Ylivisaker, the commissioner of the New Jersey Department of Community Affairs (DCA), came to appreciate what NAPA was doing during the Medical School negotiations. Especially, he took a liking to me, and we developed a friendship that lasted many years until his death in 1992. Ylivisaker's DCA fulfilled a promise to finance the first phase of housing and related community development (a school was planned, and other similar neighborhood necessities) with a grant he signed on the last day of his tenure as DCA commissioner. He signed the contract on the platform of the train station in Newark.

We went to work by first setting design criteria and timetables for any sponsor who wanted to develop land. There were height restrictions, 50 percent of the units were reserved for three-, four-, and five-bedroom apartments for large families, and there were community space requirements. The seed money grant from Ylivisaker allowed us to hire an architect (Robert Wilson, from Stamford, Connecticut), and housing consultants (Cogen-Holt from New Haven). This was the basis of our Central Development Team, headed by: Junius Williams.

With the encouragement of Ylivisaker and the approval of the folks on the NHC Board, I resigned from the board and was hired to coordinate the team of professionals. In other words, I was going to be paid. It was the first time I was paid a decent salary to do what I had been doing for free. And I learned everything I could from the architects, the housing consultants, and the lawyers we used to learn how to do housing development.

On October 4, 1969, one year after the election, NHC made conditional designations of five groups as sponsors of parcels in the first twenty-four acres of land. The fighting was not over. Four of the five sponsors were successful, constructing more than nine hundred units of housing. A large percentage of them were apartments with four and five bedrooms. All were subsidized for low-income tenants. One sponsor was unable to rehabilitate forty-four brick townhouses, a stone's throw away from the Medical School. But the dummies at the Housing Authority demolished the brick buildings. Those houses could have been retained for the families that owned them, a racially mixed neighborhood of working-class people. They would be worth $500,000 to $750,000 each in today's market.

Other sponsors eventually built another thousand units on land farther away from the new Medical School. My deputy director, Bill Yuen, who took my place and honchoed the work over the following three years, while he got his law degree at Rutgers, told me the second round of sponsors were on their own. The state refused to fund NHC after 1972. Bill is now practicing land development law of one kind or another in his home state of Hawaii.

Lessons Learned

What can we learn from the experience of the Newark Housing Council? The core group amounted to ten to twelve folks, eight of whom were from NAPA. We learned how to forge meaningful coalitions, how to be patient in building this group, and how to create meaningful change from opportunities afforded with the help of professionals. I learned how to manage a nonprofit corporation, and how to develop houses. We created an institution that could sustain change over a period of time, which resulted in substantial wealth in the process for several nonprofit black-led developers. These were new skills for most of us, and a new plateau in power.

But clearly, some aspect of street skills was necessary. We had to beat back Willie Wright when he tried to take the stage, outfox Don Melafronte when he formed a community group to run us off our turf. People could holler, but we hollered right back. People could maneuver, but we outmaneuvered them. People produced crowds to overwhelm our resolve, but we produced bigger crowds. It taught me a lesson about power: always remember the bridge that brought us over—an organized community, tough, disciplined, and ready to take action.

Our work created respect for our ability to produce among the network of power brokers and political agencies at the state and local level: we obtained seed money and mortgage commitments in excess of $30 million for the nine hundred units in the first phase of twenty-two acres. I was privileged to have been a part of that process, and to have benefited from the growth and reinvention it allowed. Even though the state refused to fund the Housing Council after 1972, and some of the same narrow selfish interests within the Newark community reappeared on the scene during Bill's tenure as director of NHC, NHC was able to assure that other church-based nonprofits were able to build on the land designated in the Medical School Agreements.

I didn't run again for the Model Neighborhood Council. City hall made it hard for me to keep my support on that council with its promise and delivery of jobs. We never once used the joint veto, didn't even try because I couldn't get a clear majority, as we did on the Housing Council. After I left, the people on the MNC didn't let outsiders come to the meeting, and the communications going out were essentially controlled through Melafronte. How could we make a federal program serve the people? Not through citizen participation. We had to control the arm that controlled the group, and that meant taking control of city hall to put our mayor into the ultimate position of power.

Comparing CFUN and NAPA

How to compare these two models for Black Power, growing up in Newark at about the same time? Baraka and CFUN, NAPA and JW were equally important and absolutely necessary in our growth and development as power people. Even though I didn't like cultural nationalism, Baraka's leadership developed an organization that focused on support for the big issues like Model Cities and the Housing Council, and the municipal elections in 1968 and 1970. On the other hand, Junius Williams, NAPA, and friends were successful in institutionalizing the protest of the street into nonprofit structures, well financed and with a clear mission, especially with the work done by the Newark Housing Council. Model Cities was only partially successful in this regard, but a tremendous learning experience nonetheless.

At the same time, George Fontaine, Jim Walker, and Gus Heningburg, with the support of NAPA and other organizations, were equally as successful with creating and maintaining a third institution: the Newark Construction Trades Training Council (NCTTC), a nonprofit organization that trained about six hundred black and Latino males for jobs in the construction industry, saw to their placement on public construction jobs, and fought with construction unions to grant them union membership, beginning with the construction of the Medical School. It is another story that begs to be told. Well into the twenty-first century, the pool of black skilled craftsmen used on any major job in northern New Jersey was composed of men who were trained, and in some cases forced upon the construction trades unions, through the mandate in the Medical School Agreements and the work done by NCTTC. These workers are now retiring, and there is no equivalent pool of minority workers trained to take their place.

As the years have gone by, I have softened in my appraisal of CFUN. People in CFUN had a right to their own definition of "soul," to follow whatever leader they felt comfortable with, just as we did in NAPA. More good than harm came out of 502 High Street. Like NAPA, CFUN gave a lot of people something larger and more challenging to use as a benchmark for personal development. Baraka helped me; I helped Baraka in turn. The brothers in the BCD were there for me, although I wouldn't think of trading them for Jerry and Earlene, who protected me because they loved me, not because they were told to do so. The BCD was a large, disciplined, well organized presence;

Jerry, Earlene, and all of NAPA represented the tip of a community that could overflow with passion at a moment's notice, but one that would protect and nurture its own. I was happy to be in their embrace.

Street Power, Suite Power

I tell my students now in the Abbott Leadership Institute that the power of the streets and the techniques used to develop it is always necessary but may not be sufficient. Having access to the suites gives more direction and opportunity to people in the streets. We cut the acreage of the Medical School and obtained land for housing and jobs based on street power. But then we converted those hard-earned skills from protests and takeovers, into nonprofit corporations that produced housing for people and jobs in construction. But still those street skills were necessary to hold onto our gains: people from within and without the community tried to take the spoils of our hard-fought victory, and so we had to maintain and show our hard edge when necessary. The power in the streets must accompany the power in the suites, and vice versa.

NAPA and CFUN were examples of the growth in awareness of power possibilities beyond just stopping the Empire through protests. In the 1970 election, would CFUN be as successful in harnessing the energy of all these street organizations to create an even larger platform of opportunity for black folks in Newark, where both sets of skills would be utilized to elect the first black mayor and black majority on the city council?

10

ELECTION OF THE FIRST BLACK MAYOR

People get ready,
There's a train a comin'
You don't need no ticket,
You just get on board

—CURTIS MAYFIELD, "PEOPLE GET READY"

Tune-Up Elections

In 1968, the United Brothers (CFUN) fielded a slate of three candidates for a special City Council election. Donald Tucker was the candidate for the East Ward position and Ted Pinckney the Councilman-at-Large candidate. Later, when a third seat opened up, the United Brothers endorsed Leon Ewing. Ewing, a bail bondsman, was at first thought to be too close to Addonizio and certainly was not one of us. But the decision was made to endorse him anyway. After the election, I wrote about the results in an unpublished essay.

> On November 5, 1968, black communities all over the country were focusing attention on the [city council] election held in Newark. The stakes were high because this was seen as a test run for the voting strength of the black majority existing in Newark. If the black community could elect three black candidates for city council in a special election, the chances of electing a black mayor in 1970 were just that more encouraging....

Unfortunately, many onlookers were very disappointed. None of the three black candidates was elected.... How could three whites be elected, one of them proclaimed an extremist by Governor Hughes, and under state investigation for his vigilante activities, in the city of Newark, where 19,000 new nonwhite votes had been registered in time for the election?... Imperiale won with an impressive 29,400 votes, while Leon Ewing, the highest black candidate, received 24,862 votes, 79 votes short of Anthony Giuliani, a Newark policeman and a law-and-order candidate.

I'll tell you how we lost: Too much Black Nationalism. Too much Karenga. Too much militancy. Too many Black Power speeches at a convention called for the purpose of selecting candidates. In 1968, many voters were not even content with being called "black," and the image of our candidates was that they were black militants.

Secondly, the three candidates suffered from being lost on the ballot. The United Brothers/CFUN did not have a mechanism to educate the voters to help them find our candidates seven rows down from the candidates for President of the United States. Lots of black people voted for president, but half the people who voted for president in the South and Central Ward failed to vote for any city council candidates.

And finally, many voters went to the polls expecting to cast a vote, only to find their names removed from the voting rolls—some because they had been moved by urban renewal or highway construction, others because their address was simply not listed. We weren't organized enough to effectively challenge illegal voter purges, and most ordinary black folks didn't want to stand in line for hours to resolve the address issue on their own.

We had a Black United Front, but it wasn't broad enough, or deep enough. Maybe we hadn't taken the time to make alliances with groups and organizations that knew how to attract and bring out the ordinary voters within the black community. And maybe the people with electioneering skills were not as important as the nationalists.

Building for the 1970 Election

So in addition to all the work in building institutions to implement the Medical School Agreements, and protesting other injustices like Route 75, we had to improve our act for the 1970 election.

Ken Gibson let everybody in the United Brothers know that he was running for mayor, based on his surprise showing in 1966, garnering 15,000 votes and forcing a runoff between Addonizio and Carlin. The problem was that most people had little confidence in Gibson as a candidate.

George Richardson, who had been a Democratic Party State Assemblyman, would have been a better candidate even though he lost to Irvine Turner as councilman of the Central Ward. But he publicly denounced Black Power. He embraced the concept of direct action in the early '60s. His stand against police brutality cost him his job in the Addonizio administration and his position on the line for state assemblyman with the Democratic Party. But he was instantly rendered obsolete by his disavowal of the rest of us in 1969. Ken Gibson, on the other hand, a man who was somewhat active with civil rights and community organizations, was left standing there under a spotlight that gleamed, "I Got 15,000 Votes!"

Ken was very quiet. Some of us, me included, interpreted his quietude as personal inner strength. Many people said he was a chump and backed away. But who did we have as the alternative? Well, there was Harry Wheeler, my cochair in the Medical School Fight, who had tried to hog twenty-two acres of land. But additionally, Harry was haunted by an accusation that he stole money designated to buy the children's milk when he was a schoolteacher. Anyway, in 1968–1969, after the Medical School Fight, he took himself out of the game by taking a mid-level job in Washington with the Department of Health and Welfare.

Then there was Oliver Lofton, the Director of Legal Services, who distinguished himself as a member of the Governor's Commission and as a member of the Medical School Negotiating Team. He took a job in DC at the Department of Justice. (Harry and Oliver both came back to town some time in 1969, but it was too late for them to be considered by our organization.)

So that left us with Ken Gibson. Maybe it was good to create a candidate with a not-so-militant image. I asked him if he wanted my help and he said, "Yes." When approached, CFUN agreed for me to be his campaign manager.

I had never run a campaign, but I was an organizer. My job was to create momentum by mobilizing the constituency we had, which I was positioned to do. But more importantly, I gave Ken credibility. The resistance community was the group who had the greatest doubt about Ken, and here we were about to sponsor him for election for mayor. Once the community saw that I had committed to work for him, several people at least shut up. Others went along, even though reluctantly. The deal was that I would arrange gatherings of churches, block clubs, tenant groups, street organizations—wherever there were people already organized and within speaking distance of our collective voice. When we had raised enough money and cast the net far enough, we would bring in a professional campaign manager.

I set out to make this happen sometime in early 1969. Baraka was fund-raising and bringing high-level visibility nationally for our candidate. He set up a meeting with Ken and Mayor Richard Hatcher, the first black mayor of Gary, Indiana, and with Jesse Jackson in his Operation Push in Chicago. Ken asked me to go with him, along with Joe White, a publicist and Ken's friend, and Earl Harris, who had been elected to county freeholder in the past. Baraka met us in Gary.

On the Campaign Trail

Our trip was amazing! Richard Hatcher was the first black mayor of a major city in the country, elected in 1967. He was a serious young man, very gracious and willing to share. He had black people all around him, coming in and out of his office looking official but relaxed; and his chief administrator, who ran the details of his office, was a black woman. We had never seen anything like this before. Because of Baraka, he took us at our word that Ken was the right man, and he and his team spent long hours answering our questions about his campaign and the problems Ken would face once he was elected. I listened to hear if there were things I might do as campaign manager to shape up our troops in similar fashion.

Next stop was Chicago, driving distance away, where Jesse Jackson hosted us at Operation Push. Every Saturday, Jesse had a rally in what looked like an old movie theater where as many as a thousand people came to hear him and his guests talk about black issues. It was reminiscent of the civil rights mass meetings and rallies down South. No democracy, just strong black oratory and great music that fed the people the hope they needed to make it through the week. And it was free of charge. (Of course, in the Baptist tradition, there was a collection at the height of the emotional moment.)

That Saturday was a triple treat: We got to hear Jesse, who had broken his ankle or his leg and was hobbling around very athletically with a crutch, but also Carl Stokes, the first black mayor of Cleveland, Ohio, and Cannonball Adderly, the great jazz alto saxophonist who was recording a new album with his sextet, featuring his brother Nat Adderly on cornet. I thought I had died and gone to heaven! Cannonball Adderly was my favorite alto saxophone player, next to Johnny Hodges, as a young saxophone player at Armstrong High School. The album was called *Country Preacher*, and it included pianist Joe Zawinul's eventual hit, "Mercy, Mercy,

Mercy." I sat on about the third row, directly in front of the band—man, oh man, oh man!

But the rest of the program was equally as fascinating: watching Jesse orchestrate every moment of everybody's time on the stage, hopping around in his cast, watching Carl Stokes mesmerize the crowd in his tailored suit and his smooth, polished delivery, watching Jesse try to get Carl off the stage, watching Jesse integrate the music into the rest of the program. And just feeling good because I was in Chicago with all those black people in a niche they created for themselves. Would Ken facilitate the same in Newark once he got elected?

At some point it was Ken Gibson's turn to go up on the stage. To the delight of the crowd, Jesse introduced him as "The next mayor of Newark, New Jersey." Ken said a few words, told the people he was going to be the first black mayor of Newark, for which he got enthusiastic applause, and sat down. Good move, because Ken was not a great speaker, but he came across as sincere. The show went on, and then it was time for Jesse. Jesse approved of Ken in his own rhetorical style, which got the crowd up again. Jesse's main purpose was to upstage Carl Stokes, which he did, but he had to work hard because Carl could speak. But in the end, this was Jesse's flock.

This was great theater in the context of the new "Age of the Black Mayor." We realized we were a part of something bigger than Jesse's rally on that one day. And so we came back to Newark, supercharged.

First Blood

We rented an office across the street on Springfield Avenue, on the second floor, within walking distance of 502 High Street, CFUN and Baraka's headquarters, and began having meetings there. One evening, I was giving a report on the campaign activities I had scheduled for that week. Honey Ward, sitting next to me, was unhappy about something I had designed. Even though he was the Ward Chairman and was supposed to be in the know, I in turn thought his particular idea didn't make sense. I told him, "That and a nickel won't buy you ..." I intended to say "cup of coffee," but before I could get the words out, he hit me in the jaw. I came back with my right to hit him, but he was on his feet, blocked me, and took me down with a right cross. I was on the floor, trying to see straight. Honey was at one time a middleweight Golden Gloves champion.

People at the meeting held him back. I slowly got up, picked up the cane I used because of a sprained ankle, which haunted me on walking tours during the campaign. Baraka and some of the other people in the meeting got Honey out of there. I sat on the couch and let my head settle down a little bit.

The next day when I went back to NAPA, I told the folks what had happened. As expected, my people wanted revenge, especially Earlene and Jerry. But I told them to cool it; we couldn't afford word getting out that we were fighting each other in the Gibson campaign, because there was too much at stake. Just let it go. But the next day we had our first public event planned, at the headquarters. I could see this was not going to sit well, and I was worried about what Jerry and Earlene might do. As the crowd gathered, the two of them eyed Honey. Back in the day, Honey had guys who were ready and able to fight and do so quite well. But by this time, the group was older, less dependable, and Honey couldn't take Jerry one-on-one. I was just hoping we could make it through the night. I saw Honey making his way through the crowd toward me. When he got up to me, he apologized. He said he shouldn't have done it, we shook hands, and that was it. I quickly told Jerry and Earlene, and just like that, it was over. The only thing left was a poem about the nonfight, written by Baraka and published in one of his books. Oh, well, I got the honor of spilling first blood for Ken Gibson in the campaign for Mayor. And being mentioned in a Baraka poem.

My Future Assured?

At some point Dan Armet replaced me as campaign manager. I had mixed emotions, but that was the deal. By that time, I was executive director at the Newark Housing Council, and behind in my work because of the campaign. But I had extracted a promise from Ken before Dan arrived. I told Ken, "Some people have asked me to consider running for councilman of the Central Ward." I told him I would rather stay with him. "But if you win, I want to be director of the Model Cities Program." He asked me to stay on as manager, and he agreed to the Model Cities appointment. I'm glad I asked him when I did, but wonder what might have happened had I chosen to become a candidate.

So when Dan came aboard, my role in the campaign diminished. And that was a bad thing, because out of sight, out of mind. I thought I would have a position of importance as an advisor of some kind, but as Ken became more popular, and as the idea took hold, the campaign developed a life of its own. I had helped give his campaign that vitality and credibility, but—oh, well, Ken's election was more important than my feelings. But I realized I never really knew the man to whom I committed myself.

The Black and Puerto Rican Convention

On November 14–16, 1969, CFUN sponsored the Black and Puerto Rican Convention, which was designed to formally select the "Community's Choice" for mayor and city council. Of course, like at most conventions, the choices had already been made before the public meetings, although there was an opportunity for people to be nominated "from the floor." For the hundreds of people there, it was more of an opportunity to galvanize the community around candidates they knew, and to get on board with CFUN for the ultimate trip of our lifetime. There would be only one chance to elect the "first black mayor."

This Convention was different than the one in the 1968. First of all, the words "and Puerto Rican" were added to the name of the Convention. About four to five hundred delegates attended. But the cultural nationalists were not as visible this time. Baraka had asked Bob Curvin and others to be in charge. Curvin said:

> While the first convention had been dominated by Baraka and the more separatist leaders of the Black community, the 1970 Convention was organized by a broad-based committee headed by myself and leaders of the Urban League... the National Council of Negro Women, a representative of a Black doctors organization, members of CFUN, and a number of Black and Puerto Rican leaders. (Robert Curvin, "The Persistent Minority: The Black Political Experience in Newark," Princeton University doctoral dissertation, 69–70)

While Curvin may be correct in the names or organizations who chaired the group, it would be inaccurate to call Baraka or CFUN "separatists." However, it was in everyone's interest that CFUN downplay the cultural nationalism.

Ken Gibson emerged as the "consensus candidate," along with Sharpe James (South Ward), Dennis Westbrooks (Central Ward), and Donald Tucker, Earl Harris, Ramon Aneses, and Ted Pinckney as candidates for the councilmen-at-large positions. The main discussion centered on the platform, which all our candidates agreed to be bound by. I remember running one of the sessions on housing and land use, while other leaders prominent in the community conducted similar sessions based on their field of interest or expertise. The convention came forth with some very interesting platform items:

- The cost of education and welfare should be completely taken over by state and federal government (more state money was ordered for schools by the New Jersey Supreme Court as part of the "Abbott remedies" in *Abbott v. Burke* some twenty-four years later).

- Revenue Sharing (a federal funding mechanism) should give "extra consideration" to real estate tax–overburdened cities like Newark.
- Schools must teach black and Puerto Rican history beginning at primary level, history "written by black and Puerto Rican writers, and approved by the community."
- The school district should be "divided into districts with duly elected governing boards for each district"(community control of schools).
- More blacks and Puerto Ricans must be appointed on the police force, and
- Police officers must live in the city.
- Establishment of an effective Police Review Board "to investigate and hear community complaints concerning police activity."
- Teachers must live in or have background related to the community in which they are teaching (mandated in the No Child Left Behind Act, federal legislation thirty years later).
- Schools need "an all-day program for pre-kindergarten children" (pre-school was ordered in *Abbott v. Burke*).
- "Free lunches for economically disadvantaged children" (mandated by the U.S. government's Title I program years later).

From the examples cited, the reader can see that there was some real thinking and democracy going on in our workshops. I remember seeing the passionate faces of the session leaders as we came forward at the last plenary session, to unite the convention around these demands upon which the candidates were duty-bound to accept. This platform and the hope that was intrinsic within is what make me excited every time I read the document.

During the campaign that followed, I don't remember hearing very much about these issues and solutions. Ken's main statements were about delivering services (he was big on garbage collection), honesty in government, and he promised he would not tolerate traditional "machine politics." He ran as a "reform" candidate, as he saw it, while the people at that convention wanted reforms way beyond conventional notions of "good government."

New Role

My role in the campaign became coordinator of walking tours in the neighborhood and literature drops for the candidates. CFUN, because of the tremendous appeal of Baraka, was able to bring college students from all over the East Coast to work on weekends right up until Election Day. He also brought in the stars, like Stevie Wonder, which gave us media attention. Because I was coordinating a literature drop on one Saturday in April 1970, still limping with my cane, I missed the opportunity to get on the flatbed truck and play my harmonica with Stevie. I consider that to be my greatest sacrifice for Ken Gibson's election.

Victory!

Ken won the election on May 12, 1970. Because there were so many candidates, there was no clear majority, and thus under the law applicable to Newark, a runoff was required. George Richardson ran in the first election without our support. Ironically, the man partially responsible for Ken's career as mayor got the least amount of votes. At some point, he left Newark and now lives in New York City. The Irish candidate, John Caulfield, Fire Director under Addonizio, supported Ken in the runoff election, while Anthony Imperiale helped Addonizio.

The runoff was black against white—the most racialized campaign in Newark's history, as Addonizio used Baraka as a scapegoat to draw votes away from Gibson. Ken kept his cool. The federal government made sure Addonizio went to trial during the runoff, charged with corruption in office as mayor. He was whipped daily in the media, and it drove away some of his supporters, many of whom were white. They didn't vote at all.

So on June 16, 1970, history was made in Newark. Ken Gibson became the first black mayor of a major Northeastern city. Along with him, Earl Harris was elected councilman-at-large, and Sharpe James and Dennis Westbrooks were elected as South and Central Ward councilmen. The remaining six members of the council were white.

I will never forget the night of that election. There was a mass of about a thousand people out front of Symphony Hall on Broad Street, and a bus chartered by Jesse Jackson. The cops gave up trying to control the crowd, which was loud, happy, peaceful, and constantly growing. The people were there to celebrate the greatest spectacle we had ever witnessed. People got on top of the bus and the whole crowd sang the Delfonics hit, "Didn't We Blow Your Mind This Time, Didn't We." More people heard the news and made their way downtown.

Meanwhile, Addonizio supporters rampaged in the North Ward and took their anger out on newsmen sent to cover their reaction. It was the end of a very short era in power at city hall for the Italians, but not the last we would hear from them.

I went inside Symphony Hall but couldn't make my way to the stage where I wanted to be. It didn't really matter in the greater scheme of things. I was committed to this experiment in power and just happy to have played a role in making it happen. Words from my future pastor, Reverend Matthew Zimmerman, much later in my life, come to my mind to reflect the moment: "I believe I'll run on and see what the end's gonna bring!" But the words were certainly true for me then.

11

THE KEN GIBSON YEARS

I can't play my music
They say my music's too loud
I kept talkin' about it
I got the big run around
When I rolled with the punches
I got knocked to the ground . . .

—THE ISLEY BROTHERS, "FIGHT THE POWER"

But what was I running to, or from? Black people were against white supremacy, and we were for Black Power. But after the election victory, what did this mean? What did it mean for me as a radical organizer, comfortable with the power we generated in the streets, but wanting to come in from the cold to become a part of this great experiment in political power I helped create?

Model Cities Director

The only job I wanted, and wanted passionately, was the combined position of director of Model Cities and Community Development Administration. In 1968, in an unpublished paper called "Black People and Federal Programs," I wrote:

> This brings us to the discussion of Model Cities. In Newark, it represents $75 million over a period of years. Also, some two hundred professional and para-professional jobs will be created in the

agency alone, not to mention those created by the programs (lev-
eraged by Model Cities funds). It was designed for big-city mayors.
...Thus Model Cities will absorb many other federal programs...
heightening the trend toward centralization (of federal dollars to
the mayor's office, nationwide).... Obviously black people should
be interested and try to do something with this potential resource.

This was a real powerhouse within City Hall, and so upon my return
from vacation in Bermuda with Ruth, I set out to get it, working my way
through the new layer of protectors and gatekeepers who controlled
access to the mayor-elect. Finally, I got the meeting I wanted. Somebody
asked me, "You're only twenty-six years old—what makes you think
you can handle the job as Model Cities Director?" Ken was listening. I
reminded them of my role setting up the Model Neighborhood Council
and the Newark Housing Council. They couldn't deny my track record.
It was an age for young soldiers taking on huge responsibilities.

Ken honored his earlier commitment, despite reservations written
all over his face, and against the advice of some on his transition team
and close friends. In the third week of July 1970, I became the youngest
Model Cities Director in the country.

Don Melafronte told me much later that Ken was also aware of my
position in the community. I was a "gift to the militants," he said, a
smile on his face. That could have been a factor in Ken's decision—to
balance all those white men Ken had placed or intended to place in
our new government. All totaled, Ken appointed five white men and
three black men, including me, as his first cabinet. The hardest for the
black community to accept was the appointment of John Redden, an
Irishman, as his first Police Director.

So I got my dream job. Increased my status. Improved my ward-
robe. People said, "Look at him: he's twenty-six years old, making
$26,000 a year—a grand for every year of his life." I liked the attention
and the money, never having made that kind of money in my life.

But I was more interested in the power, starting with the jobs that were available in this empire created by Don Melafronte, based on flexible federal money. I could shuffle the deck and create new programs and jobs, while all the other departments were bogged down with Civil Service and unions. Most of the people in the city hall jobs couldn't be budged. Civil Service had not captured Community Development Administration (CDA), by Melafronte's design, and I kept up the fast footwork to keep us "unclassified" for the more than two years I occupied the chair.

Initially, I got jobs for those in NAPA who wanted them, and even some jobs in the traditional departments in city hall when available. Jerry O'Neal "pitched garbage cans" (as a sanitation worker) for the city for a number of years before he left town. Earlene and Bebop went into the Interim Assistance Program (IAP), which did rat and pest control, and built a few parks under a federal grant. I sent other young people to IAP, where they became a part of an organization created by Don Bernard called the "Git Down Society." People today remind me that they got their first job working for me in IAP, like George Hampton, recently retired vice president at the University of Medicine and Dentistry.

I wanted to build more houses. I converted Melafronte's two development corporations into one, called the Housing Development and Rehabilitation Corporation (HDRC), and named Bob Holmes, a young lawyer I recruited at Harvard Law School, to run it. Bob now teaches at Rutgers Law School. "Project Rehab" ultimately oversaw the rehabilitation of more than 1,500 units of moderate- and low-income apartments by private developers, mostly in the West Ward.

Also, I funded the Welfare Rights group to run a day-care child care center, under the direction of Janice Day. I saw Model Cities (and city hall in general) as a series of opportunities to convert energy from protest to community building, as I outlined in chapter 9.

Plus we needed troops to maintain our position in city hall—always fresh troops—and hence I wanted allies and young people around me at all times. The youth were to be trained to be the vanguard of the next battlefront, whatever that was. I knew within my heart that the Gibson experiment in city hall would attract enemies, so I intended to teach these young people how to fight on this new battlefield. In the meantime, they had jobs and were learning new skills.

People asked, "What does the Git Down Society do?" The answer was, "We git down!" That seemed like a young, hip thing to say at the time, but the allies of mediocrity within city hall didn't like it. "GDS," as it affectionately came to be known, was perceived as some standing army for me, which more and more put me in the crosshairs of those who wanted me sidelined.

Ken Gibson's Vision

Ken Gibson quickly assured everyone that "I'm the mayor for all the people," sending a message white people needed to hear. "But Ken," we grumbled among ourselves, "all the people didn't elect you." The first black mayor projected himself as conciliator, the end of a long hot summer of racism and violence.

But those of us who came together from our base of street organizations wanted to hear, "At last, our time has come!" Both messages were compatible, but Ken believed in only one. He no longer felt it important to meet with those of us who had championed his election as a group. Amiri Baraka called for such meetings, but I believe we had just that one. It was the mayor's office, very short and perfunctory, where he constantly reminded us that, "There is only one mayor, and that's me." This was a theme that carried way beyond that gathering. "We wanted him to be mayor," Baraka said after the meeting, "but nobody thought he was going to try to run the city all by himself."

The people closest to him were not those of us who had helped him get elected. Put more bluntly: Ken favored white people more than black people as his closest aides and confidants. In his first term, there were Dennis Sullivan, Jack Krauskopf, Ira Jackson, and Pete Curtin; most of them from out of town, all young white men with college degrees and liberal Democratic Party credentials. They were his "aides" and had no line or department responsibilities. They "consulted with the mayor on policy issues." This meant they were into everybody else's business. Later, there were Tom Massaro and Al Faiella, both with paramount access to Ken and large portfolios as Ken's housing redevelopment and economic development officers, respectively. And then there was Tom Banker, who really ran the office of the Business Administrator under Elton Hill. Although they were not all there at the beginning, or all at the same time, these men had more power in city hall than anybody black on Ken's staff throughout his sixteen years in office.

The closest group of black folks to Ken were his buddies, the people he grew up with in the neighborhood. Elton Hill, Pearl Beatty, Dan Blue, and a handful of others. When Ken was first elected, Elton Hill was a carpenter at the Newark Housing Authority, and Ken made him Assistant Business Administrator. While working in City Hall, Elton earned his college degree, and was promoted to Business Administrator in Ken's third four-year-term. In his first term, Pearl became the executive secretary of the Insurance Fund Commission and let the contracts for city insurance policies. Ken eventually had her appointed chairman of the board at the Housing Authority, and saw to her election to the Board of County Freeholders on the Democratic Party line. Dan Blue became the director of the Newark Housing Authority in Ken's second or third term.

There was another level of black folks in city government. Earl Harris was elected councilman-at-large on the Black and Puerto Rican Convention Community Choice ticket, and in his second term in 1974, became the first black City Council President. In 1970, Ken appointed Harry Wheeler as Director of Manpower (job training) programs, and used Harry as his representative on certain speaking engagements.

Harry, like George Richardson, ran against Ken but dropped out in the eleventh hour, pledging support for Ken. Earl, Harry, and several others in lesser roles within the bureaucracy were veterans of the original Black Political Class that got Irvine Turner elected as the first black city councilman in the Central Ward. They brought with them insider skills, which enabled them to maneuver and manipulate within the new administration. Earl made new alliances with the majority white councilmen in his first term of office. He and Ken both slowly backed away from each other. Earl figured he didn't need Ken as much, and Ken didn't trust Earl's ambitions. Such was the nature of city hall hardball politics among those who were once friends.

I Hire My Team

Shortly after my job was announced, I became involved in a conflict with my new boss. That Sunday, somebody rang my doorbell with a fierce urgency. I opened the door, and there stood Donald Tucker, in a huff and sweating profusely. On the way up to the second floor, where I lived for the next eighteen years, Donald began his story. "Junius, Ken won't give me a job. Ken said he wasn't running an employment agency for defeated candidates." I didn't understand why Ken took that position since Donald was one of the candidates on the Community Choice ticket for councilman-at-large and came close to winning. I agreed to talk to Ken.

That Monday was my first day on the job. In the mayor's office, I raised the issue on Donald's behalf. Ken stood firm, repeating what Donald told me about not hiring defeated candidates. "Ted Pinckney also wanted a job," Ken told me, "and I told him 'no.'"

I asked Ken to reconsider. "Think of the impact on you in the community if you don't give Donald the job, and we need Donald on the city council in 1974." Only three of our candidates were elected in 1970, on a city council that seated nine. "We need him in a position where he can run again." Ken was initially unimpressed, but I wore him down. He gave me permission to hire Donald. I made Donald Tucker my third in command, putting him in charge of monitoring the many programs we operated under CDA with a staff of four or five program monitors. He was happy. He could move around and be seen. That was our plan, and it worked to get him elected to City Council in 1974. Donald Tucker died still owing me for that one.

Next I hired Dave Dennison as my second in command. My friend Paul Ylivisaker, then at the Eagleton Institute in Princeton, heard about my appointment and called me to say I would need a good administrator, planning, and grants manager to help me while I was doing the overall administration, the political work with the mayor and city council, and public relations work, including that which was needed within the community. I hadn't thought about that, and on Paul's advice, I hired a young black man from his former shop at the Department of Community Affairs who had the title of state Model Cities Director. Dave could write proposals, had experience in staff management, and knew federal and state program guidelines. His job was to ride herd on the planners and support staff, and monitor new and recurring applications to federal agencies in health care, education, housing, manpower, and law enforcement. I trusted Dave, and our personalities and skills complemented one another.

We were in the age of federal programs. Not since the Reconstruction era had there been so much money poured into the black community by the federal government. It was guilt and fear money, and so there was a mad scramble by the cities to see which one would get the most money, and who would control it once it got home.

Additionally, since Ken was a novelty as the "first black mayor of a major Northeastern city," even the Republicans under President Nixon wanted to be supportive. They couldn't afford the bad publicity if he failed, so they all gathered at the altar with more money. Government money was like a loose-fitting shoe: all we had to do was put it on and lace it up. But there was never enough to make up for the depleted tax base created by the industrial and professional exodus to the suburbs. So our job in Model Cities and CDA was to rake in as much as we could find. And we got real creative about it, more than doubling our initial Model Cities grant of $5.6 million. When added to mortgages for Project Rehab, we projected our overall value at more than $60 million federal dollars during my tenure as director.

Finally, I hired Larry Coggins. I liked Larry from our work together doing Get Out the Vote (GOTV) for Ken on Election Day. Ken didn't have anything in mind for Coggins to do, but wanted Larry's campaign management skills available at the time of his next election. To me, he was a tried and tested community organizer, and so I put him in charge of the Model Neighborhood Council, the citizen participation group I cochaired for its first year. I knew there was respect and affection for me on the council because of my history with them. But I was in a different position now. The council needed some personal stroking and tender loving care, for which I didn't have time to do on a regular basis. Some of their egos had to be stroked, and some individual ambitions for power had to be managed and handled by expert maneuvering. This was part of my community base, and I wanted the people to stay in my corner. As time went by, they helped me sniff out the hound dogs on my trail all over city hall.

In addition, the Neighborhood Council became my muse for developing new programs. It's one thing to tell people "You can participate," but another thing to expose them to real options so that they can make a meaningful, educated choice. I trusted the council with information, and let them travel to see how other Model Cities programs were creatively planning the use of federal dollars. We had high travel expenses, because there were about six committees of up to eight people each traveling all around the continental United States and Puerto Rico visiting other community development programs. So as a result, their discussions at the monthly meetings were about real issues, not complaints. If we heard something from them that was interesting and doable, I put the planners to work on writing a proposal for funding. As a result of their travel and investigation, the Model Neighborhood people grew in knowledge and self-confidence. They became a source of ideas, instead of a disgruntled group ready to cut my throat.

The Ghost of Don Melafronte and the Handwriting on the Wall

But I had an initial problem upon my arrival at the job. In hiring me, Ken called me "capable" along with a lot of other nice words. But Ken was overly impressed with Don Melafronte. Ken wanted me to use the former director as a consultant to "show me the ropes." I agreed to use him for one month. But Melafronte walked into the meeting proposing a contract for one year, to which Ken quickly agreed. Ken was calm as always, and I figured that he and Melafronte had probably talked before the meeting. There was no way I could hold my head up and truly be in charge of CDA with Don Melafronte in the house indefinitely. So I picked up the phone and called Bernice Bass, a woman of great intelligence, political savvy, and caustic wit, who had a weekly talk radio show on WNJR, the black-oriented popular AM radio station in Newark at that time. Every Sunday night at 9 p.m., the political and churchgoing black folks in Newark tuned into Bernice's one-hour program, called *News and Views*, to listen to her thrash the people she didn't like, or laugh and flirt with the ones she did. If there was anyone she hated, it was Don Melafronte. So I told her the bitter pill Ken had asked me to swallow, and had to endure a long lecture on what I should have told Ken. But on the air the next Sunday, she called Ken out: "Why is Ken Gibson hiring Donald Melafronte as a consultant in the Model Cities Program?" And it went downhill from that point forward. I was at home, glued to the radio, laughing my head off! That Monday, Melafronte on his own initiative withdrew the contract. But it told me about Ken and me; about how willing he was to play ball with the man who masterminded Addonizio's racist mayoral campaign. It showed me where our relationship was headed, but I made up my mind to show Ken what an asset I was. This was *my* job.

I made a mistake in judgment about positioning myself with the mayor. Nobody had told me the old city hall idiom about being close to the mayor to "get his ear." The pundits use this as a measuring rod: who gets the office closest to the mayor's office, who gets in to see him without an appointment, and who gets to hold his hand, earliest and most often. Once Ken told me I had the job, I presumed that was a mandate to go out and make things happen. And with Melafronte potentially no longer in the way, I figured I had clear sailing. I settled into the job, from my office on Branford Place three blocks away from city hall, where most of the staff was located. I needed to be there to properly administer a large group of people, I thought. I came over and talked to Ken periodically about our plans. I showed off my staff, especially Dave Dennison, and our command of the new language, familiarity with what was going on, and planning (fund-raising) possibilities. But at those report-out sessions, there was always a look in Ken's eyes like he really didn't understand what I was talking about. Since I had no office in city hall, I was not on hand to reinforce the message and assure him I could be trusted.

But I enjoyed my Branford Place office alongside my troops. I didn't belong in the big house, but out on the kibbutz. Actually, I didn't enjoy being around Ken. He made no effort to befriend me, and though I wanted to be included as one of his go-to guys, he clearly didn't want me too close. So I felt more at ease away from him, which left plenty of time for my detractors to run into Ken's office and undo my tenuous relation with the mayor.

In this respect, Ken and the black people close around him reflected their working-class suspicions about others with middle-class education credentials, especially those of us not born in Newark. Even though Ken and many of his cronies were from down South originally, and Ken had an engineering degree he obtained going to school nights from what is now the New Jersey Institute of Technology, there was a distance between this set and anybody who didn't grow up with them in the immediate hometown neighborhoods. There was a bond outsiders couldn't penetrate.

The Movement earlier helped me to overcome and close the gap of suspicion, since I wasn't raised in Newark and went to "white" schools. In NCUP and NAPA, people like me put ourselves sometimes in harm's way, and the neighborhood people appreciated that. They knew that if we had college degrees, we had other choices. But in Gibson-land, the taint of jealousy and distrust was there, and I always felt a need to prove my loyalty to Ken despite the role I played in his election, and the work I did as Model Cities Director. I made Ken look good. The problem was I looked good too.

Gibson and his confidants were in a position of power for the first time in their lives. A dangerous thing for the working class with no ideology, said Larry Coggins, the former Communist revolutionary, at some of our top staff dinners together. "They've been beaten down all their lives, having to take s—t from the white man, so we all better watch out." We laughed, but there was truth to Coggins's analysis. Here they were, introduced to power not through the politics of confrontation with its vision of self-empowerment for the masses of people, but suddenly thrust into a job under a man they had grown up with, but without a clear ideology for change. A little power is a dangerous thing.

And so upon the election of Ken, there was no need to back-burner their idiosyncrasies. They could let loose all their suspicions, petty jealousies, envies, grudges, hunches, and doubts upon those who were outside the circle. I was perpetually under their critical scrutiny.

Elton Hill and the Control of Jobs

As with all new mayors, and especially the new black mayor, the honeymoon is short before he is faced with the onslaught of the great expectations of the people. Early in the game, upon the advice of Earl Harris, Ken put Elton Hill, his best buddy, in charge of all hiring in city government. Well, not really. Elton certainly didn't hire the lawyers for Corporation Counsel, nor the accountants for the Finance Director. Nor did he hire police and firemen. Since most of the regular jobs were governed by Civil Service regulations, in practice, the hiring edict was aimed primarily at me in Model Cities.

In my quest to fill jobs with capable people, Elton became an obstacle. His power over my organization increased from the ability to "see that certain persons were in place" to actually approving all persons hired within CDA by the end of 1970. The new Employment Czar immediately put people we wanted to hire on check. My appeals to Ken were ignored, and so I stopped asking. And Elton felt he had to show this college-boy Yale lawyer who was in charge. If you were black or white, and even if you came to the job with great skills, you were treated with suspicion and hostility if your candidacy bore even the suggestion that you were "somebody Junius Williams wanted to hire." He even denied a local young woman a job in my evaluations unit, who, upon notice of hiring by us, had quit her job in Boston.

So I had to get around him. I sent people I wanted to hire to Elton through people Ken couldn't deny. Ken was enough of a politician early on to know that he had to build an organization filled with people on his payroll. Despite an early proclamation that he only wanted one term, most of us knew he would come back for more. And so he appreciated stalwarts in the neighborhood like Wiley Crawford and Terry Richardson, two friends from the Model Neighborhood Council. I sent people I wanted hired through these two men on more than one occasion. I also used Al Shapiro, the City Planning Officer who technically worked for me but who had an independent relationship with Ken. As long as Al got an employee he wanted in his department who could really do the work, instead of some political hack Elton might otherwise send, he was up to the task. There were others as well. We never lost a passenger on this, our underground railroad, and accumulated quite a flock of qualified people. I laughed; Dave, Coggins and Donald all laughed, but it wasn't funny.

But sometimes, Elton worked to my advantage. When people came to me for a job who I didn't think could handle the work requirements, the pace of production, or willingness to work with the community, I quickly sent them to Elton. Sometimes they came back with a slip from Elton (his favorite means of communication with me) saying, "This will introduce _____, who will serve as your _____." You win some, you lose some. I would make room for that person, bury him or her in the back of the room, and made sure they weren't in the mainstream of information to report back to Elton or the other Gibsonites.

Ken and Baraka on Jobs

Amiri Baraka had a right to expect that his people would be hired, given the pivotal role he played in Gibson's first election. But on the other hand, there was such arrogance and disregard for formal job requirements coming from some of the people he sent that it made it hard for me to completely discount Gibson's reluctance to hire them. It seems to me with hindsight that the two of them should have worked it out directly. Ken should have taken him to dinner and said, "Baraka, you have to send people qualified for the jobs available; I will see to it that you get two from column A, three from column B over X time period, as jobs come available." But this is not the way it was done, and I understood it better, by and by: Gibson was out to isolate Baraka and had no intention of helping him maintain an independent political organization by providing jobs for his army. There was nothing

I could have done to forestall this except disguise some of his more qualified and easy-to-work-with people, as I did in other cases. Had Baraka asked, I would have told him, "Send me qualified people, over time, and I will find a way to get them in." It would have been good for both of us to have each other as allies. Perhaps I should have suggested it? But I wasn't politically astute enough to see the need for that kind of alliance for my own protection. At that time, I had a pretty big head—and so did Baraka.

City Hall Politics

There were other wars to be fought on the home front. Aside from the people who wanted jobs, we were the targets of those departments that wanted federal dollars for their pet projects. When Gibson took over, Newark was almost bankrupt. There was no way to finance the deficit through federal grants, but the Model Cities money could be used for virtually anything the city felt it needed, so long as it was tied to the Model Neighborhood Area. And there were "citywide" dollars, under the mandate of the Community Development Administration. Consequently, the Police, Fire, and Public Works Directors all had their eyes on Model Cities/CDA money for police cars, fire trucks, and garbage trucks. I was targeted as unreasonable and uncooperative for not listening to their plight. But in my mind, this was a crazy way to spend Model Cities dollars when people in the community needed jobs and opportunities for self-empowerment through creation of recreational, health, housing, and other programs. Unfortunately, Ken's management style left all of us hanging: "You guys sit down and figure something out." I did. We used our knowledge of the federal agencies to attract additional dollars, such as Law Enforcement Assistance Administration (LEAA) grants for police-related work, and other money for the other guys. Still, this bunch was unsatisfied.

And then there were the aides who had nothing to do but tell Ken I was "building an empire over there" and that they were uniquely qualified to rein me in. Empire it was, but it belonged to the mayor. And qualified, they were not. I wasn't about to let "Ken's white boys," as we called them, take over Model Cities. I was just a little too arrogant and independent for them—consequently, they had me in their crosshairs from the beginning.

But I didn't play this game alone. I had a team with whom I shared power within the agency. Every week Donald, Dave, Coggins, and I met over dinner, usually at the Treat Restaurant or one other that I can't remember, both of which have been torn down. We spent long hours together planning, analyzing, plotting, and evaluating what we put into motion. Sometimes, it was about plans to get more grants. Increasingly, it became how to stay alive in city hall, since it was apparent that it was us against the rest of the Gibson administration. The nature of the intelligence I gathered from my supporters changed. No longer were the Gibsonites saying that I was "too young to handle all this." Instead, Terry and Wiley told me Ken thought I was "too fast"; that the mayor "couldn't keep up with me." We always produced; never lost a grant or missed a deadline for submission. No matter how well we performed, to the accolades of the Feds and people in the community, nothing I did was acceptable to City Hall. And we managed always to stay one step ahead of our detractors, who, over time, became legion.

I asked myself a thousand times: "Why?" Don Melafronte spelled it out for me in a conversation I had with him thirty years later:

> The people in City Hall that worked for Ken said, "I got nothing! This guy Williams, he's got it all." They were dealing with a [property] tax–based budget, locked into it. CDA was designed to be off budget; flexible; could change budgetary lines; [create or eliminate] jobs.

He went on to explain that it was less of a problem for him when he was CDA/Model Cities Director because the mostly white administrators in city hall under Addonizio didn't bother him for jobs:

CDA was a black thing with a white guy running it. Who wanted to be involved in "Rat and Pest"? [Deputy Mayor] Paul Reilly got a million requests for jobs at the Board of Education. Even Mayor [Addonizio] didn't want anything to do with federal programs. My generation was not attuned to federal programs... but you, J.W., are coming out of the War on Poverty World. They ask for jobs. Your generation understands quickly that J.W. had all the free money!... It wasn't so much the rank and file as the leadership Ken created, [especially] the four white guys who made you vulnerable [Ira, Jack, Dennis, and Pete, Ken Gibson's aides]. (Interview with Don Melafronte, July 19, 1994)

I didn't fall on my face as predicted, but wore flashy clothes, smoked a cigar, and drew compliments like, "Best Project Rehab (housing rehabilitation program) in the nation" from HUD officials in Washington. In 1972 I became first vice president of the National Model Cities Director's Association, with plans and national support to challenge for the presidency the next year. I got legislation passed by city council that was needed to submit and receive grant applications, while Gibson couldn't get anything passed. I wouldn't let the aides play in my sandbox, and I was loved and appreciated by the community, now as an administrator they could still trust.

I learned to downplay my speeches around Ken, and stayed in the background more than I did before. But in those first two years, we kept turning out product, and the media sought us out. Even though I made Ken look good, it didn't earn me any points.

With my staff, I had the ability to keep on increasing the money we raised. With Dave, Coggins, and Donald, I had the ability to run ahead of Ira, the other aides, and all the other hungry department heads who wanted control over our resources. With Coggins, Earlene, and Wiley Crawford, I maintained the allegiance of the Model Neighborhood Council. With Don Bernard, I had the youth in the Git Down Society. I thought we were on a roll.

The Hammer

But the hammer had already begun to fall. Elton Hill extended his control over the agency with the right to overrule employee terminations by me. By the middle of 1972 he assumed the right to promote or deny promotion. The mayor took away health planning and allowed duplicate criminal justice planning and drug prevention planning under some other office. The Finance Director achieved oversight but not total control over my fiscal operation. In addition, Ken asked me to resign as chair of the HDRC, the CDA housing corporation, which was in charge of Project Rehab, which had plans for new construction on land I negotiated with city council.

This one hurt the most. Everybody knew HDRC was my baby. I had too much power, and Ken was cutting me down to size. It broke my heart, but I understood: It was time to find another job.

What I didn't know was that around this time, Ken asked Melafronte to meet with Dennis Sullivan, his aide. Ken was scared to be seen with Melafronte, I suppose, after Bernice Bass outed him two years before. Melafronte shocked me with news of a conversation between him and Dennis Sullivan in 1972, set forth roughly as follows:

DENNIS. J.W. isn't with the program, but Ken doesn't know how to get rid of him.

MELAFRONTE. All Ken has to do is to fire him.

DENNIS. The mayor thinks there will be too many community repercussions.... Model Cities will be going citywide soon, and the Mayor wants J.W. out. (Interview with Donald Melafronte, June 8, 1994)

In fairness, Dennis Sullivan says he has no memory of such a discussion. And for the record, Model Cities was already "citywide" through the vehicle of the Community Development Administration, of which I was already the director.

Ken was thinking, "How the hell am I going to get this guy out of here?" And I was thinking, "How the hell am I going to get out of here?" Then something happened to rock my world even further and made me change my plans about resigning. It also gave the mayor the excuse he wanted.

The Model Cities Audit

HUD audited our programs every year, and at the end of 1971 the outside HUD auditor "questioned" $300,000 of our expenditures. Anyone who knows government programs understands that a question raised by an auditor can be resolved through adequate additional information and negotiation. In the beginning months of 1972, we were in such a stage, and I was confident the questions would be resolved favorably. So confident that initially I paid very little attention and let Dave Dennison and Fleming Jones, my comptroller, take care of it. In context of the millions we raised, $300,000 did not seem to be a lot of worry about, especially since the expenditures in question could be explained.

But Congressman Joe Minish was running in a new district, which was redistricted to include parts of Newark, and he wanted to show how vigilant he was with the taxpayers' money. And so, one day in 1972, I woke up to front-page headlines in the *Star Ledger* screaming, "HUD Questions $300,000 Spent on Model Cities Program." I was so shocked I remember sitting on the side of my bed in disbelief. This was on a Saturday. And to my amazement, the Sunday paper, the edition everybody read across the state, carried an even bigger front-page version of the same story, well over 1,500 words.

I sat on the side of my bed and cried like a baby. I didn't want to go out of the house. The article suggested, without actually saying, that Minish had discovered misappropriation and theft of funds. My explanations were given only a paragraph or two deep within the second article.

I was devastated. I got a few calls from friends. Somebody told me to make sure I went to the mayor's picnic that was coming up that same Sunday, and to hold my head up. I went and did the best I could, but I felt the judgmental stares, the icy smiles behind which said, "Uh huh—they gotcha, Mr. Big Shot. You thought you were such a hot s—." Only one or two people engaged me in conversation at the picnic. Most people just spoke and kept on going. I was a dead man walking. And I never got a call from the mayor, asking if he could help, or at least, "What's this all about?" or "How are we going to work this out?" That Monday at city hall, I put on a pleasant face, picked my head up, straightened my back, and tried to make the best of it.

But I was beginning to get mad. All I had was my reputation, and "I'll be damned if I'm gonna let some congressman take it away from me!" I ultimately said. All plans to resign were put off. I didn't want anybody thinking I left under a cloud of an impending indictment, which the city hall rumor mill had already propagated. I was dealt a vicious body blow, but I'm a fighter, so I got ready to fight.

Fighting Back

As I studied the audit, I saw that some of the questions focused on issues that should have been brought to my attention by Dave, or by Fleming Jones, who was my comptroller. I was pissed because nobody had told me about some of these items, and nobody had cleaned it up in time. But all the questions raised by HUD had answers that would have relieved the impasse.

There was good reason to have my own comptroller. With the tense relation I had with Anton Jungherr, the Finance Director, there is no way the Model Cities programs would have thrived. Jungherr had to show me he was in charge: I was a black man, not used to bowing and scraping, and he a white man, not used to a black man who didn't bow and scrape. I fought him to the last day to keep my program from being controlled by his minions, who would have delayed all my requests for payment. I can't prove it but I believe I saw his handwriting on the audit exception that claimed we didn't follow "city procedure." Our procedure was city procedure when Melafronte was in charge. There were audits then; why was I so wrong now? The audit didn't claim that the money was misspent and certainly didn't allege that any money was stolen, just that we should have gone about purchasing goods and services in another way.

Should I have been blamed for the allegations in the audit? I called myself not pointing fingers at the staff. Ever watch these kinds of exposés where one insider tries to say, "It's *his* fault"? That would have only fueled a media feeding frenzy, ending up with counter-accusations back at me. So first of all, I made up my mind that the buck stops with me. Win or lose, I would accept the acts and omissions of my staff. The public position I took was that we suffered from "sloppy bookkeeping" and that we had supplied adequate answers to the questions raised by HUD; there was no evidence of fraud, waste, or mismanagement; and therefore we didn't deserve the public black eye so many people were hell-bent on giving us.

The Fight Turns in My Favor

Second, I wrote up our responses to the audit in good journalistic fashion and called the Editor of the *Star Ledger.* The *Ledger* wasn't known for being friendly to "the people" in terms of getting articles printed, but I demanded to speak to the editor, Mort Pye. I wanted equal time to put my responses before the public. I was pissed, and blurted out my point of view in a telephone call. I accused him of complicity in the two-day ambush his paper had initiated on behalf of Minish. It must have pricked his journalistic ethics, or at least his sense of a good story: here was the opposing point of view in a conflict that up to this point had been one-sided. He told me to bring whatever I had right over. It probably surprised him that I had done a real press release, didn't rely on my staff but on my training in writing articles from the days of NAPA, NHC, the *Amherst Student,* and all the way back to the *Spirit of Armstrong.* He read it while I was standing there, handed it to someone (either Chick or Andy) and said in his short, curt fashion, "We'll do something with it." I left annoyed, not expecting much. But on Wednesday, the next day, there was a front page article below the fold putting forth my entire rebuttal to the audit exceptions, point by point, ending with an accusation that set the tone for the battle to come. I said: "Congressman Minish was on a witch hunt!"

My phone rang off the hook, in the office and at home. "Now I see what's going on," most of them intoned, and offered to help. I said to myself, "Funny, because earlier, you were willing to flush me down the toilet without taking the time to hear my side of the story." But to the callers, I merely said, "Thank you."

From that day forward until Mort Pye retired in 1994, I never had trouble getting an article in the *Star Ledger.* All I had to do was type the release, hand it to Mort, who handed it to Chick or Andy, and it was usually printed as written. He trusted my content, and I never violated the trust. Nor did I abuse my privilege with a lot of extraneous puffery.

But one call received in the wake of my rebuttal to Minish was cautionary, coming from Honey Ward, the old Central Ward Democratic leader, who had become my friend after the fight in Gibson headquarters. He told me to be careful how I went after Congressman Minish. He thought I should have kept quiet and let the storm blow over. I thanked him, but told myself while he was still on the phone, "No way!" I didn't care about consequences at that point. He was after my reputation, and I was going after his.

And so Minish struck back in the *Ledger*: He announced a formal Congressional Hearing before him in Newark on the findings of the audit. "You want a shoot-out at the O.K. Corral?" I said to myself, "That's fine with me!" Before the scheduled hearings I prepared myself with Dave and Fleming Jones. I was a lawyer and an advocate; I had never tried a case in court, but I sure had argued and won my case in many community battles. With Fleming on-site to help, I would have all the details before me. If Minish wanted a public brawl, I would give it to him.

Come the day of the event, at the Federal Building in Newark, the room was filled with spectators and the press. Joining Minish at the table in the front of the room was Congressman Rodino, Newark's other congressman and Minish's good friend. Peter W. Rodino and I both nodded in mutual recognition. He smiled, I didn't. He looked a little sheepish being there. He never asked a question, to my memory. There on the side was the stenographer, and seated close by was the GAO attack dog, who dragged up the old HUD audit on Minish's behalf. Minish was prepared to go. I walked in, took my seat at the table, and looked around for my trusted comptroller, Fleming Jones. Fleming wasn't there and never showed. In fact, no one from my office was there but me. I was all alone.

I found out later that the GAO chief auditor told Fleming to "take the day off." It would have been good to have Fleming to help with the details, but by that time I had studied the audit, and knew our responses. Minish read from a list of staff-prepared questions designed to make me look incompetent and dishonest. Minish was not very good at what he was doing, and I ran circles around him with the facts. He may have been a congressman, but he was no match for me in a debate. Public relations–wise, it was a draw. The press carried it like a call and response: he accused, I responded. There was no smoking gun. Anytime you earn a draw in the media with a hostile U.S. congressman, you've really won.

So why didn't I fire Fleming Jones, you might reasonably ask? By that time, Elton Hill had control of not only who I hired, but also who I fired.

The Turning Point

With the help of a media consultant, Dick Call from Los Angeles but in Newark to generate publicity for our successes in the Model Cities Program, I went to television interviews with some on-air hosts and met the top executives of WPIX, WABC, and WCBS. Dick saw they were out to get me, wondered why the mayor didn't help me, and agreed on his own time to make his media contacts available to me. The WPIX interview was a live afternoon talk show with an audience, a kind of forerunner to the Jerry Springer show. The guest host, whose name I forget, tried to insinuate and probe into the audit, but he gave me great big softballs which I hit a country mile. Along the way I got to put in some Model Cities success stories in housing, education, and social services. In about the last twenty seconds of the interview, he said, "Mr. Williams, there are good guys, and there are bad guys... [pause]... and I have decided that you are a good guy!" The audience erupted in applause; he and some other guests came around me, smiled, and shook my hand. I smiled a big Maurice Williams smile, pressed the flesh all the way down the line. TV cameras were rolling, I was a hit, and the happiest guy in the whole world! I'll never forget that feeling for as long as I live. Nor my indebtedness to one Dick Call. (What a name for Hollywood, eh?)

I came home; more telephone calls. Minish, I could feel, was on the ropes. All I needed was one big event to knock him back to the suburbs where he belonged. The team and I planned and announced a community rally, to vindicate the Model Cities Program, to vindicate me. My friend, well-known attorney Ray Brown, agreed to be the keynote speaker, along with other community leaders, Model Neighborhood people—our goal was five hundred people, including staff and community.

And then I got a phone call from one of the mayor's minions. "The mayor says *do not* have the rally." I was stunned and silent for a moment. Up to this point Ken had stayed in the background and let others do his dirty work. Minish was his camouflage, behind which he could engineer not only my departure, but also my complete discrediting in the community. Here was a man whose personal ambitions I made my own; who I helped by running his campaign when no one wanted to be bothered with him; who, subsequent to his election, benefited from the publicity and money I brought to his administration through my successes with federal programs; who probably knew Minish was going to use me as a whipping boy and just let it happen. And now he was telling me not to get my Just Due? I very quietly told the voice on the phone, "Go back and tell the mayor, I intend to hold the rally." It wasn't long before I got a call back from the same person: "The mayor says that anybody on your staff who goes to the rally will be fired."

I couldn't jeopardize people's jobs, so I put out the word through my division chiefs. By now they all knew that Gibson wanted me out. About four hundred people showed up at the rally, including some staff members who put integrity and their friendship with me above their own economic well-being. I will always remember them for that. But none of the team (Dave, Larry, or Donald) showed up.

Rumors of My Untimely Demise Are Not Exaggerated

Nobody got fired—from the staff, that is. But the next day, Gibson finally called me into his office and asked me to resign. I asked him for time to resolve the audit. He said no, that would take too long, but he gave me thirty days "to think about it." During this time I made copies of everything I needed to protect myself. I got ready for the other shoe to fall, but apparently Mr. Minish had had enough of me, or, more likely, had been advised that he wasn't gaining any votes in the black community by continuing the assault on me.

At the end of December 1972, I marched into Gibson's office, told him I had no intention of resigning, and so he fired me on the spot.

During my last month on the job, Ken hired Dave Dennison as Director of Planned Variations, a citywide grant from HUD, which should have come under CDA. The mayor chose to break up the power in the house that Melafronte built. He put Model Cities/CDA under someone else. So, had I stayed, I would have been in competition with Dave Dennison, the man I brought to Newark.

On the day of my dismissal, a friendly CBS-TV newscaster gave me an opportunity for one last shout-out. I looked around. I was the only one standing there. No one rushed to my side to say, "It's terrible what Ken did to you; it's terrible that he's resurrecting all these Addonizio people like Melafronte and others and giving them new life; it's horrible that he's pulling the agency apart instead of using it as the great fund-raising machine and advocacy organization it had become; it's too bad that some of your friends left you out there alone and betrayed you." Nobody was there but me. Why? Because the people I would have turned to in the past now had jobs in city hall. I had gotten some of them these jobs, one way or another. Even friends who I didn't hire had a stake in Ken's administration in one way or another. So I shut up, and went about the business of restoring my life. It was time to do something else.

About one year after my dismissal, while coming off the old Eastern Airlines Shuttle in Washington, DC, a short white man came up to me and said, "Mr. Williams, you don't know me, but I was one of the auditors on your program in Model Cites." I stiffened, not knowing what would come next. He continued, "I was approached by the prosecutor in Newark at that time and asked if there was anything there that could be used leading to an indictment." He certainly had my attention. "I want you to know I told him 'there was nothing there at all.'" He took his time, emphasizing each word. And with that, he turned and walked away, soon lost among the sea of people coming and going at Washington National Airport. As the crowd swallowed him up, I just stood there thinking to myself, "nothing, indeed." And then while walking to my destination, I thought, "How nice it is to know there are some good people in this world."

Postscript: Black Power

I was safe, on my way to recovery. But what about that which I had helped create?

In the 1970s, the energy of the Movement was absorbed by the traditional political system. The black people we elected and the people who supported them for jobs, favors, and opportunities were happier to be inside city hall than they were to continue the struggle. They thought city hall was the end of the journey and couldn't see beyond its limitations.

On the other hand, some of us vested with this momentum and energy saw struggle as a continuum. We wanted more power to gain more access to more distant levels of power, like state and federal government, and the big businesses downtown. All this required more study, different skills, and constant leadership development. Our friends in the New Black Political Class wanted to be consummate insiders, integrated into a system that worked for other ethnic groups like the Italians and the Irish. They ignored or didn't understand the limits of power based on the rules of ethnic succession for black people, established by the white power structure directing state government and private capital from their berths in the suburbs. So this new leadership should have thought of new ways to harness the power we had, which was related primarily to the people in the neighborhoods. "Hey guys, don't you remember how you got there?" The home of Black Power was still energy, fueled by black anger, even rage. Controlled and harnessed through the politics of confrontation.

Integration is the key word here. *Integration* and *assimilation* are two words I often think about even now, and shake my head in regret for the pain and futility they produced. These people, many of them my friends, wanted to be inside so bad they were willing to give up all knowledge of recent history, just to achieve a seat in the mainstream of politics in America.

Integration into the system of city government brought mostly symbolic victories: "the first black mayor," a few jobs mostly in city hall and in the surrounding governmental bureaucracies. But we inherited a tax structure that was inadequate, and our people were kept out of the world of private finance. Federal and state programs diminished in size as the memory of the Newark Rebellion receded into the collective memory of the American power structure. Integration alone was not going to make the governmental and private sectors invest more in Newark.

This desire to be on the inside didn't go unnoticed by the folks who run the country, the Empire, composed of the business and political elite of the United States, operated, prophylactically, through the Democratic Party. Hence these new elected leaders at the local level were quickly and firmly embraced by the party, and received all the attention any newcomer could possibly desire. Ken Gibson became a member of the National Democratic Council and eventually President of the U.S. Conference of Mayors. But what good did this do the city in face of the changing nature of the Democratic Party, guided by President Jimmy Carter and others to the right to become more "centrist" and thus pick up the white sectors of the population lost to the Republican Party when it appeared black people were getting too much of the American pie?

Ken Gibson was uniquely positioned to make a place for himself in the Democratic Party *and* change its rightward drift, at least on the state level. At one of our CDA/Model Cities dinner meetings before I was fired, Larry Coggins came in looking very much defeated. He said, "I told Ken he should let me organize the district leaders in Newark and throughout Essex County, to make Ken county chairman [of the Democratic Party]." Boom! There it was. Ken, as the "first black mayor," was the highest black elected official in New Jersey's history, and one of only a handful of mayors in the country. He automatically had a following beyond Newark with no competition for loyalty. Had he authorized Coggins to run district leaders throughout the city and county, including some liberal reform-minded whites and among the new Latino population, Ken could have unseated Dennis Cary and become a Democratic Party powerhouse in Essex County. He would decide who "got the line" for countywide and statewide elections (that is, "Line A," to make it easy for lazy American voters to pick candidates on the ballot without moving too far down the ballot); he would have controlled the Party purse strings; he would have had district leaders to get out the vote in every election in New Jersey for candidates of his choice. Anybody seeking election to the statehouse and ultimately the White House would have to come by him. But Ken told Larry "No," and thus a once-in-an-era opportunity went by. Later, Ken would run for governor in 1981, and for county executive in 1998, losing both races. Why? Because he had no organization sufficient to raise money and get out the vote. Had he commissioned Larry and turned us loose in CDA to get the job done, what would the history books have said?

By the middle to the end of the 1970s, Black Power as we envisioned was a dream deferred. And I was no longer in a position to awaken the minds of the people about what was happening.

12
NATIONAL BAR ASSOCIATION

Ain't no stoppin' us now
We're on the move!

—MCFADDEN & WHITEHEAD, "AIN'T NO STOPPIN' US NOW"

Reflections as a New Lawyer

In 1973 I had to become a "real" lawyer: I had to open up a practice. Remember me, not wanting to go to law school? Even after graduation from law school, there was still some doubt in my parents' minds. My father and mother had visited me at the NAPA office in 1968, the one room converted candy store on South Orange Avenue. When they returned to Richmond, my father had asked my mother, "Is that what we sent that boy to Yale to do?" I remember how proud and relieved my parents were when I passed the bar in 1969. And then they came to see me get sworn in as a lawyer, along with Ruth and my brother, Johnny, later that same year.

That ceremony in Trenton was my father's last time in New Jersey. Two years later, he died of cancer. He never saw me practice law, but he and my mother knew that they had gotten me into a secure position. I had the safety net and launching pad on terms they could understand, as old school Virginia, Jim Crow survivors, using black folk's logic. How wise and prescient they were convincing me to go to law school, and what a great gift of love. I cry as I write this paragraph because in so many ways they projected me into a life to come.

I began my law practice at 24 Commerce Street in downtown Newark. Small cases came in while I worked at the Committee on Minority Affairs (COMA), a six-month Regional Plan Association job Gus
Heningburg got for me in New York City after Model Cities. The cases
were enough to pay for the rent and my secretary Sharon's salary, and
COMA paid my salary. But after that six-month head start, I heard a
voice say, "You on your own, boy!" (God was after all, a Southern, colored God). Consistently for ten years, the little people of Newark were
my clients, and they sustained me at the level they could afford. There
were referrals from people all over, especially from folks in Model
Cities and throughout the realm of Gibson-land. They couldn't stop
Ken from firing me, but they could send me cases. They wanted me
whole, and so there was always something coming in. The amounts
paid, however, were another issue. There were days to follow when I
paid Sharon and Mr. Landlord, Mr. Electric-man, and Mr. Telephone-
man, and didn't have very much left over for me.

I practiced Door Law: I took whatever cases came in the door.
Divorces, landlord-tenant, real estate closings, and lots of criminal
work. There were a few civil rights discrimination cases, but I didn't
like federal court. I wanted personal injury cases, but black folks
thought Jewish lawyers could get them more money.

I poured myself into my practice, just as I had in the Movement
and Model Cities. I was a workaholic. The courtroom became my
forum, and criminal cases my passion. Most of my first cases were in
Municipal Court before a judge with no jury, but I gradually began
trying cases before juries.

But it was hard to develop a criminal practice in the early 1970s. The
public defender system made it possible for poor and working-class
defendants to get a court-appointed lawyer, and the big spenders went
to lawyers who were already established, like Ray Brown and John
Love, preeminent black lawyers in Jersey City and Newark, respectively.

By word of mouth, and winning, I got bigger cases. Not bigger money, necessarily, but more serious crimes, like armed robbery and even murder. My clients were always poor, and I had a reputation for taking cases for little or, in some cases, no money.

The best case I ever tried sums up my life before the criminal bar. DJL was accused of robbing a store in Elizabeth, New Jersey, and shooting a police officer. Every morning at the trial, the cops wheeled in the victim in a wheelchair, to let the jury see the evidence of my client's alleged dastardly deed. Everyone in the court was convinced DJL was guilty when I started trying the case. During the two week trial, I had a pushing and shoving match with the prosecutor over a picture that showed my client with a full beard at the time of arrest when eyewitnesses said the perpetrator of the crime just a few days earlier had only a goatee. My investigator found two witnesses that had been suppressed by the prosecutor, and I gave a two hour summation that was "great," according to the "buffalos," retired old men who did trial-watching as a hobby. The jury came back, lined up in front of the judge, and declared my client "not guilty." Then the judge gave the jury a tongue-lashing, telling them they had committed a "travesty against justice." The jurors were horrified by his attack. As they hung their heads going out of the courtroom, the only two happy people in the court were DJL and me. And some of the buffalos, who gave me smiles of approval.

I just knew this was the case that would shoot me to the top of the criminal law profession. "Judge Tells Off Jury" screamed the headlines of the Elizabeth daily paper. Then they had quotes from the prosecutor, the injured police officer, the judge, all damning the results. And who was the lawyer that pulled off this amazing verdict? They never even mentioned my name. It was a brilliant win, but those looking for the lawyer that beat the police, prosecutor, and judge against all the odds in Union County had no idea who to call. I had just spent two weeks in court, lost five pounds, got behind in other cases, not to mention the people who went somewhere else because I couldn't return their calls—and I got no play for beating the state and keeping an innocent man from going to jail! And to cap it all off, DJL said, "Thank you," but didn't finish paying me the second half of the fee he had agreed to pay. I had proceeded to trial without tucking all of Mr. Green into my shallow little pocket, and got stuck with the investigator's fee as well. After the trial was over, how was I going to sue a street vendor and expect to get paid?

In short, the life of a black attorney in solo practice practicing criminal law can indeed be brutish and quite short, without other options. I grew tired of it. It got to me after a while, the lack of money, and the constant battles against the odds; I'm a team player, basically, and I like being able to depend upon other folks while I'm in battle. Had I been in a firm, with two or three lawyers to help talk me through the matter, cover for me when I had to be in another court, handle motions while I did research or even worked on another case, then maybe, just maybe, I would still be in the game.

I never actually quit criminal defense work, but simultaneously I looked to other areas of the law. I represented some young men who were protégés of boxing legend Muhammad Ali. I let them use my office to set up their businesses based on licenses Ali gave them to sell products bearing his name and likeness. Eventually they did very well in boxing promotion and other businesses, but never once looked back to take me with them as their lawyer when they got big. I represented a man, D.W., with a casino game that some men in the gambling business had tried to steal from him. One day I received a ton of moving papers from a recognized law firm in Newark with a request to a judge for an order declaring that D.W. had signed away all his interest in the game. Within the allotted time for an answer, requesting no extension of time, I did the research and writing and had D.W. in U.S. District Court in Trenton. The opposing counsel called to discuss the case disposition. During the conversation he wanted to know, "What law firm did you work for? And where did you say you went to law school?... Oh!" They were surprised. I was a young, sole black practitioner, from

Newark, a person they had never heard of, and I evened the playing field just like that. I negotiated a good settlement for D.W., but the thieves forfeited payment when the game proved to be unmarketable. Their corporation had no assets upon which I could levy, and the judge, despite good law to the contrary, refused to allow me to "pierce the corporate veil" and go after the perpetrators individually. Up to this point, for a period of six months or more, I had financed the defense and prosecution of this case. I couldn't go any further, and despite the protests of D.W., who had no money, I did not (could not) file an appeal.

Such was the psychological nature of my practice for the first few years. Every time I thought I hit a home run, the ball died in deep center field. But I was in no way about to go out of business. The cases and business opportunities kept coming in.

And all the time I was learning. I learned how to run a business, attract clients, manage my money, budget for the future, and keep good records. As a sole practitioner, you have to be a rainmaker and do the work as well. So I learned to do research quickly and efficiently, and to write all kinds of complaints, briefs, motions, and other pleadings. Remember, there was no computer to store documents and files. Every pleading had a hard copy template, saved from the last time something like this came up, or taken from *New Jersey Practice* or some other legal form book. And then it had to be typed by my secretary, on a typewriter, thankfully, with a correction key.

My writing was my most prized deliverable. Judges didn't have time, and I didn't have time, for puffery. Today I pride myself on getting to the point quickly, to dispose of the argument in lean sentences.

"Is That All There Is?"

These words are from the rock-and-roll lyricist Jerry Leiber of the talented songwriting duo Stoller and Leiber and sung in the sultry voice of Peggy Lee. It sums up how I felt about practicing law after a while. I had been in one of the best laboratories for the development and use of power in this country, and here I was confined to a solo law practice. The work was challenging, and the financial rewards were beginning to appear below the bottom line. But it just wasn't enough. I craved for more than just the economic benefits, and looked for other ways to satisfy my need for personal fulfillment.

Because of my political exile in Newark, the courtroom was the only forum I had in the early 1970s. I had to adjust over these years, no longer the center of attention, no longer on the cutting edge of city government or in the street in some confrontation. "I must be at this point for some reason," I thought to myself. Times had changed, and the nature of advocacy had changed.

So I had to focus out of town to become engaged in something bigger than the day-to-day existence of a trial attorney. I became active in the National Bar Association (NBA), the oldest and largest organization of black attorneys in the United States.

Welcome to the National Bar Association

I first went to the NBA Convention in July 1971, while still working for Mayor Gibson. I think I was on a panel of some kind, talking about urban problems. Then in the winter of 1972, while still in city hall, I attended a Model Cities conference in San Juan, Puerto Rico. After working hard all day long in the hot Caribbean sun, even Model Cities Directors got the night off, so I went to a casino. I spent my limit on the blackjack table ($50), when I bumped into O.T. Wells at a crap table, winning money and holding the crowd with his personality and humor. O.T. was president-elect of the National Bar Association. We remembered each other from Harvard Law School, where we had been invited as speakers. I stayed at the table until O.T. decided his luck had changed, and then joined his entourage leaving the casino.

We went to another night club off Calle Condado, the main street.

A band was playing, but it was late. I pulled out one of my blues harps, got the right key, and began to play along with the band while sitting at the bar. O.T. said, "You play harmonicas, man?" I told him I did. He listened for a minute as I rolled off a blues riff, and after calling me a "harmonica-playing mutha-you-know-what," he rushed me up front and told the band leader, "I got a well-known harmonica player in the audience, and you got to let him play."

The guy told O.T., "It's quittin' time, and I'm getting' outta here."

O.T. said, "I'll pay you extra if you play one more song so my man here can play." O.T. pulled a wad of bills out of his pocket, and before I could say "Wow," I was on the stage throwing down on some blues. O.T. tells the story that we stayed all night, and the story gets more and more elaborate every time I hear it. I only remember playing one or two songs, but O.T.'s version sounds better. By the time the bar finally closed, O.T. and I were friends.

I Join the NBA

O.T. told me, "You ought to come to the next National Bar Association Convention," which in 1972 was in Miami. I had gone to the NBA Convention in Atlanta the year before. The NBA is the oldest and largest organization of black attorneys in the country, and probably in the world. O.T. got me on the program, doing a seminar on something to do with Model Cities. My seminar was small compared with whatever was happening next door. I could hear loud voices of protest coming through the wall into my room. It was a familiar sound, and I wanted to be over there, but I had responsibilities where I was. Later I learned that this was a meeting of the Black American Law Student Association (BALSA) who were upset about notions of respect coming from the leadership of the NBA.

But I had come into the organization on another level, as the mentee of O.T. Wells. He introduced me to the movers and shakers of the

NBA, all men except for a few women lawyers. Most were a generation older than me. This was the only group of black professionals I ever became a part of, and I felt comfortable with them right away. There was something very familiar and welcoming about who they were. In the generation of black lawyers that preceded me, most had gone to black colleges and black law schools. I had forfeited a certain sense of belonging and community nurturing when I left Richmond and went to Amherst and Yale, and so it was great to live it vicariously with these black men and women. This was like a big family of black professionals, who came to vacation with their wives and families each a year and attended seminars on various points of law. I made friends easily, and fell right into the jokes, the laughter, the "hiking" on one another that I grew up with in Richmond.

The Common Black Professional Experience

At that time in our age group or older, we all had Jim Crow in common. Jim Crow forced us together, and even though some of us wanted to be white, we thrived as a separate culture. Jim Crow forced us to enjoy each other, because alas, we were not white. We thrived, separated from the dominant culture, because the value of our culture was more pronounced as a means of survival and self-fulfillment. By the 1970s our culture was even stronger because of the Civil Rights and Black Power movements. Note well: this was not the Black Power set. But even the biggest Uncle Tom lawyer in town relied upon black culture to survive.

First of all, most of them had their own practice and attracted mostly black clients. There weren't many jobs open in the corporate firms for black lawyers. There were some opportunities in government, and in colleges and universities. But the overall template was work-for-yourself. This made them an independent bunch of individuals, mostly men, who practiced as sole practitioners or in firms of two or three lawyers. Most of them were trial lawyers, and of that majority, most practiced criminal law, handled accident cases and divorces, and did real estate closings. Many of them were quick thinkers and made their living convincing a jury of something. The men liked good whiskey and bragged a lot about women they claimed they had. The few women lawyers looked at the men and shook their head as if to say, "You lying, and it sure wasn't me!"

The men and women of the NBA loved black music, humor, and dancing. Because of Jim Crow, class distinctions were blurry until black professionals started moving into the suburbs because of the successes of the Civil Rights Movement. So black lawyers through the 1960s and into the '70s still celebrated being black—in church, in the barbershop, in the local bars, in schools, in fraternities and sororities, and at work. Being conscious of being separate and distinct minimized the class boundaries and gave us something to be proud of.

But class distinctions did exist. Some of these lawyers made big money, and they let everybody know it through conspicuous consumption and all the black bourgeoisie attitudes that came with it: the clothes they wore, the whiskey they drank, the high-maintenance wives who spent their money, and the money they spent at the conventions. These black lawyers saw themselves as the "talented tenth," and although they danced the same dances as the poor and working-class black folks, the dance partners were preferably middle-class, of the opposite sex, and being danced at some fancy gathering, like the NBA. There was indeed one common culture, just subdivided according to how much money you made. But as a race of people, looking beyond the issue of class that divided us as described, it was clear we were on the cutting edge in this country with our culture much celebrated through music and humor, and our politics still producing dividends.

So most of the people I found in the NBA in the early 1970s had not been so integrated into the world of white people that they had lost their "flava." And that was so important to me, because I just love being cullud!

The NBA was an institution that had withstood the test of time. Lawyers from a handful of states who were pioneers as lawyers founded the NBA in 1925, in Iowa, of all places. All the lawyers who litigated the related cases lumped together as *Brown v. Board of Education of Topeka, Kansas*, had been members at one time of the NBA. Those alive and well at that time still came to the conventions, like Thurgood Marshall, James Nabrit, Oliver Hill, and Constance Baker Motley.

In the NBA I found a home because there were enough people sure of who they were, people too busy letting their own light shine to worry about how bright mine was shining. There were advocates, businessmen and women, politicians, judges, government lawyers, and academics who made room for one another and enjoyed each other's company, even when there was disagreement about lifestyle and values. Maybe it worked because we saw each other for such a short period of time, and only once a year, but I found a place where I could use my talents and have fun at the same time, without worrying about losing my job, or losing my sense of who I had become. In the NBA, my self-confidence was renewed. I could laugh, learn, be appreciated, and appreciate those I came to respect and admire.

Planning the President's Convention

In Miami, O.T. Wells became the president of the NBA. He calls himself "The last of the imperial presidents." He made me "assistant regional director," although no such office existed in the NBA Constitution. And in early 1973, having recently opened my new law office, I got a call from O.T. that changed my priorities.

He told me that the convention had been scuttled in Los Angeles because of some problems with the Los Angeles lawyers who were planning the event. The new site was now San Francisco, the date was in late July, and guess what, Junius: "You're in charge of planning my convention." I must have said, "What, are you crazy? Have any arrangements been made? Who has agreed to be your speakers for the seminars?" OT told me that the Hyatt Regency Hotel had been booked, and maybe one or two main speakers. But the rest was left to me.

On an act of faith he gave me the responsibility for the final act that would define the NBA legacy of O.T. Wells in the minds of thousands of lawyers, law students, and their wives and significant others. "O.T., I could have done you in!" But instead, it got me hooked on the NBA, probably forever, unless they do something after this book to really piss me off.

From my law office on Commerce Street in Newark, and at my own expense, I made calls to people I had never met, from names O.T. and other NBA folks gave me. I threw myself into the task with all the passion and zeal I had previously done with NCUP, NAPA, the Medical School Negotiations, NHC, electing Ken Gibson, and running Model Cities. Work that I enjoy challenges me, makes me come alive. I wrote letters, made return calls, got to know lawyers over the phone. Think about it: there were no email, fax, or cell phones—just office telephones and snail mail. My job was to get multiple speakers for panels, which was the basis of the education engine that was the NBA for the hundreds of lawyers who would enter this brand-new Hyatt on the bay in San Francisco. And oh, yes, somebody should have told Ruth and me that it was cold in San Francisco in July! We came dressed for Los Angeles weather and got frozen to death—had to buy topcoats.

In those phone calls and conversations leading up to the big date, the lawyers I met by telephone were indeed evidence of how far we had come as a people. I contacted lawyers in entertainment and sports law, various government practices, and all the new exotic topics that were now opening up to black lawyers as a result of the politics of the '60s and '70s, like securities and health law. I was able to secure commitments from prominent lawyers in every field imaginable—some of them black, some white. And I made lots of new friends along the way.

The New Young Lawyers

The convention was a success. O.T. did in fact shine, in his own open, gregarious, ostentatious, imperial way, so much so that the young lawyers who were increasing in number because of gains created by the Movement were grumbling and mumbling loudly about our future with the bar. We enjoyed the fun and friendships, being able to rub shoulders with the glitterati of the entertainment and sports industries that our lawyers could produce. But we wanted a bar association that was more professionally organized, with accountability beyond the one year held by the president. Yes, we enjoyed the seminars and plenary speakers, but this was not the full picture that most of us saw. Something had to be done to project the collective power that was the NBA, and that meant changing the image of America's oldest and largest organization of black lawyers.

Some of the young conspirators began to meet. We were the beginning of the second attempt to formulate the Young Lawyers Section of the National Bar Association. For whatever reason, the group that came together earlier didn't stay organized, and so it was left to us at the convention in San Francisco a year later to make it happen. I became the first chairman, principally on the strength of the contacts I made with lawyers within my generation when I was planning the convention for O.T. But I was not alone in the mission to give the NBA a makeover, based upon a vision of professionalism and power we felt was potentially ours. There were people such as Shelvin Hall from Chicago, now a judge on the Illinois Court of Appeals; Buddy Blakey from Louisville, Kentucky; Al Lester and Golden Johnson, friends of mine from Newark; Arthenia Joyner, from Florida, now a state senator; Janice Orr, from Washington, DC; and many more. Forgive me but space prohibits me from calling the roll.

Note that there were a lot of women. Women always make the best revolutionaries; I'm always happy that they bring me along. Some of these same young women lawyers got together in the following year to begin the Women's Division of the NBA, to promote their own interests in an organization long dominated by men. But in 1973, the cutting edge of the NBA was the Young Lawyers Division. We decided to run Arthenia Joyner for treasurer. The incumbent treasurer was a man named C.C. Spaulding, the heir to the North Carolina Mutual Insurance dynasty. We wanted a young, vibrant, independent treasurer to bring some checks and balances on the office of the president. Translated: we couldn't topple the old order all at once, so we decided to hit 'em in the pocketbook.

With the backing of this new organized group of young lawyers, Arthenia was elected the treasurer. I was elected to the board of the NBA, and remained chairman of the Young Lawyers Division. In Chicago in 1974, I became fourth vice president. The word got around: "the Young Lawyers are on the move, so be careful with your ambitions." Joyce London (Alexander), later appointed the first black female U.S. District Court magistrate in the country in her home state of Massachusetts, hosted our first campaign party in her hotel room. It was not a suite because none of us could afford one at that time, so we pushed the bed up against the wall, and had so many people crammed into her single room with our boom box blasting that the folks were spilling out into the hallway. Heretofore, NBA lawyer parties were glass-clinking receptions, held in the suites among the older elite, or in the reception rooms on the lower floors of the hotel. After 1974, we partied! And on the strength and loyalty of our following, I ran successfully over the next three years for the third and second vice presidential spots, and finally for the office of president-elect. During that one-year period, I crisscrossed the country, using my listening ear developed as an organizer in the movement, looking for leadership in my age group that should be supported and in turn would support us, developing an idea of who "my people" were in this period of the fast-moving '70s and gaining a national perspective of the issues that affected the profession and communities. And I did it at my own expense. My law practice always subsidized my politics. Isn't that the way it should be?

And so in 1978, I was sworn in as president of the National Bar Association at our annual convention in Hollywood, Florida, at the age of thirty-four. I am still the youngest person ever to become president.

I am happy I was patient before running for president-elect. As I rose within the ranks, I developed allies among the older generation of lawyers. They saw me working on committee assignments, heard me speak, and understood what I was all about. I earned their trust, and they were willing to listen to my ideas, which weren't too much different from theirs. Because I had developed not only a following but cultivated young people with whom I wanted to work, I had young people ready to carry out leadership assignments the day after I was sworn in.

"The Year of Affirmative Action"

My theme was "The Year of Affirmative Action." I became president during the time when civil rights gains were under attack and being slowly eroded by the political right in this country. In places all over, like Newark, the organizational bridge that had brought us over was slowly crumbling, but most of us didn't see it. And so, I traveled the country, talking and teaching young people about the need to "stand strong" in support of affirmative action plans in colleges and universities in the face of the *Bakke* case, which introduced "reverse discrimination" into the lexicon and hierarchy of American values.

But under my presidency we did more than preach. With the help of Robert Archie, a Philadelphia lawyer and chairman of the Commercial Law Section, we intensified the NBA push to have Fortune 500 companies hire black firms as outside counsel. This was not new, but we took it to new heights: in my closing convention in 1979 in Los Angeles, we had at least seven or eight general counsels from the largest companies in the country on-site to interview black firms in my suite as president of the NBA. Tens of lawyers crowded in, drank my liquor, and met the top lawyers of the companies that would in some cases become their new clients. Even today, I get "thank yous" from lawyers whose firms grew as a result of the business they got from companies that day.

Other opportunities emerged to enhance black lawyers in the legal profession. The NBA earlier persuaded the White House to allow the organization similar privileges afforded the American Bar Association: we reviewed the credentials of the minority judges and attorneys nominated for the federal judiciary. I created a Judicial Review Committee, headed by my friend Sam Jackson, then of the law firm Stroock and Stroock and Lavan in Washington, DC, but formerly an assistant secretary at HUD under Nixon. The *NBA Bulletin* said of this effort:

> On the issue of the judiciary, the National Bar Association led the minority effort to increase the number of minority judges selected for the Federal Bench. . . . As a result of this concerted effort, Anna Diggs Taylor, Joseph C. Howard, Joseph W. Hatchett, Nathanial Jones, and Gabriella McDonald were nominated for federal judgeships.

But it was because of Annette Adams, a.k.a. "Peaches," who became the assistant chair of the International Affairs Committee, that I scored my most lasting achievement and victory as president of the NBA.

The present-day African nation of Zimbabwe was formerly known as Southern Rhodesia under British colonial rule. After years of guerilla warfare, in 1979 white Prime Minister Ian Smith prepared a constitution that purported to pass power to the black majority, but which in reality did not. You had to read the fine print, and that's what lawyers do better than most people.

Peaches told me that John Peyton (later president of the NAACP Legal Defense Fund until his untimely death in 2012) and other members of our committee had done an analysis of the "Muzorewa Constitution" to show that the colonialists would use a house Negro named Bishop Abel Muzorewa and this constitution and stay in power forever. After meeting with John Peyton and another lawyer who had helped him, we quickly agreed that this should be an NBA document on the matter of independence of the new nation of Zimbabwe. But how to make it worth more than a document to put on the shelf, or in somebody's files?

I got on the phone at my office in Newark and called my friend Irving Davis, formerly the International Affairs chairman in SNCC. Irving Davis was a nationalist and an internationalist. Irving knew everyone that needed to be known on the African continent. I showed him our paper, his eyes lit up, and he immediately told me, "We got to take this to the United Nations!"

Irving saw the potential power in what we had done, more so than the lawyers who were around me. We wanted to drive a wedge between world public opinion and this barely camouflaged effort by the white settlers to stay in power in southern Africa, a move that would have been acceptable to the United States and other Western powers. Calling a press conference would not work. No one would come. A press release might get some play, especially with the black press, but why not stage a world event right here in our backyard, at the United Nations?

Irving took copies and went to work. Within a few days he had me scheduled to present the full paper before the UN at a meeting of the

Organization of African Unity (OAU), to be held at UN Headquarters in New York City.

I went to the UN on the appointed day with members of the NBA International Affairs Committee. It was my first time, and I soaked in the pomp and circumstance of the surroundings and of the occasion. Here were people of all colors, some with headphones, listening as my speech was translated into I don't know how many languages. I read the entire report, and everybody listened. John and the committee members had painstakingly dissected every paragraph of the constitution, showing that black Africans would control none of important features of government. It was easy reading. It was not that Africans and others didn't know the deception, but here were lawyers, black lawyers, spelling it out on an international stage in the language of the law. My heart races and fills with pride every time I think about that moment in the UN; proud of my friends in the NBA, each of whom played a role in making this happen; proud of the connection I had made with Mother Africa. I was happy for the NBA because this was indeed a first for the organization. And I was thrilled that I, as a great-great-great-grandson of unknown enslaved Africans, was standing in the United Nations with a gift for the people of Rhodesia/Zimbabwe in their struggle for freedom.

When I finished, there was great applause and a rush toward me to shake my hand. In the swirl that followed my presentation, I saw and felt what Brother Malcolm must have experienced when he went to Africa: there were Africans of all sizes, shapes, colors, and dressed in all kinds of garb, from European business suits to flowing African garb symbolic of the many cultures. From Egypt to Ghana, from Libya to Zaire, to the unseated delegations representing the independence movements in places not yet free, like South Africa—everybody wanted our paper. I met enthusiastic people in the delegation from the Zimbabwe African National Union (ZANU), who especially wanted the document to send or take back home to the guerillas fighting for independence in Zimbabwe. Here was the argument they had been making, just in more detail, done in the language and in the format imperialists understood. I still think of the moment and get chills. Thank you, even now, Irving, John, and Peaches for making that such a full moment.

Neither the happening in the UN nor our analysis got much press in this country. The *New York Times* carried a small article, but it made front page of the *Ghanaian Times* the next day. My friend Sati Mould, who I had met through a client in New York, wrote me and said, "What have you been doing . . . I read about you in the paper in Accra [Ghana], and I knew you were alright!" And you can bet your bottom dollar that the people in the State Department read it, and understood it. The *NBA Bulletin* sums up the move:

> March 29 [1979]. The National Bar Association today urged President Carter to continue to adhere to the United Nation's Security Council sanction against Rhodesia. NBA President Junius Williams cited Rhodesia's historical and continuing subjugation of the African majority; the fallacy of the recently adopted Rhodesian constitution and the inconsistencies of the Case-Javits amendment which recommends that the current U.N. sanctions be lifted.

It is my understanding that President Carter used our analysis in deciding to uphold sanctions against Rhodesia, urged upon him by a member of his staff who was also a member of the NBA.

In the face of the rising tide of international public opinion, the Constitution was scrapped, and in 1980 Rhodesia became the independent nation of Zimbabwe. The NBA was by no means responsible for the heavy lifting that won freedom from white colonial rule. Most of the credit is owed to the people themselves. But I would like to think we had something to do with helping them along the road to freedom and independence.

The 1979 NBA Convention, Los Angeles

All good things must come to an end, and for the NBA president, it's at the annual convention at the end of his or her one-year term. My convention in Los Angeles in 1979 was like a who's who of important people in the United States, and in the emerging African nations. I told John Crump, our executive director, who I wanted as speakers and special guests to celebrate what we had become as a bar and what I had done as its leader. Andrew Young, still in his position as U.S. ambassador to the United Nations, was the banquet speaker. Bill Lucy, treasurer of the American Federation of State County and Municipal Employees (AFSCME), and Malcolm Corrin, president of the International Congress of Business Opportunity (ICBO), also came to help me celebrate. During my presidency, Bill Lucy had me speak at the Coalition of Black Trade Unions conference in Detroit. I came into a big church, right from the airport, dragging my suitcase and briefcase from some other engagement, tired as all get out. But when I saw all those mostly black folks, and heard Bill warming up the crowd and listened to all that gospel music that was playing behind him as I made it on up front to the pulpit, I threw away the speech, and just spoke. I don't remember what I said, but they loved it, and so did Bill. It was on the subject of fighting for our rights to affirmative action. I finished my speech, got my suitcase, and made it on back down the aisle to go to the airport, with the sounds of the applause ringing in my ears. It was a heady feeling, and I wanted Bill there and other friends like Malcolm to be with me.

Then there was my friend Wiley Branton, dean of the Howard Law School, who I asked to emcee the Friday-night banquet. Wiley was a prominent civil rights lawyer in Arkansas, and told some of the best jokes I still remember, like the one about a law school dean being the same as a fireplug for a dog.

Also, the African ambassadors and the representatives of the governments in the making were there, such as Johnny Makatini from the African National Congress in South Africa. The Nigerian ambassador, who I met at Turk Thompson's, agreed to help me introduce an idea of bringing black professionals to Zimbabwe. I don't remember the names, but I do remember they were glad to establish a relationship with an organization of black lawyers who appreciated who they were and what they were trying to do.

The California people added two political major-league hitters. Mayor Tom Bradley, the first black mayor of Los Angeles, and Governor Jerry Brown, both of whom gave remarks.

Louis Farrakhan

My keynote speaker at the opening session was Louis Farrakhan. I met Minister Farrakhan when I was a law student at Yale in New Haven, Connecticut, where he was the imam at the local Muslim mosque. In 1979 he was the national spokesperson for the Honorable Elijah Muhammad. I called him, got through his Chicago bureaucracy, and he remembered me. After we talked, he agreed to come.

This was a new moment for the NBA, one quite challenging for conservative lawyers, some of whom were old enough to be my parents. Civil rights, yes; but a spokesman for the Nation of Islam, the organization of Elijah Muhammad; the organization Mike Wallace on CBS had called *The Hate That Hate Produced,* in the person of a man the Empire had cast as the most controversial black man in America? So when the dais was announced, Farrakhan and I walking side by side, there was a hush in the audience. In fact, there was absolute silence, where at other conventions there was generally a buzz about the dais guests. I had never felt that chill before. Had I gone too far? I kept my head up, a smile on my face and we walked to the platform together.

The place was packed at this the first plenary session, and that was a bit unusual for a popular place like LA. But here was something unusual, and the lawyers flocked to the great hall to see this man the media branded as verboten, but that their popular president had dared bring to Los Angeles.

I introduced Louis Farrakhan, telling the New Haven story. Unfortunately there is no record of my speech because the company who had the convention recording contract decided not to turn on the tape until Farrakhan got up to talk.

Before a hushed audience, he arose, shook my hand, smiled warmly, and began to charm the members and guests of the National Bar Association.

I should never have worried about his reception, because he was in his element. He thanked me for reaching out, reconnecting after all these years, and asked, "What does a black Muslim minister have to do with the National Bar Association?" And then over the next hour, he told us. His theme was "justice," and to talk about justice, he had to walk us through the history of injustice. He was interrupted by applause at least twenty times; he joked, cajoled, used his characteristic sarcasm when talking about those who run America without once calling white people out of their name. He had the audience laughing, talking back, cheering him on as he made the connection between blacks of all stripes and how we must work together and overcome.

Was it a new set of solutions? No. Was it a unique political analysis? Not really. Was it different from what Jesse or any of the other civil rights leaders would have said? Yes, because it came from a man that had been targeted for us to hate by the Empire, especially by his own people, and he just wouldn't let us do it. I have been to thirty-nine NBA conventions, missing only one in the last forty years because of the sickness and eventual death of my mother, but I have never heard an audience response like the one given Farrakhan on that morning. The standing ovation lasted for well over a minute. And he pushed my stock way up! Thirty-four years later, I get compliments about that convention, and "the speech that Farrakhan made."

Reflections on the NBA

My leadership rise within the organization and my presidency was a coming together of a lot of people and interests, intersecting with historical and current world events, all comingling in imperfect fashion. This was perhaps best exemplified by my convention that culminated (and highlighted) my presidency. I told you, all NBA presidents think we are the most unique.

But the convention in many ways was anticlimactic. Over a four-year period, I had used the skills of an organizer to put myself into a position inside the NBA to make it one of the most influential organizations in the country at that time. The NBA was my salvation, kept me from wallowing in self-pity about my unfortunate demise in city hall in Newark, and put me on a national and even international pedestal.

My voice as a radical thinker found new avenues of expression, especially in support of Zimbabwe. I made new friends all over the globe for following my instincts and relying upon my contacts that took the organization and me way beyond traditional NBA boundaries.

At the closing convention, my brother, Johnny, my mother, and Ruth shared the moment with my two daughters, Camille and Junea, then ages three and one. Camille, my oldest, had traveled with me to LA before the convention on one of my pre-convention inspection tours. I had the wonderful experience of taking my then–two-year-old on a plane for five hours across the country, by myself! After the takeoff, when she cried, I had fun entertaining her all the way out, and back, and getting a little sleep when she slept. It was the greatest experience I had as a father up to that point—just to know I could take care of my daughter's needs for three days without Mama's help. I tell you again, reader, "It don't get no better than that!"

13

RUNNING FOR MAYOR
IN 1982

Very superstitious, writing's on the wall
Very superstitious, ladder's 'bout to fall . . .
When you believe in things you don't understand
Then you suffer . . .
Superstition ain't the way

—STEVIE WONDER, "SUPERSTITION"

I left the NBA with a full head of steam, and had nowhere to go. I was well known, and was respected even more in Newark after this year of publicity. Mort Pye, editor of the *Star Ledger,* had sent a reporter to cover the convention in Los Angeles, and thus people at home knew about my exploits for five or six days running. But politically, I was still an outcast.

I missed the limelight and the glory that accompanied me in the NBA. I had been on a national and international platform, hobnobbing with influential and famous people. I had been a champion for affirmative action for lawyers and judges, and I had helped influence the struggle of an African country to gain its independence on honorable terms.

So there I was, practicing law in my little law firm once again, with some nice clients, thanks to the NBA: Conrail, Aetna, and Ford, all sending me negligence defense cases. Along the way I even picked up two local banks as clients. But how was I supposed to be satisfied doing depositions for Conrail? From my office on the fifteenth floor of

24 Commerce Street, I set out to make life more interesting, consonant with my new place in the world.

I contacted my new acquaintances at the Cuban Mission to the United Nations and arranged a trip to Cuba. I returned to Newark after one week, a much more enlightened man about what Castro was doing on an island just ninety miles from the United States. It was clear to me that we had a lot to learn about Cuba, in terms of universal health care, education, caring for the mentally ill—and sharing. I ate the food, enjoyed the people, loved the music. Castro was smart to send his enemies to the United States and preserve the culture at home. And Cuban ice cream: the best I ever tasted!

My second project was more long-term. I wanted to bring black professionals to Zimbabwe to work in the country as doctors, lawyers, nurses, and dentists. My plan was simple: in 1980 the major black professional organizations met together for the first time in Dallas. I went there to introduce the concept, with the help of the Nigerian ambassador, the endorsement of my friends from the independence organization ZANU from Zimbabwe, and with interest from the Ford Foundation to fund the project. The black nurses, dentists, and lawyers were excited about the project, but subsequently I couldn't get the new ambassador from Zimbabwe to the United States to sign on. Ford waited, but the response never came. It hurt me deeply, and I never found out why.

The third project overlapped with the Zimbabwe venture. I needed to rest and think about my next move. And so I called my friend Paul Ylivisaker, former commissioner of the Department of Community Affairs. In 1980 he was the dean of the Department of Education at Harvard Education School. He got me a fellowship at the Institute of Politics (IOP) at the Kennedy School at Harvard, where ex-mayors and former federal government higher-ups went to cool out and tool up for the next big thing. The IOP gave me an apartment in Cambridge, fully furnished, for the spring semester starting in January 1981. My duties were to teach one class and to write at least one article before I left. Paul was a godsend.

I let Bob Pickett run my office on a financial basis that was good for him and me. I left my wife, Ruth, with two children and two dogs, but she let me go. I went up to Cambridge for five days a week, and came back home over the weekends. But toward the end of the semester, sometimes I stayed straight through. Ruth never made it hard on me for my decision, although I know it was hard on her. She had to take care of two small children and two dogs. (I found a miniature poodle in Weequahic Park; he and Napa became buddies). In addition she had to put up with my absence from the home for long periods. She enjoyed our children, but this would have been way too much for me to have handled alone. I appreciated her for that, because I needed the time. Harvard and Cambridge allowed me to flex my new intellectual muscles.

I taught a noncredit class to undergraduates called Urban America and the Third World, a comparison of the plight of poor people in cities in the United States with poor people in so-called underdeveloped or "Third World" countries. From my NBA experience at the United Nations, the trips to Jamaica and Cuba, I saw the need to internationalize our agenda as advocates. In order to beat back Ronald Reagan, then spreading his influence as President of the United States, we had to look to the so-called Third World as entrepreneurs, professionals, and as workers. Such was the theory supporting my venture to Zimbabwe: black people would help Zimbabweans with our skills, and they would avail us with their resources on a partnership basis.

Listen to excerpts of a speech I gave to the NBA in August 1980, while I was in Dallas recruiting black professionals for the Zimbabwe proposal. I called the paper "The Third World Connection":

If we extend our analysis a bit further, we can see that we are not the only people who must learn to cope with these realities [of

Reaganomics]. Problems previously considered urban and minority in America are beginning to appear all over the globe. The same economic decisions about investment have created cities all over the world. It is estimated that by the year 2010, two billion more people will be living in cities around the globe. This event changes the rural peasant from subsistence farmer to urban worker. These people come with hope for a better life. More and more crowd in, and already low wages are depressed even further. This process has created a displaced permanent reserve of poor and landless people congregating in cities throughout the world—some with work, but an increasing amount are under- or unemployed. At best they work for very low wages when times are good.

Thus we see when the jobs leave New Jersey and go to Taiwan, the Taiwanese or Chinese equivalent of our own Mrs. Jones sits down at a sewing machine once used by Mrs. Jones until the factory left New Jersey and went overseas.

The paper was a forecast of what I was to teach at Harvard the next year at the IOP. I had more black undergraduates taking that noncredit course than had ever been at the Kennedy school before. They were bright kids, twenty years my junior, and they had never been taught the relationship between colonialism and the growth of capitalism at home and abroad. And they made me think. During that semester, I read books, went to Harvard lectures, went to the movies, and hung out with old and new friends from many different places.

And then the Miami riot occurred, and gave me a wake-up call. Cops shot an unarmed black motorcycle rider, and the stuff hit the fan. I had to back off Harvard for a minute and get my thoughts together. This place was becoming too sweet, and I was beginning to believe I belonged there. "What went wrong in Miami?" the pundits implored, wringing their hands in disbelief. In the 1980s, weren't we past this kind of thing in post–Jim Crow America? Clearly not, I explained in my first op-ed piece in the *New York Times*, set up by a friend who was an IPS fellow at that time. It was my signature statement on race and class, and when I finished it, I knew it was time to go back to Newark. In May 1981, Ruth and my daughters came up for our final barbecue on Cape Cod, and I packed my bags and went home.

I understood that the only way to take on the political and economic forces that made the Miamis in America still explode was to climb back into the political arena in Newark. But nobody had cleared a place for me at the table in Newark, so what's a man to do?

The Politics of Frustration

I wrote a long and rambling essay to myself while at Harvard, a portion of which said:

> If we study the history of black people in America, we cannot help but notice that it ranges between periods of no hope created by tyranny and colonialism of one form or another (slavery; the KKK; Jim Crow)... and Hope (Abolition; Reconstruction; the Civil Rights Era). Our history is a blueprint of Hope and Despair, Heroism and Tragedy; Activism and Lethargy.... It is the yin and the yang of human existence....
>
> One of the moments of hope came when black people seized control of the formal levers of power in cities. In most such places it came as a result of a movement from protest to electoral politics. The advent of black people to these seats of power did not represent a structural change in the American politics. No new institutions were created, and the old ones were [left undisturbed]. But the elections in most cases proved to be "revolutionary" because of how we took power, the timing of the takeovers, and the potential for change on the American political horizon. Black people were in positions of authority and influence with

the wherewithal to make alliances, control votes, create jobs, and make opportunity possible.... But the potential was never realized, and the threat (or promise) for real change never realized.... One such city in which this scenario got played out was Newark, New Jersey.

If you're old enough, you'll remember a song by the Mills Brothers: "I'm gonna sit right down and write myself a letter..." I had a message of great urgency but nowhere to deliver it. Or maybe I felt like Paul Revere. What would have happened if Paul had no horse? Or, given the horse, no one to listen? Or once they gathered, they just didn't hear? Or once they heard, they took no action? The brother would have been frustrated, and that was me in 1981.

The Death of Independent Politics

Where was the "audience" that would have listened to my analysis of the right-wing rhetoric and furor generated by Reaganomics? The organizational infrastructure that at one time crisscrossed Newark, as wild an unpredictable as it was, was no longer in existence in 1981. SNCC died when Phil Hutchings left town. I don't recall hearing much about CORE after the election of Ken Gibson, although Fred Means, one of its former chairmen, organized the Organization of Black Educators, which was active against the Newark teachers strike in 1971. The Black Panthers were never strong in Newark, and other than the foray with the Jersey City Panthers, under Captain Carl Nichols, against Route 75, the roar of the Black Panther was seldom heard in Newark. The United Community Corporation, once a hotbed of community fervor, was now just another service agency, hanging on for dear life due to decreased funding.

Let's look at my own organization, NAPA. Somewhere after the first Gibson election in 1970, I stopped coming to the office as much. Over the next year or so, most of my stalwarts left town, got jobs in city hall, or went back to their old lifestyles. Joe, Fran, and Big Hakim moved to New Orleans; Jerry left town to live in Kentucky, where he was shot by his brother; Earlene quit her job to raise her brothers' kids; Julie got a job; Ab and Jamil drifted away. Soon there was no office. We ran into each other around town, still friends, but organized no more as NAPA.

Look also at our allies, the Welfare Rights Organization. Problems started when the Welfare Rights group got some grant money in 1969–1970. About twenty to thirty welfare mamas were hired on a training project through the Urban League from a grant arranged by National Welfare Rights Organization. Some of them would continue their advocacy at so called "Fair Hearings" and teach people how to do the same. But because of the money they received, they were no longer on welfare, so ineligible for membership. It was like they were penalized for doing better, and a new cadre of competent leadership did not materialize. "After the breakup, there was no more office. And the money ran out in 1970," said Juliet Grant, one of the active members of Welfare Rights who landed jobs in the nonprofit sector and eventually at the University of Medicine and Dentistry as a result of her new college degree and community awareness.

So after Ken's first election, there were very few independent organizations left. And as he continued to be reelected, people didn't want to fight city hall as we had done before. Most people genuinely loved the idea of having a black mayor. They made no connection between the decline in the quality of life in Newark and the first black mayor they put in office. People did not understand what was going on and just distanced themselves from the political process, because there was no education about the issues of class, economic development, and racism as factors destroying what little quality of life remained in Newark. The politics of confrontation were relegated to celebrations during Black History Month, usually through praise of Dr. Martin Luther King Jr., who became a "man of peace and love."

So what happens to a dream deferred? It sags. It doesn't always explode. More often than not, it just sags.

For Ken Gibson and his people, it wasn't enough just to have been integrated into the white power structure. They wanted no possible opposition, and no reminders of the way things were. By the mid-'70s, there was only one obstacle in his way to being the only game in town: the Committee for a Unified Newark, and Amiri Baraka.

The Loss of the Committee for Unified Newark

In 1972, Amiri Baraka had wanted to build housing for low- and moderate-income people in Newark. Eventually, he found a site in North Newark, a white neighborhood, and planned to develop 210 apartments in a sixteen-floor building, projected to cost $6.5 million. He was able to get Frank Megaro, the Italian councilman from the North Ward, to sponsor an Ordinance for Tax Abatement, and all other approvals were made by the city. Gibson was on board. Imperiale had been promised some jobs on the construction site, and had therefore accepted the project. The state Housing Finance Agency (NJHFA) granted the necessary financing of the project, to be called Kawaida Towers. The groundbreaking ceremony took place in October 1972, the cameras rolling, when at some point it became apparent that nobody had talked to Steve Adubato, the North Ward Democratic Party Chairman. As late as 2007, when I was on a panel with Steve, his eyes lit up when he angrily proclaimed, "I was not going to let Baraka Africanize the North Ward!"

Adubato publicly denounced the project at or after the press conference. Imperiale then backed out of his deal with Baraka and began picketing the site with North Ward white residents who opposed black incursion into the last bastion of white supremacy. Their resistance turned violent when a black construction worker was attacked on his way from the site. Imperiale had hundreds of people on the site every day for a while. With the support of the police, on and off duty, Imperiale blocked the few black folks who were laborers and who were willing to work on the site. The foundation of the structure was completed, but Imperiale convinced the carpenters, teamsters, and electricians unions to boycott the job.

Baraka fought back in the media, in court, and in the street. Irv Vogelman, Ray Brown's partner, won all the legal battles, but Baraka was slowly losing the war in the street and in the media. At one point, John Redden, the Police Director, resigned, blaming Baraka for the turmoil during the North Ward confrontations.

And where was Mayor Gibson? Ken never really helped Baraka, just left him out there to spin around while the pieces gradually unraveled. The Council rescinded the tax abatement. Without the tax abatement, the rents would have been too high. Ken didn't put pressure on the state Democrats to make the unions come to work. He appointed David Kerr, a Newark Police Department lieutenant, as the first black Police Director at this time. But neither Ken nor the new director was in control of the police force at that time. And Baraka did not have enough troops to compete with Imperiale to control the streets in the North Ward.

This housing development would have institutionized Baraka at another level in the pantheon of political power, giving him another kind of legitimacy, a continuing cash flow, and a renewable resource: housing for those in need. The 210 apartments meant 210 families that owed their housing to Baraka, not the mayor or anybody else. Along with the other social and educational programs he had designed and implemented, he would have become a formidable force in Newark at yet another level of power: he would have transferred from People Power to power based on position and money.

But one by one, the pillars of his organization began to fall. Because of rising interest rates, the New Jersey Housing Finance Agency told Baraka he would have to strip the project of many of its attractive community amenities, and eliminate the two-bedroom apartments. Baraka said "No." People tried to buy him out of the project, but again he said "No."

Kamozi Woodard, in his book titled *Nation within a Nation: Amiri Baraka and Black Power Politics,* reports more information I did not know at the time:

> Within a few months (after the failure of the housing efforts), the funding for Kawaida Towers, Kawaida Community Development, the Project Area Committee, and the African Free School was withdrawn, and those programs were dismantled. The Newark Housing Authority demolished the buildings that housed the PAC office, CAP's theater and television studio training program, the headquarters for the National Black Assembly and the African Liberation Support Committee, and classrooms for the African Free School. In 1976, the NJ HFMA buried the $1.5 million foundation of Kawaida Towers....
>
> Ultimately, Amiri Baraka repudiated black nationalism [and became a communist].... His rejection of nationalism marked one of the most definitive points in the conclusion of that phase of Black Power. (254)

Yes and no. There was more to Black Power in Newark than nationalism and Amiri Baraka. But suffice it to say, we lost one of the most effective independent black organizations, which, despite the contradictions imposed by cultural nationalism, helped propel us into the modern era of power through organization of the majority black population into an effective electoral base in 1970.

Ken let third parties, with killer instincts more sharply defined than his, do the job he wanted done. Ken and Steve Adubato were too smart to show Ken's hand. It was not a clean kill, but a protracted public mauling of an integral part of the team that made Ken Gibson who he was.

Building a New Base from Remnants of the Old: The Leadership Development Group

Soon after I came back to Newark from Harvard, I set up the Leadership Development Group (LDG), which met at Essex County College (ECC). I wanted to share my developing vision and get some people to buy into it; I wanted to be a part of something that would take us to the next stage of politics, inclusive of the redefinition of city hall. My first class, The Third World Connection, a refinement of the class I taught at Harvard, attracted a mixed group of community advocates, old Movement workers, and young people. I developed a little following and over the next two years taught a few different topics, but all focused on the new face of power as practiced under Reaganomics. We talked about racism, then and now: the Klan versus the burgeoning prison-industrial complex designated for black and brown drug dealers. We discussed economic underdevelopment in the city and throughout the country, and compared the United States to Third World countries. And we talked about our "new leaders" in the 1980s who blamed the underclass of black and brown people for their failure based on wrong individual choices. The classes helped clarify for me and a lot of people the misinformation put out by the Empire, and by our own leaders who bought into the propaganda.

And so it was easy for me to attract a constituency at this time from among the same people who were dissatisfied with the quality of leadership we all endured under Gibson and the New Black Political Class. Their politics were confined to elections for perpetuation of Ken and his followers in office, while the state and nation galloped to the political right. The narrow "Negro Nationalism" they practiced just wouldn't do.

LDG became a little oasis, something we really looked forward to every week. Our classes outlined the theory, and all of us wanted some way to put our new awareness about power into action.

City hall loomed large because it was a mechanism that could leverage that kind of power, to forge new relationships in an age where power was slipping from our grasp. Should we form a new street-based organization to pressure the New Black Political class in city hall with our points of view? Or challenge city hall itself with candidates for office?

Even though I believed the have-nots could rise up in anger, because they had done so in the past, most recently in Miami, it would offer a set of dangerous confrontations between black folks, mainly the youth from the poorest parts of town and the still-majority-white police force, directed by a black mayor. This would never do, and would set us back and set the city back a hundred years. I had no intention of stimulating that kind of conflict.

Therefore, with all that was upon us, in terms of hardships and political undoing of the gains made, it would take a seat in city hall, with all its resources and legitimacy, to activate the people in a manner more than in an isolated, temporary, emotional fashion. Somebody had to be willing to do the work to translate the message of loss and anger around issues such as poor education, dilapidated housing, and the litany of other woes people thought the new administration would cure, into an action plan for the '80s to challenge the Empire for resources and real control of the city. Somebody would have to challenge the private sector in its movement of jobs not just out of town but out of the country. Somebody would have to organize to redirect the politics of city hall to fight Reaganomics and the forces of globalization that were consolidating to consume the world, putting people of color in danger wherever they reached for resources (goods and labor) and markets (for their finished goods). It meant education, organization, mobilization, and election politics. We had to translate all that potential anger into an effective political force, directed at Essex County, the statehouse in Trenton, the halls of government in Washington, and the private sector in-state and out of state, to get us on course to save our communities.

There was only one seat that could cause all of that to happen in any reasonable amount of time, and that was the seat then occupied by Mayor Kenneth Allen Gibson. So I decided to run for mayor, with the encouragement of my friends and supporters.

I decided I couldn't become a councilman and be one of nine, my voice marginalized and isolated into meaningless speeches at late-night meetings in city hall. As it turned out, there was a seat vacated when South Ward Councilman Sharpe James ran for councilman-at-large, setting himself up to run for mayor in 1986. I never thought about that seat, although I lived in the South Ward and probably could have won. Traditional city council politics is always like a male locker room. And as a councilman, I wouldn't have the bargaining toys like jobs to gain a majority on council. So, to educate and organize, and to gain the silence or buy-in necessary, I needed to be in the big seat.

The Contrast between the Ideal and Reality

I listen to myself now, talking about leveraging power to fight the President of the United States from the mayor's office in Newark, New Jersey, and it sounds so very bizarre. Did I really think I could mobilize people on issues so distant from their everyday experience? "I need a job," someone would say. "Yes, ma'am, but your job that used to be here is in Taiwan," I would answer. "We have to join together to change the way corporations do business! How does that sound to you?" I was working with a knowledge base that took me years to acquire, and a year to pass on to the students at the Leadership Development Group. I suffered under no illusions that the new politics implicit and explicit in our conversations about the "Third World connection" would translate directly into a platform or set of issues I could use to run for any office. The campaign would have to be "regular," that is, shaped and structured like any other campaign with short sound-bite slogans and short explanation of the platform. Education and organization of the people was one of my long-term goals, but in bite sizes. We needed to combine the power of the streets with that in the suites, aimed toward the world of economics. This was my vision.

And then another voice rings in my ear, asking, "Did you really think the Empire would let you win with these kinds of ideas? And if you won, did you think they would let you function one day without wearing you down, making your life miserable, even taking your life? This thing you challenged in your mind, Williams, was far bigger than an LDG class, and you planned on taking them on from a visible perch in city hall?"

What I had I mind couldn't be done from a street corner organization on South Orange Avenue, or from a one-man law firm on Commerce Street, or from a one-person seat on city council. It had to be done through controlling the formal reins of power at city government level, and it had to be done at that moment. Despite the challenges, the answer I got at the time was, "Junius, go for it!"

Practical Considerations

So much for emotional commitment to a progressive political theory. Could I win the election? There was a major player in the race other than Gibson: Earl Harris, then the president of the Newark City Council, a wily veteran of city and county politics since the 1950s. He became the first black person elected to the position of president of the city council, a feat that took the support of three white councilmen who couldn't stand Gibson. Earl Harris was the personification of the "beyond race" candidate—perhaps the first black man in Newark to achieve that status. He could use the bully pulpit when he talked to black folks, and championed issues interpreted to be "black," like rent control (though all tenants benefited). And he could talk to white people about his main campaign theme, "law and order."

When Earl said he was going to "take back the streets," white and black folks knew he was talking about black street crime, not organized crime, nor white-collar crime. And more and more black folks too accepted this as necessity. Black people would cheer just as loudly, maybe even more than the whites on the other side of town. Ironically, Gibson's police force was already locking up their sons and daughters, but Gibson wasn't using the rhetoric of the New Right. So for the 1982 election, Earl had to one-up him with a call for police dogs.

My image of police dogs was etched in my mind through the still photos and television footage from Birmingham in 1963. And I remembered the confrontations against Imperiale right there in the city council chambers in Newark in 1968–1969 when he was on the city council during Addonizio's years as mayor, clamoring for police dogs in Newark. One day NAPA had almost fought Imperiale's thugs on the steps leading out of city hall after one such council meeting. NAPA was outnumbered, and hostile words were exchanged; but for the intervention of Julie Saunders's daddy, the only black cop on duty that night, there would have been a major rumble going down the steps to Broad Street.

So how the hell could a black man be for police dogs, knowing what they symbolized and actualized in the black community?

There were people in City Hall at that time who were openly or secretly supporting Earl, and he had the support of several white political leaders.

Earl's black supporters were those who had been "in with Ken" but for some reason were now out. After twelve years in office, mayors have enemies, and these were the many who flocked to Earl, who in turn promised them salvation, or anything else they wanted to hear. "Let the people say Amen." Amen.

Ken Gibson as Formidable Adversary

Ken, on the other hand, was much more of a shrewd politician than the man who fired me almost ten years before. City hall was almost

309

all black, except for certain white people he maintained at high places. Ken's patronage empire included the federal programs, the property tax budgeted Civil Service positions through turnover, the Board of Education, and the Housing Authority. Lots of families owed their livelihood to Ken Gibson, and he was beginning to act the part of "big-city mayor." He had a political machine, and anybody who wanted to beat him had to be strong enough to overcome the hundreds of minions, and eventually thousands of voters Larry Coggins could put in the street on Election Day.

Ken was content with being mayor, even liked it, without ever figuring out how to use power. Somewhere in his first term, I think Ken gave up on trying to actually run the city. Instead, he decided to hold the office as long as he could. In 1981, Councilman Sharpe James told the *New York Times:*

> Many things have happened in Newark that if they happened under a white administration, [the conclusion reached would be that] "Hey, whitey don't care.". . . Now, people don't know what to do. They don't know how to fight a black administration.

It was indeed the feeling that we were a leaderless city with people in charge who didn't care that gave me the slogan I needed in 1981. Junius Williams would provide "Leadership You Can Believe In."

My constituency was composed of those who were dissatisfied with Ken and Earl, Movement people from the 1960s, tenant organizers, and young people in college or just graduated. These were people who believed in the prospects of a people's movement that could triumph through the raising of enough sentiment to bring the left-outs and have-nots to the polls. We would campaign on a theme of leadership because overall, that's what we needed. As far as I was concerned, it was the "Gibson-Harris administration." I worked that construct effectively, I'm told. But I'm getting ahead of the story.

There was an added dimension to this election. A man named Joe

Frisina mysteriously entered the race and ran for mayor. Joe had tenure at city hall as the Tax Assessor. He had no track record of activism or of being active in electoral politics, but he was Italian, a resident of the North Ward. Many believe Ken had Joe enter the race to take white votes away from Earl Harris. Joe had just enough money to put out literature and no real issues to speak of. And how do you run against your boss, Ken Gibson, and come back to your job afterward (which he did) as though nothing happened? Joe was what is called a spoiler. Joe Frisina ran, lost, and nobody ever heard from him after that. Unlike me, he never intended to win.

Running for Mayor

My plan was to trump Gibson with "community organization." I had very little money, but a good reputation in the community. We had lots of energy, and I knew the people in the neighborhoods. I would go to the tenant organizations, and the block clubs, which still proliferated. I would organize a cadre of churches that had to be dissatisfied with the way things were. I would excite students, high school and college. In other words, I would do everything we had done twelve years before when we elected Ken the first time, and split the Gibson-Harris base. Except there just weren't many community organizations to rely on.

There were real issues that had to be vetted: more affordable housing construction on all those vacant lots, the need for jobs to be created or negotiated from the public and private sector, police brutality and lack of police accountability to the people who needed a police officer when they called, the failure to properly use money allocated for public housing repair. Ours would be an ordinary campaign in many aspects, but with issues with extraordinary potential. People had to get back to the notion of having high expectations about the role of the people in changing the priorities of the federal and state government and private industry.

There would have to be a popular electoral rebellion, and I was sure we could do it. After all, hadn't I been a leader in the Movement right here in Newark; hadn't I been a popular Model Cities Director; hadn't I been a national figure—no, an international figure—as head of the National Bar Association? John Crump once told me that NBA past presidents "often overstate the value of their own importance."

"But you gotta believe, Crump, you gotta believe!"

I campaigned hard, and dove inside the Newark I knew: the tenant organizations, the block clubs, and the few black churches untied to Gibson or Harris who would let me talk to the congregations on Sunday morning. I had LDG class members. I knocked on doors throughout the black sections of town, conceding the white vote to Harris and Frisina, mostly in the North Ward and East Ward. I did have a few supporters in the each ward, like Joe, an old district leader who worked for the Department of Sanitation. He listened and believed. He made me believe in the power of the rainbow. I campaigned a little in the East Ward with Joe by my side.

There were a few debates. I did well picking out the contradictions of twelve years of Gibson and Harris and the little progress for the average working man and woman in Newark. "Where was the effort to create jobs? Why not rely more on the talents of the people of Newark?"

"The young could help the old, the old could teach the young, especially in after-school programs." "Neighbors could join together and work with the police." "We don't need police dogs; we need to reorganize the police force and put civilians at the desk, and put the police we already have in the street." "And we need to reform education, teaching young people first and foremost to believe in themselves. How? Again, with the support of the talent we have right here in Newark! How? By holding teachers and administrators accountable, and bringing in talent from the community to teach and inspire." "Newark would have to create more jobs and business opportunities by making

Newark more attractive as the transportation hub of New Jersey: the Port of Newark, the airport, and the railroads. We need an administration that would advocate for jobs for the ordinary people in Newark in those places, and others in the downtown economy. The Gibson-Harris administration had done none of this, had twelve years to do the job, was uncreative and unimaginative, so they had to go!" Whew!

By and large, that was my speech, honed over weeks of effort so that I knew the best lines that got the best response. More catchphrases, less thoughtful analysis. One time I knew I did well at one of the debates when Earl Harris looked at me and said something like, "I'm gonna kick your [butt]!" I wasn't worried about that—he was too old and I was well covered in that department. Wherever I spoke, I got support because there were people just tired of the no-leadership syndrome everyone felt. I am able to teach when I speak, to help people see the big picture and make connections; I excited people with possibilities, not with rhetorical flourishes, and made them want to work with me. I thought from the reactions I was getting from the people we touched that surely they would pass the word and the insurrection would occur.

But I couldn't reach beyond the people who came to those debates, or the tenant association meetings, or the block club gatherings. Why? Because I just didn't have the money I needed. I expected thousands of dollars to pour in because I was smart and I was telling the truth. Instead of thousands, I sometimes got hundreds. My childhood friend, Arthur Ashe, came over to spearhead a fund-raiser for me. It attracted few people, but he gave me a very nice donation.

Why didn't I get the money? Because by this time there were too many people whose political and economic interests were tied to Gibson, and the ones who were on the outs with him, for whatever reason, were by and large supporting Earl Harris. "You should have run for councilman, Williams." "We like you, but..." It became a mantra I grew accustomed to hearing.

The Elected School Board Issue

There was another issue I should have jumped on, but didn't. Amiri Baraka wrote me a note pledging his support. He told me I ought to take up the issue of an elected school board. Ken created the issue because of his abuse of power.

Ken had asked all the people he appointed to positions such as the Board of Education to give him an undated letter of resignation. He tried to get rid of his school board appointee Brenda Grier by filling in the date on her already-signed letter. She took him to court and won. Hence, a movement formed to take the power of appointment away from the mayor, a movement that gained momentum but was beneath my radar screen.

In looking back, that was my issue, but I just didn't sense how strong the sentiment was. The referendum for an elected school board was on the same ballot people used to vote for mayor and council in May of 1982, and the voters took away Ken's power to appoint school board members. There would come a time when I understood the power of this moment, but it wasn't in 1982.

Would I have won had I picked that issue to run with? I may have gained the attention of a small but growing number of people, including the Teachers Union and the service employees unions at the Board of Education. How much money would the unions have given me? How many voters would they have stirred up for me?

Everybody has his or her own agenda; I don't know if I would have fit into theirs. Nobody asked me to be their champion, but they could have used the attention I was getting as a mayoral candidate. Maybe I'm tipping you off, reader, to the existence of a whole "nutha" world out there about which I was blissfully ignorant.

New York Times Endorsement

Three days before the election I got a surprise endorsement from the *New York Times*. At least we thought it was an endorsement. The editorial was called "A Difficult Choice in Newark." After talking mostly about the aloofness and decline of quality in the Gibson administration, the lack of qualifications of Harris to become mayor, the fact that Gibson and Harris were under indictment for the no-show job given to Mickey Bontempo, a former city councilman, and the fact that Joe Frisina demonstrated not much more than "congeniality," they finally looked around and saw me. They said:

> Junius Williams is a former president of the National Bar Association who managed Newark's Model Cities program during Mayor Gibson's first term. He was dismissed, following a critical Federal audit of his management. But political considerations seem to have given that critique excessive weight.
>
> Mr. Gibson still banks on his national reputation, and Mr. Harris enjoys formidable local support. Mr. Williams alone has tried to use this campaign to educate the voters about Newark's current problems. In an unpromising lot, he is the most promising. (*New York Times*, May 8, 1982)

Well, it's nice they saw the Model Cities audit in proper context. But what really confused me was whether I was considered "promising" among all four of us, or just the least unpromising of the entire lot. So, vote for me as the "lesser of the unpromising?" Or don't vote for any of them? Like I said, Williams, sometimes you think too much.

We made copies of the article and used it was an endorsement, even though most people in Newark didn't read the *New York Times* anyway.

Four days before the election, I wrote a letter to the board of the NBA, meeting in Atlantic City, New Jersey. I said:

I had intended to be with you tonight in Atlantic City but am at this time working to help finalize my field organization [for the election]. I am [sending one of my associates to visit you] because I am in need of your help at this the eleventh hour . . . a CBS-TV poll said I was the only candidate picking up support, and doing so at a rapid rate. I am confident that I will be in the runoff on June 15th, as either number one or number two. From there I shall emerge victorious as the next Mayor of Newark, because people *do* want change after twelve years of Mayor Gibson.

I never really saw that CBS poll. I do know that there were a growing number of people who took me at my word, that I did represent "leadership they could believe in."

So on election day, as the mostly volunteer little army went out to stand at the hundreds of polling places to support our cause and cheer me on to victory, I felt very good about my chances. I didn't have the machine Gibson had, or the money Gibson and Harris put on the polls to hire mean, nasty, and knowledgeable folks to corral the vote for their respective candidates. I knew all this somewhere in the back of my head, but I was hoping for a miracle, an insurrection. The way we did it in 1970!

I rode around to visit a few polls by myself. I remember being at the polling place in the South Ward in the firehouse on the corner of Bergen near Lyons, where I heard a conversation that told me the truth.

LADY: I'm worried about the fact that both of them [Ken and Earl] got indicted.

SOMEBODY WHO KNEW ME AND SAW ME STANDING THERE: What about Junius Williams, why didn't you vote for him? He's clean.

LADY: Who is he? I never heard of him.

At that moment, I knew I hadn't penetrated deep enough to reach the core voter, who was indeed looking for an option. I didn't have enough literature, enough workers, enough organization to find that lady at church, the beauty parlor, or on her job. When she came home from work, she didn't go to the debates, and didn't hear me or see me in action. She didn't listen to the few radio sixty-second blasts I managed to get on the air in the last few days of the campaign. She didn't see my signs, up for less than a day before Gibson or Harris supporters tore them down; she hadn't heard the debates on cable TV. After the election was over, Mr. Wes (Wesley Weaver), my favorite tavern owner, told me he heard me on TV and said, "Wow, I wish I had listened to you before I made up my mind—I would have helped you out!" I hadn't reached him or the lady at the polls because I didn't have enough of what it took to hit the mother lode.

Election night was sad but necessary. After being on that corner, I was no longer excited, not knowing what to expect. ABC-TV wanted to cover my campaign on election night—they must have seen the CBS poll? Or believed the *New York Times* endorsement meant something in Newark—and so they paid for me to get a bigger space: the old Wiss Piano building on Broad Street, downtown. This was the kind of space I thought I would have had from the git-go, but here I was renting on a daily basis for the official broadcast of the agony of my defeat. My family was there, Johnny from wherever he was living at the time, and Mother came up from Richmond. I said all the usual things politicians say when they get crushed. People pledged their undying loyalty, clapped the night away. And I went home to hide under the covers.

But in retrospect, I had achieved something in defeat. (Don't we all say that?) But really, I got almost five thousand votes (4,996, once the absentees were added in), spending only about $30,000, mostly my own money from savings, coming from some money my sister Connie left when she died. I got outspent more than ten to one by Gibson and Harris. Joe Frisina, Ken's spoiler, got 8,500 votes, and Ken and Earl got 21,000 and 11,500 respectively. Fifty percent of the eligible voters turned out. There had to be a runoff, since nobody got a majority of the votes cast.

Post-Election Promises

Both Earl and Ken called me, asking for my endorsement. I couldn't support Earl, with his talk of police dogs. And all Ken wanted me to do was *not* support Earl. I sat out the runoff, which Gibson won.

Whether you consider me foolish for even getting into this arena, or not, a lot of people took notice of me. Seeing how well I did with little money, and using a little organization with a lot of heart and soul, they thought it best that I never got another chance to become mayor. Of such is the substance of this story of mine.

14
PUBS AND LEGAL SERVICES

I been in the right place
But it must have been the wrong time;
I'd have said the right thing
But I must have used the wrong line...

—DR. JOHN, "RIGHT PLACE, WRONG TIME"

Essex Newark Legal Services Project

One day after the election in 1982, I was sitting in my office, minding my own business. I was busy looking out the window at Newark Airport from my fifteenth-floor office at 24 Commerce Street, wishing I were on one of those planes gracefully gaining altitude, flying away from reality. My secretary buzzed me and said I had a call from Jackie Rucker, an attorney and chairperson of the Essex Newark Legal Services Project. Jackie told me that ENLSP was looking for a new executive director, and wondered if I knew anybody who might be interested. At some point, she asked me if I was interested. I had to think about it for a few days, but I finally told her "yes." Here was what I had been hoping for, a job that would take me away from all those individual cases, each with its unique set of problems. For the first time in about ten years I would get a salary and become an administrator of a staff of lawyers who represented "the people."

And this job would give me freedom of movement to meet people and involve myself in issues. Oh, I was running for mayor again. I

319

thought God must be telling me something: I was supposed to get this position.

So I took the job. But there were conflicting as well as complimentary aspects of this gift. You see, I really believed in Legal Services. I enjoyed using my skills as lawyer, organizer, and administrator to make the program better. I enjoyed creating remedies for poor people where few existed before. So going in, and especially once I became entrenched, it was more than just a platform for visibility.

Changes at Legal Services

My problem started when I made organizational changes. I insisted that the lawyers carry a full caseload, and dress as lawyers, not as hippies. I called regular staff meetings, insisted on better record keeping, directed lead attorneys to do case reviews in each area every month for me to see who was doing what and what progress was made, and assigned one attorney to arrange staff training, especially for new and fairly new attorneys.

With board approval I designed some new programs, like Community Legal Education, using my network of community contacts to "get the word out" about Legal Services, and about people's legal rights in various areas. My attorneys and I went out and talked to people, including grade-school students. I commissioned a Volunteer Senior Citizens Paralegal Program for seniors to counsel elders on their rights and remedies under law. We had a staff newsletter, a two-hour radio call-in show on WNJR-AM, the popular black-oriented radio station, and a cable television show called *Legalities,* all to emphasize entitlement and remedies. Through the media and our outreach efforts, Legal Services got more attention than it ever had before. And my in-house administrative moves presented me with a methodology for staff training and accountability.

The increased visibility increased our caseload, but we had fewer attorneys due to Reagan administration cuts in the program.

Some staff wanted to shut off services at a certain point. But instead we increased the number of volunteer attorneys from one hundred to three hundred during my tenure, partly due to the work of our board members, a contract with the Garden State Bar, the black lawyers NBA affiliate, and a relationship with the Essex County Bar.

As I brought change, I made enemies. Some lawyers and support staff didn't want more work. After I examined the caseloads and applied my experience practicing law, I concluded that we hadn't reached the saturation point if attorneys and staff made adjustments in how they handled intake. My objective, which I told them coming in, was to make this not a social services agency but a law firm for the poor.

I had to fire a few of the staff for nonproductivity, and some lawyers resigned. Fortunately, I hired some people who were loyal and in fact carried the bulk of the "new work" I "imposed" on staff, according to my detractors. Dean Despotovitch, head of the General/Consumer Protection section, and John Porter, head of the Housing Unit, were two such attorneys, and Sandy Bolden became my right arm as director of Community Legal Education. (Sandy is now Sandra Cunningham, New Jersey State Senator from Jersey City.) Together these and a few others helped with my "big projects."

The Homeless Individual Welfare Rights Suit

Of all the cases I personally handled, the homeless individuals' right to city welfare gave me the greatest personal satisfaction. We found out that the city welfare agency had a policy of refusing payment to homeless individuals, the number of which was on the rise in the early 1980s. They were typically men without families. It was easy to find clients for this suit, but many of them were distrustful and so disturbed by their own personal demons created by years and years of living in the street, it was difficult to sign them up as clients. But our investigative staff was good and we were able to bring our clients into Judge Bedford's court. After hearing testimony from them, and hearing the city Welfare Director admit that she saw no reason why they were turned down, Judge Bedford ordered the homeless men to apply for emergency and general assistance.

This case drew attention and even an editorial comment from the *Bergen Record.* Some people attributed the increased flurry of excitement to my own political aspirations, but the editorial board of the newspaper concluded it was a case with great merit.

Had I really just been using Legal Services just to run for mayor, I would have left things the way they were, avoided the risk of upsetting the staff, and just used the pulpit it provided to see and be seen. The fact is, I really enjoyed the challenge of being the administrator of Legal Services and making it better for our clients.

The Joe Pine Show

One of my staff members came to me and told me she had been invited to appear on a television program to talk about her work at ENLSP. Despite her desire for the spotlight alone, I decided to go with her on the *Joe Pine Show,* on Channel 9. But I made a mistake. Joe Pine asked, during one commercial interruption, "Is there anything else you would like me to cover?" Partially in jest I said, "Yes. Ask me if I'm going to run for mayor again in 1986." We both laughed, and sure enough when the cameras came back up, he asked me! I gave a politicians answer: "if the people call, I shall respond," or something like that. I crossed the line, and I regret it to this day. I regretted it even more in the context of events that were to follow.

The Education Picture in Newark

Except for the *Joe Pine show,* I kept my politics separate. On my own time, I joined the People United for Better Schools (PUBS). To understand how significant PUBS was for things to come, both for me at Legal Services and beyond, you need a primer on the politics of education in the Newark Schools District up to 1983–1984.

The Newark Education Picture

As black people from the South migrated to Newark in the 1950s and 1960s, the mostly white teachers and administrators never felt that black and later brown children would amount to much. There was conflict between parents and educators about who should teach the children, and who should run the schools. There were more education advocacy groups in Newark than advocacy groups of any other kind, some more vocal than others. In chapter 6, "The Newark Rebellion," I talked about the Parker-Callaghan fight, when Mayor Addonizio tried to install a white high-school graduate as the School District business administrator (then called the Board Secretary) over the choice of the black community, a black man who was a CPA. Parents and education advocates wanted more black educators, and a curriculum that reflected the needs of the majority black school population, including Black Studies. By the 1980s, there were more black teachers and administrators, and the head of the Newark Teachers Union, Carol Graves, was black. But most of the power over schools and classroom teaching still remained in the hands of white professional educators.

The Parker-Callaghan fight could have been a moment from which a plan evolved for comprehensive school reform. But two things happened: Addonizio backed down and kept the then–Secretary to the Board in place, and the community leadership went onto the stage-one

323

fight against the Medical School. There's only so much the same leadership can do, so education reform was stuck on the issue of race: "We want more black educators!" But what about curriculum and teaching methodology? A common vision for school reform never developed the way it did in the Medical School victory. It was not until the Black and Puerto Rican Convention platform in 1969 that we saw elements of a vision for real school reform.

On the issue of education, Ken Gibson meant well. He promised to make the schools "better." Once elected, Ken created a twenty-seven-person Education Task Force, and separately, began placing his people on the Board of Education, three each year, for as long as he could. He thought he picked good people, and some of them were—but they failed to provide leadership in defining a new direction in education for the children of Newark.

So there was a vacuum, and power does not like a vacuum. People instinctively rush to fill it.

The Newark Teachers Union

In 1970, before Gibson was elected mayor, the Newark Teachers Union (NTU) went on strike, calling for higher wages, fewer work responsibilities (no hall, cafeteria, and playground monitoring), and binding arbitration. The black community saw the strike as an attempt to do less and make more money, adding insult to injury to the perceived poor job teachers and principals were already doing for black kids. When Ken came in, his new appointees to the board reflected this attitude and didn't want to honor the 1970 contract, so the union went on strike again in 1971.

Gibson wanted his board appointees to hold the line on any increases to the union. The community scattered, with many voices raised in a deafening roar, but with a demand that the teachers resume their nonteaching duties dominant in some quarters. On the other hand, the teachers union was on the defensive, but determined to hold the line on what they had already achieved.

Ken never brought together his board appointees, community leaders including Baraka, who was at the peak of his strength in 1970–1971, the Education Task Force, and parent groups. Consequently, the union made its demands for enforcement of its contract based on the needs of its members without having to address a clear articulation of standards for improvement and specific measures of accountability coming from the community and city hall. In 1971, after the longest teachers strike in the country, they gained what was considered by pundits as one of the "best teachers contracts in the country."

So what's so wrong with that? I believe unions have the right to collective bargaining, and the hiring of additional staff to do "nonprofessional duties" meant jobs for lots of people from the community. But there was a perception that the majority of teachers just didn't want to be bothered with these children. Thus race was the other dimension to this strike, and colored relations with the NTU for many years to follow.

The black community ended up with eye candy. In 1971 the Board of Education changed the names of a few schools to reflect the nationalists' need for "black identification" (which only further polarized blacks from the whites). In name only, several schools were declared to be "community schools," but parent participation was neither desired nor respected by city hall, the board, or the union. The Board of Education listened to hundreds of people and absorbed protest energy for still more demands for school name changes, and people waved black flags symbolically in the name of education reform at long, angry, and loud meetings. Over time, the meetings got shorter and less emotional as the people lay down their swords and shields. Many community advocates got jobs in city hall, at the Board of Education, or elsewhere in Gibson-land. Others just gave up. PTAs were never as strong again.

The Politics of Education

During this period, I remember sitting at meetings and in my office at city hall or at the raucous Board of Education meetings, feeling that something was wrong. I remember hearing then Board of Education President Jesse Jacob proclaim somewhere during the second teachers strike, "Free at last, free at last; great God almighty we're free at last," imitating one of Martin Luther King's speeches in the Southern Movement. But what were we "free" from, or "free" to do?

By the end of 1971 the Board of Education was majority minority (four blacks, one Latino, four whites). From that point forward, the complexion of the board grew darker and darker as Gibson continued to appoint his people, trying to find the right combination to turn the school district around. But there was a perception we were losing ground with our schools.

In frustration, Ken and the board came to see the Newark School District as mayors in Newark had done previously: a five-hundred-pound gorilla waiting to be exploited for jobs, contracts, and political power. Education reform was high on his priority list, but it seemed more elusive than real. To make sure his board voted the way he wanted on jobs, budgets, and his education priorities, Ken appointed people who worked for him somewhere in Gibson-land. But that didn't stop some of his people from becoming rogue elephants. So the mayor resorted to the undated letter of resignation. When Brenda Grier failed to obey Ken's decision to hire Columbus Salley as Superintendent of Schools in 1981, Ken filled in the date of her resignation, and Brenda, he thought, was gone. But Brenda fought back, and a judge ordered her reinstatement. Ken subsequently loss of the power to appoint Board of Education members in the general election in 1982, when the people voted for an elected school board, as discussed in chapter 13, "Running for Mayor in 1982."

It is in this context that I came into the picture in late 1983 or early 1984.

The Organization called PUBS

Every movement, every organizational effort, every surge by people trying to get power has left its signature on the fabric of the city. People United for Better Schools (PUBS) was such an organization.

PUBS was the "Brawl for It All," named appropriately by James Benjamin, the president of Local 3. PUBS looked and felt like a movement for education reform, but when I look back at what really happened, it was an election campaign to control the Board of Education and to begin the process to get rid of Gibson. There was talk about better schools, but our major goal, even those of us who wanted movement purity, was to get rid of Columbus Salley, the superintendent, by winning control of the elected school board.

I asked former Board of Education President Carl Sharif recently, "What was wrong with Columbus Salley?" Answer: "Nothing. He was a bright guy and would have gotten the job done. But he was too attracted to the politics, which put him in Gibson's circle."

What caught my eye about Salley, and others of us who joined in what was to become a feeding frenzy for his removal, was his Truancy Task Force. I saw them in action on occasion in the streets of Newark, rounding up young black kids who didn't come to school, treating them as criminals, putting them in the backs of vans that looked like police paddy wagons. And the truant officers were just as heavy-handed as the police. To me, somebody needed to ask why these kids didn't want to attend school. Maybe because they weren't learning anything, and were more often demeaned. Despite the other things he designed that might have been good, the most visible aspect of his plan was a police approach to education that matched a "let's get tough with crime" initiative put out by the Reagan White House. The kids were easy targets. School reform was more complex.

Had Salley sat down with all the stakeholders in town and shown us the objectives, a plan, and the timetable for achieving change, there might have been a different story. He would have had the community on his side. But instead he was arrogant, and adopted a know-it-all approach.

What Was PUBS?

PUBS was a coalition that included community people, labor unions, and local politicians that had a commitment to bringing parents and community folks back into the issues of schools and school reform. People who were involved included Charlie Bell, who I had worked with at the Housing Council; Marcia Brown, who was then a community activist not long in Newark; Richard Cammarieri; and others. We all felt like a good fit even though we were skeptical of the unions at first. So I gladly went to my first meeting, sometime in late 1983, while still employed at Legal Services as the director. PUBS by night, Legal Services by day.

I didn't join PUBS to enhance my election possibilities, but it wasn't lost on me that PUBS presented some potential allies when the time was right. I didn't ask anybody to support me in exchange for the name recognition and skills I brought to the table. And I did bring both. I wrote a song for the campaign. Actually, I took the music from an old Robert Johnson blues called "Sweet Home Chicago," and composed new lyrics.

In addition, my band and I played and sang it at the Robert Treat Hotel before 1,500 people, mostly teachers and school district service employees, at the campaign kickoff in February 1984. We brought in a drummer and a bass man, and Joe Scott played piano as the working band for the afternoon. Janet Van Kline and I did the vocals, and I played my harmonica. After a four-bar funky blues introduction to the music, I knew we had a fun-loving, down South, fat-back and cornbread crowd, even before the words came out. And after that, we just let it run! People laughed, danced, sang, picked up the words, and fed it back to us:

Go home, Columbus Salley must go home
You done messed up all the children,
So leave the schools of Newark alone. . . .

That's when everybody there knew we had something going on that was beyond just another campaign. There were all the speeches by the usual suspects, but the thing people talked about was "Junius and the song about Columbus Salley." To this day, people who worked at the board during that time, most now retired, come up and tell me they were there on the day we played the "Blues for Brown, Stecher, and Brown," our candidates for the three seats coming available on the Newark Board of Education. James Benjamin liked the song so much, he wanted a recording. So we went into a studio on Staten Island run by a friend of Joe Scott. Benjamin and his brother took a copy of the tape, put it in a car with a loudspeaker on top, and played it all over Newark, but especially in front of the board office building at 2 Cedar Street. The campaign was in full gear.

Marcia, Richard, and I really sank our teeth into this campaign, because it gave us an outlet for our outrage at what was not happening at city hall. It was a campaign like I had recently run for mayor, but more broadly based and better funded. We believed there was a real commitment to hiring more administrators of color and the development of a new curriculum and teaching approaches; and fairness and democracy at the board and meaningful parent engagement. It had the feeling of home, an unbelievable comeback for Movement politics through the vehicle of a political campaign.

Carl Sharif ran the campaign, and on Election Day, I ran the South Ward election headquarters, which is the heaviest-voting black ward. I had learned my GOTV skills from Larry Coggins in the first Gibson election in 1970. And we indeed "got out the vote," especially in the South Ward for our team. The Team of Brown, Stecher, Brown won, and everybody was, of course, excited. Oliver Brown was the pastor of Roseville Presbyterian Church; Fred Stecher was a labor leader; and Edgar Brown (no relation to Oliver) was President of the Vailsburg PTA. Nine thousand voters participated in the election, about 11 percent of the overall voters in Newark at that time.

But our celebration was short lived.

Board of Education v. Edgar Brown and Oliver Brown

One day after the election, the Board of Education decided not to seat Edgar Brown and Oliver Brown, stating they were in conflict of interest, having earlier brought a lawsuit against the Board of Education claiming irregularities in the hiring of Columbus Salley. The board selected the next two highest vote-getters and Fred Stecher, because he was not involved in the lawsuit. With Charles Bell already on the board, the win would have given PUBS four out of nine seats on the board, and that was too close for the opposition. The board represented too much patronage and business to give up, so they cheated.

It was time for PUBS to lawyer up. PUBS asked Vicki Donaldson to represent Brown and Brown. I agreed to represent the voters whose voting rights had been violated, from my position as Director of Legal Services. My clients, Wilnora Homan, George Tillman, and William P. Rutan, were all eligible under Legal Services guidelines. With the murmur of dissention coming from some of my board, I went to court on their behalf.

On April 24, 1984, we went before an administrative law judge to settle the matter. The room was full of people. The Legal Services brief was tight and anticipated all the issues: the standing of these plaintiffs to sue as voters, declaration as a class action, the violation by the defendants of plaintiff's right to vote, the violation of plaintiff's due process, the entitlement to injunctive relief, including a demand for a new election if Brown and Brown were somehow found disqualified for office. If you think, reader, that I am trying to impress you with all this legalese, you damn right I am! The team of Legal Services attorneys—Dean Despotovitch, John Porter, and Junius Williams—were at the top of our game as trial attorneys.

The judge cited the Legal Services brief several times, and we won the case! The board filed an appeal, but in the end dropped it. Brown and Brown were seated.

That night, at the Terrace Ballroom, more than a thousand people gathered to hear the team leaders proclaim victory and to talk bad about the bad guys that stood in our way. It was an exciting moment, and always nice when you're on the winning side. But among the fanfare, only one lawyer was called to the podium and given accolades for winning the case—and that lawyer was not me.

Meantime, Back at the Ranch (Legal Services)

I remember telling Reverend Oliver Brown, "It was too bad *both* of us weren't recognized because I did a lot of work." During the conversation I could see in his eyes that Vicki, as far as he was concerned, was Diana Ross and I wasn't even a Supreme. He apologized, but there was no real sorrow. Vicki accepted the credit. But I didn't have time to nurse that feeling of déjà vu. I came under attack at Legal Services for having been involved in the lawsuit, and it took a deadly twist for my career as director.

My Contract Is in Jeopardy

It started in June 1984, with what I thought would be a slam-dunk of a review of my performance evaluation by the ENLSP Board personnel committee. But instead, I was met with some rather harsh questioning, led by someone on the personnel committee I shall merely call The Attorney, a black lawyer I thought to be my friend. He and others followed, questioning my management style, my failure to hire enough attorneys, my failure to communicate with staff, my responsibility for low staff morale. My friend Halim Suliman left the meeting and called me to say that he felt there was a chance my contract would not be renewed beyond December 1984.

I was caught by surprise but I understood the source of two-thirds of the complaints against me: those board members who listened to disgruntled staff who saw my administrative moves and demands for accountability as a threat to their easygoing, relaxed, social-services-agency approach to the law. Still others on the board were Gibson employees and wanted my head for winning the homeless individual and especially the Brown and Brown cases. There was overlap between the two factions. But the third group was truly a mystery, personified by The Attorney. He was one of a few black lawyers I thought I could count on. For whatever reason, some of the black lawyers on the board thought I was too "controversial," I heard it said. But what was conveyed by body language was just as instructive: "Who does he think he is, anyway?"

The matter of my contract was an issue before the board for four months. There was a majority committee report, expressing all the reasons I should be dismissed: I created a morale problem; I was too political; there weren't enough attorneys; the publicity generated was for me only. I took my time and answered each charge, listing my accomplishments on behalf of ENLSP; that we were short of experienced attorneys because of budget cuts that started before I got there; that the Board of Education case was within the purview of Legal Services since I represented voters who were Legal Services eligible, not PUBS, not the successful candidates; that I raised about $78,000 outside the federal government grants; that I developed a powerful relationship with the court (Legal Services lawyers were allowed to bundle their housing cases to be handled first in Landlord-Tenant Court so that our lawyers wouldn't have to wait all day in court until each individual case was called); a good relationship with the private bar (hundreds of private attorneys volunteered to take cases, and some made contributions through various fund-raising efforts); a good relationship with community groups, and yes, along with increased visibility and information about legal rights through our Community Legal Education series came more poor people with problems. The reforms I made were designed to take care of that need.

Before this fight started, I had decided to leave ENLSP because I felt the time had come to go back into private practice. I had done what I could. But once again, just like under Gibson twelve years earlier, I had to fight for a job I no longer wanted. I hadn't paid attention to my own Rule Number 1: always have an exit plan, and leave yourself enough time enough to execute it.

And as it turned out, I won. On September 27, 1984, I was voted a one-year contract extension by a vote of thirteen to twelve. Two of the board members who worked for the city were threatened with the loss of their jobs if they supported me, but one voted for me anyway. However, one board member who was Jewish was unable to attend the meeting because of Rosh Hashanah, the Jewish High Holiday. She tried to vote against me by telephone, but the bylaws did not allow for such. Thus the board president, Jackie Rucker, disallowed the vote. I thought my lifeline at Legal Services had been extended.

But the president immediately resigned from the board without signing my contract. I begged Jackie to sign the contract and to stay on, because the vice president was in opposition to my contract renewal. When Jackie left, the vice president refused to sign the contract and went on to rule the motion for my contract out of order at a call meeting of the board on October 4, 1984.

Along with other board members as plaintiffs, I went to court to have the thirteen-to-twelve vote validated, and to compel former Vice

President Morgan to sign the contract. Also at issue were the negative votes cast by three board members who did not reflect the sentiment of their constituent organizations, who were in support of my contract extensions. The organizations, the NAACP, the Newark Coalitions of Neighborhoods, and the United Community Corporation, were parties in the lawsuit urging the seating of three replacement members in the board, which would have increased my majority. Additionally, we discovered that two of the naysayers made too much money and did not meet ENLS guidelines.

Chancery Court Judge Harry Margolis, who I had appeared before at least a dozen times when I was in private practice, after reviewing the pleadings of both parties, ruled that the thirteen-to-twelve vote was illegal because it was held on the Jewish holiday, and that the one board member should have been allowed to vote. And he took no action on the other allegations. I appealed, of course, and lost the appeal just as quickly as I filed it. I didn't understand how a date that I didn't set and a consideration that was not countenanced in the bylaws was used as the basis of my undoing. But such were the decisions.

In the subsequent meeting, with this person voting, and one vote switching for me and one against, the result was a fourteen-to-fourteen tie. Based on the tie vote, my contract was not renewed.

Good Ol' PUBS

My friends at PUBS, the union members and the community delegations, were there at the November meeting and raised a lot of hell at the vote. But they had no power to overturn it. So upon the loss of the appeal, I was out of work. I knew my friends at PUBS, now comfortably in power at the Board of Education, would gladly take care of me, right? After all, hadn't I written the campaign song, run the South Ward get-out-the-vote, and jointly won the lawsuit to seat Brown and Brown? Vicki Donaldson, my cocounsel, was appointed by the board to be board counsel (lawyer for the Board of Education). So I asked them to let me handle cases in my capacity as a private attorney. Edgar Brown, by then sworn in as a board member at least in part because of my work, said they would "think about it."

When I didn't hear from him, I called Charlie Bell, back in as board president. He said, "There was some talk about you becoming chief of staff."

I told him, "There may have been 'talk,' but nobody talked to me."

He too said, "I'll get back to you."

I finally called my friend Clara Dasher, vice president in the Newark Teachers Union, with whom I had served many fun-filled and monumental years together on the Board of Essex County College. "Clara," I said quite pointedly, "I need some help here." I told her what I wanted, and she too said—you guessed it—"I'll get back to you."

By this time, I saw the handwriting on wall. I was no longer necessary to PUBS, and off the radar screen. And once it became apparent that they were supporting Sharpe James for mayor, it was clear I would get nothing from them. I was the competition to be eliminated. I had never asked them for help to run for mayor, mind you, but supplying me with cases in support of my proposed new law firm would have given me time to raise money and further develop my organization for 1986.

It seemed I had seen this movie before. And they achieved their objective: I didn't run for mayor.

Winners and Losers

As is always, there were winners and there were losers coming out of this series of events.

Winners

Steve Adubato: in the haste to get rid of Columbus Salley, the PUBS union and community leaders invited the fox into the hen house. Steve

Adubato had nothing to do with our election success, and very little involvement in education issues before 1984. But PUBS had only four board members and needed five to get rid of Salley. Hence they added Eleanor George, a "protégé" of Adubato's who sat on the board, to give the fifth vote. Adubato extracted a promise to support her for her reelection bid and became in essence a member of PUBS.

But he became bigger than PUBS. He increased his influence by his ability to manage and win small elections with good turnouts from the North Ward. By keeping the elections small, usually with a 5 to 7 percent voter turnout, Adubato (and initially) Lou Turco, the East Ward councilman, determined who won the elections to the Board of Education and therefore had great influence over the affairs of the district. Through the years, the majority of the board elected has been black or brown, but the man who engineered the election of most of them is white. Currently, his handpicked candidates constitute a majority on the board. As I pen these words, there is a movement afoot to end his dynasty, but look how much damage has been done.

Losers

Coalition Members: over a short period of time, community leaders and advocates Amiri Baraka, Marcia Brown, Carl Sharif, Kabili Tyari, Wilbur Haddock, and others were ostracized, ignored and/or pushed aside. The concept of PUBS as a central organizing base to bring the community and parents back into the educational arena was traded for traditional insider political leverage for the unions and Bell and a few others.

Black Power: although all the black mayors since the 1984 election have complained about low turnout in school board elections as a reason for turning the school board into an appointive one instead of an elected one, none of them has taken the easy way out: run some candidates and beat Steve Adubato at his game. Since 1984, none of them has developed the organizational capacity to win in these small elections.

Instead, mayors Gibson, Sharpe James, and Cory Booker have sought to make peace with Adubato and his North Ward machine for help in school board and other elections.

Troubling also is the vision that the Newark Public Schools belongs to a coalition of power brokers, and not to the parents and children who attend the schools. With power in the hands of so few, where is the accountability for real school reform, and the impetus to get more people engaged in the election process?

Locals 617 and 3: Service Employees Unions Locals 617 and 3 saw to the improvement of rank-and-file salaries and benefits at the Board of Education beginning with the first year of the new PUBS majority. A good win for them. But most of the people in the two service workers unions lived in Newark, and so they were parents as well as workers.

Trade unionists could have developed parent leaders in schools as insurance to protect the interests of their children in Newark, and in Trenton, where decisions were made about school finance, which in the long term affected their jobs.

The Children of Newark: instead of using this organization as a means to bring about school reform, PUBS became a political group that saw the board as had the previous mayors. And with no countervailing power to hold the new PUBS majority to the promise of school reform, the children's education performance got worse. Hence the state came in and took charge of the Newark School District, wresting it from the hands of PUBS in 1995.

There are two lessons to be learned from these experiences:

First of all, "Don't forget the bridge that brought you over." In 1995 the state took the power away from the Board of Education, citing many improprieties, especially the failure to improve schools for the kids. This ended local control of education until this day. Despite the claim of incompetence made by the state about local leadership when they took control of the Newark Public School District initially, the schools still only graduate 55 percent of the high school population, depending on which numbers one uses. At the time of takeover, there was yelling and gnashing of teeth—a few noisy demonstrations. But there was no real organized parent community to which the elected Board and administrative staff could turn for sustained pressure on the state government in Trenton. Most people didn't want a state takeover, but didn't appreciate how the remaining partners in PUBS (unions, politicians, and elected board members) allowed the district to fall so far. The state prevailed because there was no army in the street to protect the leaders in the suites.

Also, PUBS was the last great united front in Newark. When the people's component was effectively dismantled, there was no way to hold accountable the people we had put in power to represent our interests (nor to confront the new rulers, placed there by the New Jersey Department of Education). People must look at defeat more objectively: those of us expelled from PUBS should have organized into an ongoing community organization, engaging and teaching young parents about what just happened. But using myself as an example, sometimes there just isn't enough energy. Once again, it was time for me to move on and survive.

What happens to a dream undone? Does it make people tired and disgusted, and then run?

15
UNIVERSITY HEIGHTS

You know we've got to find a way
To bring understanding here today.

—MARVIN GAYE, "WHAT'S GOING ON"

I saw Charlie Bell of PUBS from time to time while he was still in power at the PUBS-dominated Board of Education, maybe passing by in the street, maybe at an event. He would always say, "I know we owe you something, and we're going to take care of you." I half smiled and nodded. Inside, I told myself, "Yeah, buddy, I know what you're gonna do for me."

There was a disturbance in the Force that had once provided a sense of order. Instinct told me, "You're out of balance, Junius, close to the first real fall in your life. Forget all the other rules and go back to the real Rule Number 1: "Get your spiritual house in order; regain the moral high ground." So I went back to church.

I joined Greater Abyssinian Baptist Church, a church at which I had campaigned in 1982. When I came in one Sunday in December, the minister, Reverend Matthew Zimmerman, had me stand up. But that was far from what I wanted. I was comfortable in the back, surrounded by some old ladies who looked after me with their warmth and humor for months to come. That first Sunday, Reverend Zimmerman preached about forgiveness, and it seemed he was looking straight into my soul. I joined the church the next Sunday. Over a period of time, I became a Trustee, and eventually Chairman of the Board of Trustees. Reverend Zimmerman brought me from the back to the front of the church, and along the way helped me regain my sense of who I was as a confident, successful, and vital member of the community.

And then there was the return of music to my life. I had taught myself how to play the harmonica in my senior year at Amherst. In 1983, Marcia Brown, now assistant dean at Rutgers University–Newark, asked me to join with her in singing civil rights freedom songs, wherever somebody asked for some music. She always spoke in a manner that guilt-tripped me into going to some little meeting where sometimes there were Marcia and I and two or three other people. But Marcia was just as enthusiastic as if there were hundreds, and so was I once we got started. Something about that music that's so infectious.

Marcia named us Return to the Source, after a speech by that name given by Amílcar Cabral, the assassinated Guinea-Bissauan freedom fighter.

I expanded the group to include singers I met at Essex County College. I was appointed to the ECC Board, and decided to take music lessons from the former bassist for Duke Ellington, "Doc" Bell (Professor Aaron Bell), and to join his music ensemble at ECC. I met talented singers such as Anthony Jackson, Letty O'Laughlin, and Joy Moore. We did blues and jazz with Doc Bell. I asked them to join Return to the Source to sing freedom songs with Marcia and me. One day I had an idea: "All black music is about freedom, so let's sing blues, gospel, and jazz as well." On top of playing my harmonicas with Doc's ensemble in places like the West End Café on Broadway in Manhattan, I brought these great voices to RTS on gigs Marcia and I set up. To this mix I added Joe Scott (piano) and Janet Van Kline (vocals), and we had a hot group that could do it all.

So here was a brand-new organization for me to fuss over, to grow, and to make money with. At some point Marcia left the group, and went back to law school. RTS performed in more than three hundred grade schools all over New Jersey through a sponsor called Young

Audiences. We toured several colleges as far west at Ohio and all the Eastern and New England states. And we performed as far south as Florida, with the NBA. I wrote two raps and produced lots of multimedia productions for schools and concerts.

I was reborn and given new strength for the next venture I was called upon to bring leadership to, with Marcia Brown and other refugees from PUBS, plus some brand-new players.

University Heights

One morning in July 1984, in bold headlines, the *Star Ledger* announced that three of the four colleges, who called themselves the Council of Higher Education in Newark, or CHEN, had a plan to expand their land holdings. Rutgers University, the New Jersey University of Medicine and Dentistry (UMDNJ), and the New Jersey Institute of Technology (NJIT) wanted more land for the development of something they called University Heights, a plan for student housing, more college buildings, and businesses related to college research or other activities.

Nothing made me see red more than the thought that UMDNJ was at it again, trying to take more land, joined by two other colleges centered in the Central Ward. Here was the revival and resuscitation of what was apparently an unfinished agenda, a door we thought was closed, a done deal undone. Nothing to me was more important than to fix the boundaries for college expansion.

In the 1980s, there were hundreds, no, thousands of vacant lots in Newark, many of them owned by the city by way of property tax foreclosure. Some of them were adjacent to each other, thus creating large buildable spaces. After the Rebellion, many landowners wanted no more of Newark and just walked away from their property, having wrested as much value as possible as slum landlords, and then as insurance beneficiaries from mysterious fires. But to Newark advocates, the accumulated land represented an opportunity for black businesses and nonprofits to develop housing, businesses, and other facilities.

So there was a confrontation of major proportions in the making. Whose side would Gibson and his people take, the colleges or the people?

Over a period of weeks, then months, we pulled together a coalition of community people. Our first meeting drew six hundred people and served notice to the colleges and the downtown business community that we were still able to mobilize the people. Alex Plinio of the Prudential Insurance Company had organized a group called the Newark Collaboration, which included the colleges, businesses, and representatives of the community, dedicated to "collaboration" to present Newark as a viable city. They didn't want a bunch of angry natives, so the word went out to negotiate.

We had new people in our inner circle of something we called the Ad Hoc Committee on University Heights: strong people like Della Williams, a sharp-tongued real estate agent; Boysie Williams, who worked in a foundry and was a Newark homeowner; Reverend McCombs, from St. Mathews Presbyterian Church; and Sylvia Jackson and her two sisters. Then there were veterans from other struggles, like Edna Thomas, who I knew from the UCC days, and Carolyn Whitley, a parent and employee at the Newark School District. But the strong organizations that carried the day in the Medical School Fight were gone, as I described in chapter 7.

We should have been able to just call the mayor, who we had put into a position of power for occasions just like this. Initially, Gibson was silent on the issue. So the community folks became the leaders in a wild, volatile coalition, and set out to force the hand of a tremendously strong group of state institutions, operating with support from downtown business, the state, and city governments.

But this was not 1968, so inquiring minds wanted to know, "How much muscle do you really have?"

We pushed hard with this community coalition, going to meetings just about every night of the week, meetings of the whole or meetings of the committees. We struggled to keep community interlopers and naysayers at bay: people who had personal agendas, people who wanted to be in charge, and people who had no agenda but just wanted to disrupt. Our meetings were always bordering on chaos. Monsignor William Linder of the New Community Corporation, a Catholic-based nonprofit community development group, and I cochaired the committee, but I chaired the actual meetings. And after a while he stopped coming.

Years of experience helped us; Marcia in the background, me up front, and with the help of our inner circle of supporters.

We took advantage of the call to negotiate. We told the colleges we wanted an opportunity to develop a community plan to balance their plan. In the 1968 Medical School negotiations, we could stand at arm's length and hurl verbal punches, and knew they would always come back to the table. We knew they were afraid of another riot. In the 1980s, there was less fear—still some, but mostly of disruption of the image that black folks were under control, so as not to frighten away new investment possibilities. But this time, our coalition was shakier. Sometimes it's important to embrace the other side, to stay real close to them—especially when your power base is likely to implode all around you because egos had not submitted to discipline. But the colleges didn't know that was the situation at that time.

What did joint planning mean? CHEN gave the Community Caucus of the Ad Hoc Committee $30,000 to hire our own planner and architect, and we had the right to join with their planner to put forth our ideas in a master plan for the area. With our own planners, we could put forth ideas to capture the imagination of our constituents. Simultaneously we would be party to whatever they planned, would see their plans more quickly than waiting for an announcement in the

Star Ledger. This cooperative approach avoided the necessity to blast them to kingdom come should we have major disagreements.

We set forth priorities for any plan in the neighborhood: preservation of housing and neighborhoods where possible, construction of affordable housing on vacant city-owned land along with commercial and other facilities, involvement of the colleges programmatically in the uplift of the Newark Public Schools and construction of new schools where feasible, a commitment to minority business development, and jobs for neighborhood residents.

A Fractured Community

Up to now, I've given you the textbook on how to educate, arouse, and mobilize the community. We made our demands; called a meeting to show we could still mobilize the masses (six hundred people is very impressive); and devised a strategy that was reminiscent of the Medical School Fight (an alternate community plan for the neighborhood) but done so in a way that recognized we didn't have much time before the egos and distrust in our group would betray the lack of discipline in the Ad Hoc Committee. We were able to join the "adversary" in coming up with something we both wanted, while carefully monitoring what they wanted. This is still a valuable formula, but added to it at the time was the need for improvisation, because things had indeed changed since 1968. How?

People fought each other at the meetings and between meetings. There were meetings and then even more meetings. There was a perpetual struggle for dominance and control of the effort, especially when folks got wind of the fact that there was some money on the table for creating plans. This might be called "The Era of the Alternate Plan." I wrote myself a little memo after one of those meetings, when I felt like throwing in the towel.

What has happened is fragmentation, chronic fragmentation.... The University Heights dilemma is instructive: The Newark Housing and Redevelopment Authority, the mayor, the colleges, and the community all have plans. City council is threatening to do one. The mayor, after fifteen years [without a] Master Plan, [has] decided to make one....

People are fighting each other over the plan. People in ignorance do strange things. People in ignorance do not trust each other, and cancel out each other's effort. The mayor says, "This is the Plan!" [The idea of a plan] sounds good, but is it implementable?

Dr. Stan Bergen of UMDNJ used the increasing dissent of some to try to drive a wedge whenever possible, always asking, "Are you [the Ad Hoc Committee community leaders] the spokespersons you say you are, that is, representatives of the entire community?" I remember Edna Thomas telling Bergen, "You need to stop raising that silly issue all the time, because nobody represents everybody. There's always going to be somebody with another opinion, even among you people!" Stan backed off ... temporarily.

We lost members when they felt they couldn't be in charge of the money and the action. Worst of all, we lost Bill Linder because of community criticism. People wanted to know if the New Community Corporation (NCC) was displacing people to buy land to build more houses. At a stormy meeting, people demanded that Linder explain the NCC land-acquisition process. When Linder didn't show up to explain, the people removed him as cochairman of the Ad Hoc Committee. NCC was indeed negotiating for land, but they had the ability to absorb the displaced tenants and even homeowners in the apartments they already built, so I saw them as different from what the colleges planned to do. To this day, I believe Bill Linder thinks I maneuvered his public flaying, but I had nothing to do with it; in fact, I didn't want it to happen. Sometimes pride can make a man see things the wrong way.

Often people were looking for a scapegoat to flog, to vent their anger. Sometimes the targets were the people who were protecting their interests, the members of the Ad Hoc Committee.

Coulda-Woulda-Shoulda

It wasn't until October 1985 that the mayor got into the planning game. Why did he wait so long? Here was a conflict that began in mid-1984. Conflicts spell opportunity because they beg to be resolved. In reviewing the diagram that purported to be his plan, all Gibson's staff did was to outline some areas for housing, retail, social-service facilities, commercial development, and neighborhood stabilization. There were no maximum or minimum space allocations for community development or development by the colleges. There were no standards for future development by the colleges or anyone else in the area marked "commercial development"; there were no requirements for minority business; no thinking about partnership in areas like education, compelling the colleges to use their resources to aid the failing city schools, in consideration for the mayor's support for college land use.

By contrast, the "Guidelines for Development" conceived by the community and set forth by our architect Ben Thompson and planner Toni Jackson called for a thousand new housing units for low- and moderate-income people, an affirmative action program to insure minority participation in construction throughout the area, and participation by the colleges in upgrading the public school system in Newark. Neither space nor priority in this memoir will permit a detailed discussion of the level of planning entered into by this community group, but someone should take a look at our plan. For one thing, our planners foresaw the damage of the city's intention to tear down high-rise public housing without building new housing on a one-for-one basis. Mayors Gibson, James, and now Booker are each in part responsible for the wave of increased homelessness among poor and low-income people in Newark, and the gradual out-migration of poor people looking for homes in other surrounding cities, which was caused by this policy, begun in the 1980s. And our planners warned of selling city-owned land to speculators, who were becoming interested in Newark but had no intention of building for the majority of working-class and low-income people.

On April 8, 1986, I received a surprise letter from Mayor Gibson, which said:

> One issue on which I am in solid agreement with you is the need for more low-income housing. I think a thousand units is a reasonable goal, and I am willing to work with you and the Ad Hoc Committee to try to realize this goal.

Ken's offer was too little, too late. He lost the election to Sharpe James a month after this letter, and so I have no way of knowing whether he was serious or not. Ironically, Ken didn't have to work with the Ad Hoc Committee. He could have simply told the colleges to ante up enough money to pay the seed money for any nonprofit corporations Ken designated, and used his influence at the state level to arrange financing for construction of housing on any amount of land he chose. Ken could have said to the governor, "If you want the colleges to expand and grow, then you must make available through the Department of Community Affairs and the New Jersey Housing Finance Agency enough mortgage commitments to construct a thousand units of affordable housing." Had he done so at an early stage in the conflict, beginning a mass operation that spelled housing, jobs, and business opportunities for minority contractors, perhaps he would have won the election and served an unprecedented twenty years as mayor. But he didn't, and the people opted for a new leader.

So instead of a powerful alternate and all-inclusive plan, we in the community had to fight for supremacy among ourselves, create a relationship that was always strained with the colleges and the city, and watch while Gibson remained aloof from the struggle until it was time for him to go.

Lesson in Disempowerment

I want to share with you three aspects of the culture of Newark as regards the power relationships that were illustrated thus far in this episode: (1) power to the people in Newark never evolved beyond a perception of win-lose, instead of a perception of win-win. There was enough vacant land in Newark in the middle '80s for everyone to build what he or she wanted in University Heights. The mayor was in the best position to assure the equitable distribution of land, where the colleges could have been assured of their perceived manifest destiny, and the community could build housing, retail commercial, and social-service facilities using nonprofit and for-profit business ventures. Instead the mayor waited too late to get involved, leaving the Ad Hoc Committee as the only group that tried to pull all the pieces together.

And (2), the community was no longer able to put aside its differences, to have the trust and discipline to hold the colleges and Gibson accountable for its felt needs for housing and related community development. In 1968, during the Medical School Fight, Harry Wheeler and I, representing the Committee Against Negro and Puerto Rican Removal and NAPA, were able to negotiate demands based on a shared vision for the groups we represented. There was trust that we would deliver in accordance with the game plan. There was discipline within the ranks. When there was outside opposition to our negotiating team from pretenders to the throne within the black community, we were able to mobilize our supporters to shut it down. Once the various movements of the 1960s died or were kicked to the curb by the new Black Political Class, as described earlier in chapter 13, community leadership was never really cultivated by our elected leaders to help them in the administration of this new Black Power. The collective memory of independent organizations grew more and more faint, and consequently, strong partnerships between the community and our elected officials never materialized to fight more sophisticated battles such as University Heights in a fashion to produce a win-win victory for all parties involved. The people in the suites didn't think they needed leaders in the streets to create winnable situations when confronted with Big Powers like the state of New Jersey, represented in this case through three colleges.

In Newark, we installed leadership, through the vote, who developed no real vision or understanding of how to play high-stakes poker in a contest with big players, like the state, the colleges, or the downtown business community. They had no vision of power other than the street fights needed to win campaigns, and didn't trust people who had larger visions like those of us in the Community Caucus of the Ad Hoc Committee. City hall always saw us as a threat or a nuisance, never as partners in the game of creating more power so that everybody could be a winner.

Finally, (3): sadly, the rank and file in our Ad Hoc Coalition, those brand-new or left over from the old days of community struggle, although well intentioned for the most part, never embraced strategies that required more sophisticated analysis: politics beyond just black versus white or good versus bad; strategies that called for more than direct-action demonstrations as a resolution for every perceived wrong. In other words, sixteen years after the election of Gibson, there was limited leadership vision and knowledge of conflict-management skills in the community. People were too quick to base struggle on their own instincts for survival, which more often than not was selfish and self-only, unlike the willingness to engage in group-based solutions, as in the days of the Newark Area Planning Association (NAPA) and the Committee for a Unified Newark (CFUN).

In this struggle and the one that occurred earlier within PUBS, there was too much emphasis placed on leaving one's opponent bleeding and left for dead on the floor. If I had to describe Newark politics I would say bashing and thrashing is normative in what is perceived as a winner-take-all struggle. Nowhere in my travels have I found this tendency as much as in Newark.

Why was this so, after all these years of Black Power? Because the leadership, and consequently, most of the followers had no class analysis to go along with racial analysis, and never sought to develop new, young leaders with skills to challenge the white power structure to get real power based on economics. The Black Political Class, personified by Mayor Ken Gibson at this time, followed by Mayor Sharpe James, defined its objectives as procuring jobs and contractual opportunities for their friends, political and personal. (Cory Booker is just as closed in his dealings with the community, but his closest associates have been brought in from out of town.) None of these three black Mayors ever sought to organize their local constituency as a fighting force to bring more economic gain into the city for more people outside of the circle of close acquaintances. Hence, the pie has been perpetually small, offering little chance for growth.

As a result, at the time of my story, people went out of the way to grab what they thought was power, which meant hollering, making their little narrow point of view known—even to the point of hurting one another—while the powerful universities and corporations, though they disagreed with one another quite often, always kept their eyes on the prize. And they learned how to play upon our weaknesses, eventually realizing that we had insufficient analysis and strategy to deal with their moves and countermoves. They simply played one of us against another, and there was no one in high office or authority to call us all to order.

The issues have changed through the years, but the interests and the failure to organize and respond to the potential power in the streets remain the same.

Building Our Demands

In 1986 and over the ensuing five-plus years, I became the developer of a nonprofit organization, set up by the community and representatives of the four colleges, to construct seventy units of low- and moderate-income housing. It was our intention to build more of the thousand units our joint plans said we needed, but the politics of housing construction did not allow that to happen. Simply put, the new mayor, Sharpe James, did not consider our effort a priority, and hence our project suffered interminable delays. While over the years the colleges constructed several new buildings for research, attracted several governmental grants to carry out their activities in the land allocated in our agreement in University Heights, we were handicapped by the acts and omissions of the City of Newark. But still we persevered, the little core group of rebels who constituted the Community Caucus of the Ad Hoc Committee.

The results? Despite all the attempts to kill this project, we built sixty-six units of housing, and sold them all. At the time, it was the most successful for-sale affordable housing project in Newark. We qualified buyers for all the units, based on their ability to pay the sales price using no more than 20 percent of their net income monthly to pay the mortgage. Thirty-three of them sold for $33,000, and thirty-three for $58,500, all of them three-bedroom units, depending on people's income. In fact, we were so "bad" (in the "good" sense) that while we were waiting for the contractor to finish, we had already sold the last few units. To pre-sell in that market at that time was indeed a tremendous achievement, testimony to the work of mortgage broker Patrice Simms, and staff member Chris Houston, both of whom were responsible for qualifying buyers.

We started with zero dollars, and parlayed our community movement into housing worth more than $5 million, with help of a lot of people in high places who believed in us, like Len Coleman, the commissioner of the New Jersey Department of Community Affairs who made the first commitment of Balanced Housing funding; Jerry Greco, Essex County freeholder and vice president of First National Bank, who saw to it that we received sufficient construction financing in three phases to build sixty-six units of housing; and Carla Lehrman, who was a creative housing administrator at the Department of Community Affairs.

But there was no loud celebration when we sold the last unit sometime in 1992. I quietly made a note on my wall in my home office, located in my basement in Irvington, where I had moved when my wife and I separated. Over the years, there had grown a distance between us. Earth, Wind & Fire said it best: "What used to be right is wrong." And so I thought it best that we go our separate ways. I didn't want to move out of Newark, but I couldn't find a place suitable for me and my two daughters, who were with me on every Wednesday and Thursday, and some weekends, but less so on the weekends as they got older. And I took them to school every day, five days a week, from middle school all the way through high school. This was the way I maintained contact with them. Just a few minutes each morning, to see what was going on in their lives, and to let them know Daddy was always there.

So in the comfort of my basement office in a wonderful house with an attached garage, and a big back yard for my girls and my dog, I just made a note, and mentally moved on, aware that I had been once again tested, but had come out a winner.

16

THE ABBOTT LEADERSHIP INSTITUTE

I could take you in easy
That's just half the fun . . .
Seeking satisfaction
Keeps me on the run. . . .
You gotta fight the powers that be!

—ISLEY BROTHERS, "FIGHT THE POWERS THAT BE"

I finally mastered Rule Number 1 from the days of Model Cities: "Always have another option." Music became my creative passion, and the harmonica was my primary outlet. I sat in with people like Little Jimmy Scott in East Orange, Ellis Marsalis in New Orleans, and jazz musicians as far away as Johannesburg, South Africa. My singing group, Return to the Source, became a growing cottage industry. And from my basement in Irvington, I practiced law, which overlapped with my work as developer for the "Upper University Heights" housing development for a time. I had a few clients, one contractor in particular. I did collection work for him, some of it for substantial sums of money, which introduced me to construction law and took me into a new arena of law called construction arbitration. As a matter of fact, because of my fee earned in one of his cases, I was able to put a down payment on my house, which up to that point I had been renting. God is good.

Music and My New Wife

My music business and Return to the Source also introduced me to the young lady who would become my wife. Professor Antoinette Ellis caught my eye at a concert at Monmouth University in New Jersey. Here she was, this fine little Afro-centric (by her dress) lady, just digging the music. One of my singers had his eye on her too, but I had to back him off. After all, I was the boss. As I got to know Annie, and we began liking each other more and more, she made it clear she was not in this for short-term dating. I had to deal with my demons and fears, and finally agreed to marriage. "What the hell are you doing, Williams?" I asked myself. "This is a young intelligent woman, and she wants kids! How you gonna get out now?" I realized that her honesty put me into a position where I had to ask God for help: "What do you want me to do?" And God told me, "You need to be a husband, and father two more children. Your job is not finished in this department yet." Another unfinished agenda.

And so eventually the marriage came, with all the ceremony that a young Jamaican woman with a large family would want. I smiled and went through it, listening to three of her four large brothers tell me what they would do to me if I messed up. Who would be my army if she messed up? My mother! It was all in fun, and everybody had a good time.

I introduced her to my church, and the good church ladies at the Greater Abyssinian Baptist Church first looked at her as a young woman who had taken advantage of their middle-aged Junius, weakened by advancing age and the promise of a pretty face. That is, until they found out she was a woman of God, and that she sure can preach! Annie got her start as a preacher at Greater, and is now associate pastor at Bethany Baptist Church, my new church home as well. She is much sought after as a preacher around the state, and is a professor at New Jersey City University in Jersey City, where she directs the Lee Hagan Africana Studies Center.

About a year after we were married, we had our first son, Junius Onome Williams. (You can bet the church ladies were counting the months.) Two years later, we had Che Adolphous Williams. Like my daughters Camille and Junea before them, I love, appreciate, and am thankful for all they give me. I am blessed to see the four of them now texting each other. As a telephone man, I find myself out of that loop.

The Township of Irvington

In 1990 I ran into my friend and former fellow Board of Trustees member at Essex County College, Sara Bost, who was then president of the Irvington City Council. Irvington is a city of about 50,000 people south and west of Newark, which should have been annexed a long time ago by Newark. Sara asked me to be the lawyer for the city council, a job called Legislative Counsel. Most of the fun in this position came in advising the council how to do battle with Mayor Steele, who was the first black Mayor of Irvington. Like all mayors and councils, they each wanted more power than they were entitled to have under the law. My job was to help push the council's interests. I enjoyed the debates—and the salary and benefits, and often was called upon to wax eloquent on behalf of my client, mostly at the council caucus sessions.

Sara decided to run for mayor in 1994, and I helped her win the election. She became the first female elected to the position as mayor in the township's history, and appointed me township attorney.

This was a great experience, partly because of the municipal law I learned. I also appreciated working for a mayor who was not intimidated by my skills, and didn't worry about whether I wanted her job. I got a chance to use my entire accumulated insider political and advocacy skills. I was her advisor on legal and political matters, and resolved legal issues among the other department heads. I used my knowledge of construction in the purchase and rehabilitation of the Irvington Recreation Center, and to finish off the Irvington swimming pool, suffering from cost overruns and a long list of construction problems.

I worked for the mayor for eight more years, in a town plagued by financial problems that began before Sara got there, but for which she was held responsible. Eventually, the state came in and took over management, including approval of budgets, approvals of all new hiring, and constant audits of the books.

I may have disagreed with her on occasion, but there is no doubt in my mind that she is my favorite mayor.

But Newark called. Once the University Heights housing was sold, the only thing that connected me with Newark was a few pro bono (nonpaying) clients and my position on the Board of Trustees of the Education Law Center (ELC). Sometime during that era I became its chairman.

The Education Law Center and *Abbott v. Burke*

ELC was the group of lawyers and community people who waged war with the state of New Jersey about school funding litigation. ELC filed the case known as *Abbott v. Burke* in 1981. The lawyers convinced the Supreme Court that the Abbott School Districts, thirty-one urban districts, should receive from the state an amount equal to that paid for operation of schools in the most affluent school districts. In addition, the court ordered "Supplemental Programs" such as universal preschool for children ages three and four, full-day kindergarten, before- and after-school programs, reading tutors in grades one to three, health centers in schools, and additional personnel such as parent liaisons, dropout prevention coordinators, and social workers. And the court ordered new schools. After much fighting within the state legislature, a $6.5-billion-dollar construction program was authorized to replace old schools, some of which had been built in the 1890s.

Each year the ELC lawyers went back to court to enforce the order, since all governors and state legislators since 1981 fought spending that much money on poor, mostly black and brown kids. I became chairman of the board of ELC sometime in the early 2000s, but running the meetings was not enough. There was a need to teach parents more about the Abbott remedies and to get them involved in making the remedies work by holding the school district and the state accountable for the success of the program. I took a leave of absence to organize a statewide parent and community support mechanism for Abbott. We mobilized what became the largest march on Trenton up to that time in support of the Abbott Program, with eight hundred people rallying at the Supreme Court and later at the State House. We got a lot of attention but still didn't get the increases we deserved.

I liked being back on the front line with the parents through the vehicle I created called the Black and Latino Education Summit (BLES). After that rally, the black and Latino leaders of agencies and action groups from across the state came together periodically to maintain an ongoing presence in Abbott politics, but foundation money was not there to support the organization. We needed the presence of a full-time organization. School districts were quick to say to the parents, "Get on the bus; go to Trenton; save Abbott." But when the Abbott money crisis had subsided, parents in each district were put on the back burner. There was no vehicle for the kind of empowerment I had experienced throughout my adult life with ongoing leadership opportunities in organizations making demands of the system. By the year 2002, there was now another generation and a half of parents who knew nothing of PUBS, nor the elected school board, nor PTA involvement, nor Abbott. I begin to think: perhaps I could be the source of training for the birth of such awareness in Newark in my next reinvention?

Transition from Irvington

I had to think of transition anyway. Sara announced one day that she would not seek a third term. With the help of friends in local foundations and an invitation to establish my new organization at Rutgers University–Newark, I came home to set up the Abbott Leadership Institute (ALI). It is a leadership development series of free classes, held on campus on Saturdays. Ultimately, we prepare ALI parents to organize to make a difference in Newark schools.

Meet the Abbott Leadership Institute (ALI)

Over the years I have realized that I work best with a small, tightly knit, and efficient group of people who enjoy hard work. I have been blessed with fine workers at ALI who understand and appreciate my style. Yanique Taylor, from Jamaica, was my first administrative assistant until she went on to earn her master's degree at Rutgers Newark. That meant I had a Jamaican wife at home and a Jamaican assistant in the office: not for the faint of heart! Yanique was replaced by Kaleena Berryman, an Arts High School and William Paterson University graduate. Kaleena covers all the bases I can't reach with my overambitious appetite, with great creativity, discipline, and passion. And then there is Michael James, who handles special assignments, like organizing pastors, recruiting parents, and taking high school students in our Youth Media Symposium (YMS) on field trips. If the job requires tenacity, give it to Michael.

We started with nineteen parents, community advocates, grandparents, and one teacher, "my sister," Mary Moye. Then there was "our class Mother," Wilhelmina Holder, a parent and now grandparent activist who is the President of the Newark Secondary Parents Council. It is a coalition of community activists mostly from high schools in Newark, all with strong personalities and definite opinions about everything. With Holder and Moye, and the help of other "veterans" from time to time and class to class, we always have something going between parents who are brand new, and parents that have wrestled with school reform issues over a period of years, each in his or her own way. We eat breakfast, talk, educate, and laugh with one another.

Over the past ten years ALI has grown by word of mouth. And now we get teachers, administrators, and college students from Rutgers, Montclair State, and Essex County College as well as parents. We have a group of "regulars" who come back with us each semester. Why? Because ALI has become the place to go for discussion and work on education practices and policies, all from the perspective of parent engagement and empowerment. Our average class is now seventy-five to eighty people, with some as large as 100 to 125, depending on the temperature of the issue. At the time of the writing of this paragraph, we have instructed more than 2,500 parents, teachers, administrators, and students (college and high school) in one aspect of education advocacy or another, at Rutgers or in community venues. Many of them have engaged in some project or advocacy on their own, or in advocacy projects designed in the ALI classes.

So what is the key to our success? My classes help people who have been mired in self-blame, distrust, and disorganization by putting them in touch with our historical roots, and with one another. And it shows those who are advocates how to go beyond emotional displays of outrage to understand the power of information.

Newark Revisited

I attract a lot of people who have already been involved in advocacy for better schools. Some people are very good at banging at the door to gain entry for rights they are entitled to have. However, few people understand what to do once the door is open and the power structure says, "Come on in and sit down at the table." Such is the situation with the Abbott case remedies and No Child Left Behind (NCLB). The advocacy skills are far different at the table than those used in demonstrations, takeovers, and picket lines, as we learned in the Medical School Fight. People today are frustrated, confused, and angry, because the advocacy process is far more complicated than they have learned. People are looking for ways to make the changes they need to have, but tend to repeat the same answers that may have been good then, but are no longer valid. As my friend and protégé Louscious Jones says, "The fight is in us, but we don't understand the nature of the fight."

Generally our community organizations like PTAs are no longer as strong as they were in the days of the teachers strikes (1970–1971). There is so much distrust and fighting among different groups and factions, and even fewer people know how to fashion win-win resolutions to conflicts and strategies for success based on organization. Newark has become a community full of fear, not of white people as represented by the Ku Klux Klan in Alabama and all points deep South, but fear coming from the culture of drugs and violence and hostility in the streets; of distrust of one another. And disdain for political solutions because too few know the successes of the past.

Fear. Hostility. Mistrust. The three Horsemen of Disorganization. All of this played out against a backdrop of the politics of me-first that so characterized the Black Political Class, coming to the black community only at election time to perpetuate their tenuous hold on office and maintain what they thought was power.

In ALI classes, we encourage a different relationship with power. We teach people the relationship among information, perception, and response. People need to:

- Collect *information* about the school or school policy that is troublesome.
- Use the information collected to formulate a *perception* of the problem.
- Get together with a critical mass of people, and share the information; use the information and initial perception to raise questions.
- Use information and perception to formulate an appropriate organized *response* to make schools better, in conjunction with other stakeholders.
- Go out with at least five people and put the response in action.

I illustrate this interrelationship and flow from stage to stage with something I call "The Dynamic Triangle of Change." The common denominator for use of information is to clear out misinformation about who was responsible for what; to create new perceptions about people's ability to do for self; and to fuel the fire to make people hunger for More.

Please don't think that the process is purely cerebral. Although information is the kindling for the fire that must burn in order for change to occur, it is outrage that has mobilized thousands of feet in face of obvious injustice, whether it be by the police, the courts, the welfare programs, or in our case, the schools. Unfortunately the rage produced by injustice is now oriented inward, toward one another, not toward the systems that oppress and exploit. In class at ALI, I am able to connect the dots for some for the very first time, and help regain our balance in the community.

One of the biggest hurdles to overcome is the person I call "The Lone Ranger." He or she understands the theory and practice of advocacy that we teach in the series. But invariably, they work alone. Why?

For the last twenty years, elements of the majority community have said to us, "You have no more excuse for failure, since Jim Crow is dead. The problem now is within the black community, and it is one of moral decay." This theory of moral dysfunction perniciously gained increased acceptance not only in the white community, but in the black neighborhoods as well, championed by some black leadership. The seeds of a "moral dilemma" have been planted deep within in the minds of the American public as a whole, and in the psyches of black and brown people in particular.

So the Lone Ranger is doubtful and even afraid—afraid not of authority figures, but of her peers. She wants nothing to do with people society has judged to be responsible for their own degradation, and who display all the symptoms of a failed ghetto existence: people who have said "yes" and don't show up, people who argue all the time, and are constantly putting their needs and their agendas ahead of the group. We have a needy population of people out there, created by all the anger and confusion and self-doubt imposed by the Empire. The lone parent advocate seeks to make an intervention with someone she can depend on: "Me, myself, and I." There aren't too many people who think they can fix their own lives, much less a school.

The "Lone Ranger" is a product of this cultural deficit.

I talk to them about it, caution them against it; "Don't go down there (to the school headquarters) by yourself—take some people with you!" When you're alone you can be isolated, minimized. "Oh, okay, Mrs. Jones," the school officials assure, "We see what you're saying, but it's not always like that." Unspoken finishing thought: "It's just *you* that has that problem," and so pretty soon you and the issue will be swept away.

I see this type of advocate at the Board of Education meetings; very articulate, strong, mostly women, on point with excellent delivery and fearless in their presentation. But they're all by themselves, at best with a friend or two. We teach our parents, "Get five parents, and you will get someone's attention; get ten, and you can change the culture of the school." Whenever I can, I meet the Lone Rangers, take their contact information, and encourage them to come to ALI class. That's one way our list has grown to over two thousand people.

To clarify the analysis of where we stand as victims of self-doubt, I came up with another invention. I ask in a PowerPoint, "Are We Still in Bondage?" featuring the songbird afraid to fly out, even when the cage door opens. We need to fly out and see how we can work together. Many of us are that caged bird, with only a sad song to sing.

My class is a little oasis for those who have dared venture out of their cage, and gotten connected with people who are similarly situated. ALI is more than a class: it is a family of people who help each other visualize solutions and work together to solve problems, such as the need to remove a principal from a school or fight for proper allocation of money in the school district as a whole. It is the members of the ALI family who have joined together to help form the Coalition for Effective Newark Public Schools to take on a secret plan promulgated by the enemies of public education to close schools, and colocate with charter schools, taking away vitally needed resources for the majority of schools in the district. The coalition is an organization of community advocates, high school students, local educators, a citywide parents organization, and unions, including the Newark Teachers Union (NTU) and the City Association of Supervisors and Administrators (CASA), the union for school administrators. Since the days of PUBS, the unions seem ready to embrace a brand of collective school reform that will help teachers, but also parents and students benefit from new forms of teaching and learning.

Satisfaction

I think I have found a niche that suits my temperament and the times. I am in a place where I can continue my life's journey as an advocate through continuing the education of others. I criticize my generation, the Black Political Class, and even some of us who consider ourselves to be advocates—for not taking time to pass on the knowledge to help generate new leadership. Through the Leadership Development

Group at Essex County College, through the music of Return to the Source, through my senior status as past president of the National Bar Association, where I have been honored each year for almost twenty-two years with a luncheon at the NBA Annual Convention in my name sponsored by the Young Lawyers Division, and now at the Abbott Leadership Institute, I do my best to Pass It On! Surrounded by people of all ages who are bright, energetic, inquisitive, and open to new ideas coming from a firm foundation, I am as happy as I can be to be who I am.

Acknowledgment

And I am happy to say that the people of Newark and New Jersey seem to appreciate me for who I am. In the last few years, I have received awards from the Urban League, the National Association of Negro Women, the Garden State Bar Association, the New Jersey Performing Arts Center, the Newark chapter of the NAACP, and Ahavas Sholom, the last remaining Jewish synagogue in Newark, and President Obama for my community service. But the big event of my recent life was staged by my friends George Hampton and Bob Holmes, both of whom worked for me back in the days of Model Cities, and nurtured to fruition by my friend Marcia Brown and my wife, Annie. About four hundred people showed up at the Robeson Center in 2007. Seventeen came from Richmond, Virginia, the Class of '61 from Armstrong High School. I had friends from the NBA, NCUP, the Welfare Rights Organization and NAPA, Agricultural Missions, Greater Abyssinian Baptist and Bethany Baptist Church, and of course parents and community people and teachers from ALI, just to name a few. In fact, there were people there from every phase of my life. There was my old fast-food business partner, Bob DeTore, representing "the white people in my life," still telling whoppers about our defunct chicken business. And of course my family, represented on-stage by my lawyer daughter, Junea, who delights in telling insider-only family stories. The planning committee didn't have all the names because some more said they would have come from all over the country. The farthest traveler? Bill Yuen, my old roommate and successor at the Newark Housing Council, flew in from Hawaii, with two Hawaiian leis made out of real flowers. I kept those things in my refrigerator for about a month, trying to keep them alive. And the tributes poured in, from the Newark City Council through Council President Mildred Crump, and from Congressman Donald Payne, who couldn't make it but sent in his words. Return to the Source, including some singers I hadn't seen in a long time, surprised me with an appearance, including our music director, Anthony Jackson, who now lives in Atlanta. We talked of making a comeback, a "Reunion Tour" like the Jackson family, which is still to come.

I didn't realize how much I was loved and appreciated until that moment. It was special—and it went on all weekend, as the Armstrong people, some of the NBA folks, and some of my ALI friends came over on Saturday and ate and partied and ate and partied until I was tired and went to bed. My wife—bless her heart—was there for me on this one on both days to make this the crowning success that it was.

I have been accustomed to being the outside player, the man left alone. Respected and listened to, but never embraced. These last few years have made me realize people do appreciate me for who I am.

Actually, there was one other time earlier when I was surprised by the love and affection of people I didn't know. In the winter of 1982, months after my unsuccessful run for mayor, the owner of Otis Men's Shop in East Orange announced on the radio that they were having a "Man of the Year" contest, honoring the man who had done the most for community service. After all the calls were tallied, I received the most votes! I didn't know anything about it until Otis called me and told me to "come on down" to get my award, which was a nice shirt and sweater outfit. I was overwhelmed. The little people, some who probably voted for me but others who may not have been registered, voted me in as "their man!" The clothes? I can't wear them anymore, but I still have that plaque, which sits near the window in my home office. I'll always have that plaque, which says:

Otis Men's Shop "Man of The Year"
Junius Williams
For
Outstanding Community Service
December 16, 1982

Once again, I tell you, speaking about both events, each forty-five years apart, "It don't get much better than that."

My Conclusion

Recently, I asked George Hampton, "Why did so many people enjoy pulling the rug from under me?"

He told me, "Because you were smart, confident, and had too much street in you! You had the pedigree, but you also had the street." And that was a little too much for some people. And that's what my life story is meant to help you understand, reader. During the '70s, '80s, and '90s, we spent too much time judging each other and pushing one another aside instead of combining the talents and skills together to make the vision of power a reality. With the Abbott Leadership Institute, and the Youth Media Symposium, I am happy to be engaged in a process far bigger than just me alone, one that is preparing tomorrow's advocates, today.

How effective have I been, and was it worth the sacrifice? Newark has changed, and I've had a hand in that evolution, even revolution. But most people are not yet where I want them to be, self-empowered and fully engaged with a clear agenda and a knowledge of their role in a process of change. My friend Joe Keeseker, former executive director of Agricultural Missions, told us a story at the Ag Missions Executive Board not too long ago. A man was making a peanut butter sandwich for his son, and got down to the bottom of the jar. As he scraped and scraped, the amount he retrieved grew less and less. At one point he thought, "How little peanut butter can I put on the bread and still call it a peanut butter sandwich?"

This can be a metaphor about me. In my present position at ALI, is teaching and giving advice to others a valid substitute for being on the front line? If I were to read my own book, I would conclude that the present front line is the battle for the influence and direction of people's minds, and so I'm still on the battlefield. What better way to continue the struggle but by teaching what I know, and learning from my students?

So I'm still a valid peanut butter sandwich. Maybe not as crunchy as I once was and would still like to be, but still vital and yummy. I am in a new stage in life, a new role in struggle, but struggle just the same.

So what will I do next? My friend Barbara Summers, whom I met at Yale, a former high-fashion model and an impressive author, told me, "I liked the political passion and intimate knowledge you bring to your writing, the way you fit the pieces together." I do like to write. But I also like the rough and tumble, the thrill of victory, the confrontation between "good" and "evil"—perhaps I'm being a little too melodramatic for a real organizer, one who has come to understand nuance, instead of absolutes?—I can't help it. And so will I be able to sit on the side and just write articles and more books?

I guess we'll have to wait and see. In the meantime, classes for the Abbott Leadership Institute are held every other Saturday, free, at Rutgers Newark. If you want to learn more, come join us. And thanks for being such good readers.

BLACK POWER AND THE OCCUPY MOVEMENT

How I got over,
How I got over . . .
Sometimes my soul looks back in wonder
How I got over!

—REVEREND WILLIAM BREWSTER,
"HOW I GOT OVER"

All children are open and ready for information; eager for commitment. Who and what will enter their minds at an early age, and claim their allegiance? Today there is no Jim Crow, but society tells young people of color through the media, in schools, and through a constantly receding governmental safety net, "Racism has been conquered. And since you're still not successful, it must be your own fault." I feel the need to help our children fight that message, starting with my own family. What does a father do to protect his children when the vehicles that afforded him protection and projection into the world of liberation politics, the Civil Rights and Black Power Movements, are gone?

My daughter Camille is now thirty-six years old, and had the courage to go back to college at age thirty-four, after joining the work world long ago and seeing there was a glass ceiling she could never penetrate with just a high school diploma. She is very smart and talented, and I don't know how she did it, but she is a friend of Beyoncé and Jay-Z. Then came Junea, now a lawyer in her own firm, representing kids caught up in the state child welfare system. She is a wife and mother, and recently made me a granddaddy for the first time. "Granddaddy" implies, "You are now officially old." But Justice Coltrane Edmund (I call him "JC") has captured my heart, and so I embrace my status.

By my second marriage, I have two boys. Junius, age sixteen, plays drums and piano, and speaks French and Arabic. He is in love with the United Nations and world diplomacy. Che, age fourteen, plays hockey and baseball, produces music, loves super heroes and Asian history, and is a freestyle hip-hop artist. Both are leaders in their high schools, although their styles are quite different.

When each set of children were little girls and boys, I told them about their heritage: "You are African people living in America. This entitles you," I told them, "to all the history of the world." They internalized this early, and so they were ready for school and the television, when the challenges came to who they were, culturally: the negative images of African people in books, classrooms, and in the media; the willful separation of themselves by other young children their age and color, who defiantly proclaim, "I'm not an African." Each one of my children is comfortable with and understands the importance of the African connection. They study African history with an open mind. Junea and Junius have traveled to several countries in Africa, and all four have been to the Caribbean.

Second, I taught them they are children of the blues. Spirituals, blues, jazz, gospel, R&B, soul, and early hip-hop is all music that comes out of the struggle by black folks in this country to be free, and reflects that struggle in so many ways. Contrast the traditional African elements like multi-rhythms, call and response, field hollers, and improvisation found in all African-influenced music with today's pop and commercial hip-hop: electronically created rhythms with messages of material pleasure, negative stereotypes, antisocial imagery, and preference for all things white. Successive generations lose primary connection with the past and with the extent of their artistic potential as listeners and performers today. We can see not only the robbery of a cultural art form from its original genius, but a denial of the culture of struggle from which the original music was born. Our music is our most significant offering to the world. Lose connection with it, and we lose a lot of that significance. I wanted my children to acknowledge and protect the blues and its progeny by any means necessary.

This is not easy to achieve in the wake of the barrage of "pop" and commercial hip-hop. When I took my children to school, almost twenty years apart for each of two sets, they remember me playing the music on the car radio, and discussing the giants who created it, the connections between each art form, and its relationship to black and American history. They remember the music quizzes in the car ("Who's that playing?" "What's the name of that song?" "What's the time signature in that song?" "What kind of Latin beat is that?"). Camille and Junea remember meeting Count Basie. They remember a concert featuring Stevie Wonder, when I embarrassed them by dancing in the aisle. They took *me* to two Father's Day concerts starring Beyoncé; and another one with Earth, Wind & Fire. Che and Junea have taught our music to their respective friends in class; Junius plays in three musical groups in school. Today, all four have iPods with an eclectic mix of music from all over the world, including soul, West African, Arabic, Brazilian, Jamaican, and European classics. They listen avidly and understand the importance of our music and its historical context of struggle to their identity. And to my grandson, I proudly proclaim, "JC, I'm coming for you next!"

Next, I taught them that they are children who come from a legacy of struggle. Anything we as a people have accomplished, like our music, has been because of struggle, done by working together to overcome forces that would enslave and imprison us, mentally as well as physically. And so they are conversant with our history in this country, and of our ancestors in Africa and throughout the African diaspora. They were never empty vessels to be filled with somebody else's story of who we were and who we are now. Camille and Junea remember meeting people like Kwame Ture (Stokely Carmichael), and sitting in the middle of 125th Street and 8th Avenue watching newly released from South African prison Nelson Mandela, and Winnie Mandela meet Betty Shabazz for the first time. Junius and Che remember meeting Bishop Desmond Tutu in Newark, and Reverend Jesse Jackson at an NBA convention.

My children learned to resist early in life, recalling demonstrations for rights at school recess as early as the fourth grade (Junius), and a school sit-in for better lunch in the eighth grade (Che). Junea recalls marches to Washington, DC, in support of affirmative action, and protests against the killing of Amadou Diallo by New York police.

By their testimony, they have formed their own worldview based on a concept of justice; they are informed and opinionated; they are articulate and unafraid to speak up; they know who they are as black youth, but do not isolate themselves away from other people of other cultures and other systems of belief. In fact, some of their best friends are white, in college and high school (lol). They are ready for the next step, and at least three of the four would welcome a Movement presence in their lives. (75 percent ain't bad. . . . I'm still working on the last 25 percent!)

But my children are privileged, protected by middle-class status. They attended Catholic, private, and public schools. Their world is not like those of most kids who are black and brown from working-class and poor families. They have been protected from the economic impact of racism by the class status of their parents, and now their own.

Therefore, I want you to meet the rest of my children, who I love as well. About six years ago, we developed the concept of the Abbott Leadership Institute Youth Media Symposium (YMS). We set out to show high school students, recruited initially through our network of parents and educators, that they have a voice, their voice is worth listening to, and that learning media skills will help amplify that voice. Each of these three steps is significant, because young people are prime targets of miseducation that has disempowered many parents.

Through the years we have developed a cadre of high school students who have learned to formulate opinions about their lives, especially about schools and the education they get in Newark. Now they are asking hard questions of the education system in Newark: "Why don't I have a geometry teacher, instead of a string of substitute teachers who are not teaching me enough for me to graduate?" And they are formulating demands of the system: "We want enough guidance counselors to begin preparing us for college beginning in the eighth grade!" Now they have a voice that is getting stronger, because they believe they have the right to a good education.

YMS students, through their advocacy, have changed school policy, become role models for grade school students across the state, and impressed adults at gatherings such as the New Jersey Black Issues Convention on several occasions. They were the catalysts for the U.S. Department of Education national youth "Listening Tour" instituted because of an analysis YMS students did of problems in their schools in Newark. "You haven't seen the best of us yet," they tell me with their smiles and laughter, brimming with newfound self-confidence.

Who are they? They go to public high schools mostly in Newark; some of them come from families with one parent, without much money present in the household; and most of their parents and grandparents never had a Movement experience like my wife and me.

They come to us with talents and a variety of personalities. Some are natural public speakers (Aisha and Brianna); some are very technically proficient (William and Israel); some have a great sense of humor (Chris), while some are very serious (Alexis); some are more eager than others to learn and listen to the music I introduce into their lives (Lamone and Montaya); some take to politics like ducks to water

(Ramon, Tyree, and Ronnie). And all have gone to a school system that fails to validate who they are as black and Latino teenagers.

How do we do it? Through restoration and empowerment. Unlike my children, who've been under my influence continuously from birth, these are young people whose first contact with concepts like power and liberation comes from their experiences with YMS as teenagers. When they first came to YMS, they had been miseducated into thinking it was their fault if they didn't do well in school, without daring to think about holding adult educators accountable for what they know or don't know. They have been trapped in a school system that describes "education" as how well they do on standardized tests; they are subjected to a disciplinary system that withholds music, drama, and interesting electives because there just isn't enough money for these children of a darker hew, as there is in suburban districts.

And so my staff and I teach them about the civil rights and other political movements, about the need for political action to change the schools that miseducate and force them to abandon their hopes and dreams. I personally enjoy teaching them about the corporate theft of black/American music, and its removal from the consciousness of all America.

I love my parents and older community advocates, but there is something so strong and solid about seeing that freedom light enter the eyes of a young person for the first time. It's fierce; it's empowering watching them become empowered, because of what they must overcome to get there. But once it clicks on, it's there forever.

They have begun to free themselves from inferiority complexes imposed by adults that surround them, some in their own households; and in doing so emerge with the beginnings of a race- and class-based analysis of who they are as young people, although they certainly would not use my language.

But they, like my children, will always be vulnerable. We continuously teach them how to fight through the projection of false values and artificially (media) created needs. In classes and one-on-one dis-cussion, my staff and I challenge some of the deadly cultural contra-dictions: "saggin'" (pants worn down below the waste); rap videos glamorizing drugs and violence; the negative and powerless imagery of females and the preference for light-skinned women over dark; the propaganda glamorizing charter schools over public schools.

And then there is the violence and the threat of violence constantly in their lives, coming from all directions—the drug dealers; the police; the half-crazed people in the neighborhood whose anger sometimes cannot be contained. So much is coming at them. Can they survive? Can they hold on to what we teach them until they get back in class two days later . . . until they grow up, hopefully go to college as we direct and prepare them, and comfortably make a place for themselves in an entirely different way of life? Newark (America) is a dead zone for young people of color until they are fortified intellectually, culturally, and politically to know how to separate themselves from the lies and half-truths that bombard them every day that tell them they unworthy.

When I was a young man, we needed a Movement to keep our eyes on the prize, to internalize the lessons we learned about the need for struggle to redefine ourselves in the context of Jim Crow. And that is what these children need, those of my blood, and my extended family in YMS. YMS and I can only go so far, just as my parents and Amherst College could only do so much for me. To whom can all my children turn to sustain the knowledge already acquired, and to help them reach the next level of their development? Who or what will come forth and absorb this energy we helped create and focus it in the right direction? At this juncture, what are the options?

The Importance of the Occupy Movement

Occupy Wall Street is the most important political movement since Jesse Jackson's Rainbow Coalition in the late 1980s. Why? Because it popularized and facilitated the understanding of the notion of class analysis and class-based solutions. They took the "power elite" from sociologist C. Wright Mills and the notion of the "military-industrial complex" from President Dwight David Eisenhower, and renamed those at the top of this economic and political pyramid "the 1 percent," synonymous with what I called throughout my book "the Empire." Then they called for unity among the remaining 99 percent, no matter what race, age, gender, or sexual orientation. Here is a movement where people from everywhere can come together around the economic issues they have in common, like jobs, the social services safety net, tax relief for the people that need it, and accountability from those who control most of the wealth in this country. They broke it down for everybody to see, and put boots on the ground through street demonstrations to try to break the hold of the banks and other financial institutions on the political economy of America.

Black Power, as important as it was for development of positive racial identity and political victories like electing the first black mayors in places like Newark and the placement of black people in other high government and private-sector positions, did not develop a class analysis. At least not as it evolved. The leadership of SNCC had such analysis, but as the concept took hold and sped around the country, most Black Power aficionados had no platform dealing with systemic inequality in our economic system. At the height of its popularity, Black Power came to mean, "Let's put a black face in a high place." Hence, the Black Political Class in places like Newark was a manifestation of Black Power, in their minds. Many of them stayed race-based in their analysis of problems and proposals of solutions, thus separating themselves from the working class and poor in the community who were also black, but could not all look forward to a job in city hall, Prudential, or Rutgers University; who could not move to the suburbs under the open housing act; or sit in the integrated restaurants, because they couldn't afford the meal.

So because there was no class analysis, the limited mobility gained by middle-class people of color because of the civil rights and Black Power era blinded this group from the disproportionate impact of racism and classism on the working-class and poor sectors of the black and increasingly brown communities throughout the country, particularly in the inner cities.

Let's visit the issue of drugs as an example. Urged on by the media that is controlled by the 1 percent, many of the black and Latino middle class, as well as their white counterparts in the cities and suburbs, see drug users and drug dealers as moral and social degenerates. They don't see drug users as people who can no longer cope; or drug dealers as ghetto capitalists in the only sector of the economy open to everybody. Nor has this middle class been taught to recognize that most of the illegal drugs in the country are sold and used by white people in the suburbs and places like Wall Street. Nor do they pay attention to the more lenient punishment that is meted out to white middle- and upper-class professionals caught dealing or using drugs. Without race and class analysis together, the true nature of the workings of the criminal justice system is beyond comprehension, and there is not enough unity among the middle class, working class, and poor people of all races to form an effective political movement to correct the injustices in the criminal justice system. There is too much blame coming from above, and too much acceptance of the harsh indictment of "unclean!" from within the less affluent communities hit hardest by drug violence and heavy-handed police response. There is a "jailhouse train" moving through ghetto communities, and even the mothers and fathers who watch their children taken away every day have very little to say.

The "criminal industrial complex" is a term that reflects the wealth and power generated by elements of the 1 percent, which profits not only from the incarceration of more than one million living souls, the majority of whom are people of color, but keeps its victims disorganized and separated from potential allies by manipulation of images and apportionment of blame on everybody but the political and economic conditions that create the culture of drugs. And the anger that is created and stored among those who suffer as perpetrators or victims of the poverty and violence in the ghetto communities, instead of directed outward against those who dominate and perpetuate this system, explodes inward and hurts the people in the communities most discriminated against, causing even more division and blame among those who should be together in struggle. Why? Because like the middle class, there is no class and race analysis to help the perpetrators and victims of crime and violence to understand what is happening in their lives.

The picture painted above marks the making of the most recent chapter of what Carter G. Woodson called *The Mis-Education of the Negro*. Actually, it is an example of the miseducation of everybody affected, including black and white middle-class people of good will. The consequence: we have alienated and become alienated from so many young people in our communities, so many potential soldiers in our next-generation Freedom Army. I look at the Bloods and Crips. Forty to fifty years ago, they would have been Young Lords, Black Panthers, or in SNCC.

How, then, can young people in the ghettos of America (and those who are not so young) identify with the call to action of any movement coming from outside their communities that directs their attention toward an outside source as the ultimate cause of their misery, when they cannot make the connection between corporate domination and the lives they endure? "We gotta get the cops to get Pookey off the corner; he's the real problem." That's as far as that argument will go.

Young people in the throes of the urban gang and drug culture are not as easily reached as my four children at home, or the few who annually come to school at YMS. They play by different rules and are trapped in a kingdom not entirely of their making. They have little experience with organization, other than gangs; see civil rights as something that happened yesterday; dropped out of school or will very soon; and have role models like Pookey who fashion delivery systems based on protecting corners or taking other people's corners to build up their economic domains.

But they are smart, and can learn. They must first understand who they are, and learn to define survival in terms that take them beyond living from one day to the next. But what a powerful addition they would make to a movement for social change. These are the people who most frighten the Empire, because they have the most to gain and the least to lose. If they wake up, and connect the dots, here will be an army very hard to stop.

The Bloods and the Crips

A few years ago, the Bloods and the Crips called a truce in Newark. It was at the time of the first Hip Hop National Convention, held in Newark at Rutgers University. Some of the conveners of the conference were instrumental in bringing the gang leaders to the table, and at some point left the conference-goers to go down to Symphony Hall for the announcement of the truce. I remember sitting midway up the aisle at this grand old music and entertainment mecca, the home of Sarah Vaughan and the like, listening as one by one, leaders from each gang went on stage and proclaimed it was time to stop the violence. They were strong, tough young men, mostly in their late twenties; street hard, prison hard; articulate and forceful with their presence. The common denominator: "We're tired of all the blood being shed." I sat there caught up in the emotion of the moment. They were tired and wanted to come in from the cold.

"But we have one condition," they told the assembled group of city leaders, including members of the city council, representatives of the mayor's office, the Newark School District, several well-known black preachers, and representatives of social agencies. "You have to get us jobs!"

All the city leaders said, "Yes" and talked about what a marvelous breakthrough this was. But in the ensuing months, very few jobs were generated, and the conditions that kept gang members from getting jobs in the private sector, like driver's licenses for those who were convicted felons, were never resolved.

Slowly, the momentum was lost. The only ones who paid continued attention to the gang leadership on stage that summer night were the police. I asked one of the facilitators of the truce what happened to the gang leadership, and what happened to the truce. He told me the cops singled out each one of them for surveillance and eventually found some reason to put them back in jail. Eventually, the truce ended as both the Bloods and the Crips went back to gang-banging and their livelihood based on selling drugs.

I cite this example because it shows this most organized layer of youth in the community can be reached, by the right people, and under the right circumstances. But can the Occupy Movement bridge the gap between races and class to enlist and entice the Bloods and Crips and other organizations, to make the connection between jobs and the 1 percent and try nonviolence as a means of protest?

I think about the impact of the local black college students and neighborhood people on the campaign by SNCC in 1965 to break out of the corner of Jackson and High streets and march downtown in Montgomery, Alabama. Without the addition of those most likely to strike fear in the hearts and minds of the power structure in Montgomery, the demonstrations would not have been as successful. I think about the impact of the rebellion in Newark on the politics of Newark after the summer of 1967. The power brokers scuffled to make concessions, and thus job training, jobs, and housing resulted in significant quantity and quality.

Given the philosophy of Occupy, and with new troops and energy from the ghettos and barrios from the cities, how far would this political tsunami roll in its impact on the current political and economic system, with young people of color directing their anger away from themselves in *organized, nonviolent fashion*, and making demands upon those who are the real center of their perpetual have-not status?

Occupy Wall Street, Up Close and Personal

I wanted to see for myself the prospects of Occupy occupying the minds of young people of color, the ones I have described. And so my wife, Annie, and son, Che, went with me to see the Occupy Movement on a seasonally cold October day in 2011. We made our journey by way of the PATH Train from Newark to New York City because I was not willing to chance finding a parking space in that area. "And I don't want to worry about a car on top of anything else that might happen," I thought out loud to my family. My son was only thirteen; my wife inexperienced with large street demonstrations, although she had participated in college resistance activities. All my civil rights and street confrontation skills and training started working overtime: "Suppose the cops get the order to clear Zuccotti Park," I thought, as they did some weeks later. Before we left the house, I told my wife and son what to wear, what not to wear; what to take and what to leave at home; once there, to always keep one eye on the police. I was going to be in my element, and protection of my family was the highest priority.

We were on our way to Occupy territory at the height of its impact on the world consciousness, through media saturation. The police surrounded the park both day and night.

When we arrived, we found an organized community of resistance. A *quilombo*, if you will, thinking back to the organized communities of escaped African slaves hidden in the Brazilian jungles in the 1700s or 1800s. But this community was not hidden, and in fact thrived on the public attention it received, which assured some degree of safety from the rash acts of Big Wall Street and the police, the guardians of the status quo. It also gave Occupy an opportunity to project its message about the economic and political divide between the 1 percent and the 99 percent. Here was a group that wanted Wall Street held accountable, and many Americans were listening. Occupy Wall Street was waking up the people from their stupor caused by years and years of miseducation.

Much has been written about the unity between labor unions and other progressive organizations with the youth in the Occupy Movement throughout the country. But nothing could cement a deal based on respect and admiration forever between Occupy and the various police departments at all levels of government. However sympathetic some policemen may have been with their calls for protecting the interests of the workingman and woman, the confrontational tactics of Occupy were basically in conflict with police mentality. Police forces are hired to protect the property of the Empire, and the idea of Empire itself. Occupy wanted to invade and physically penetrate the territory of these power magnates who were at the top of the pyramid of economic and political power in the United States, and the police were designed and programmed not to let that happen. So even though there was quiet at the time of our family visit, the tension was there. We were on a staging ground for conflict, and it was just a matter of time before Occupy moved on Wall Street, or Wall Street, through the police, moved on Occupy.

But the people I saw weren't expecting either event at the time of our visit. It was a nice day, and people were friendly, going about their daily routines. Che was checking out everything, and Annie was taking pictures for her class or for Facebook.

I remember how impressed I was with the degree and level of services: food, health care, media relations... even a library. "People had time to read," I thought. There was even a librarian fussing over the placement and the rules for returning borrowed books. And there were other rules, written on signs and posted throughout the encampment. Rules about cleanliness, privacy, and of course the library. I wondered who enforced the rules in this democracy.

I was now in my mind thinking back to my days with SDS, and the NCUP project in Newark. "If no one takes the initiative, how do things get done," I always thought. And in taking the initiative, isn't that "leadership?" If every act (or omission) has to be reviewed by everybody, how do we get time for the big issues politics, and organizing . . . and doesn't too much group input destroy the will to jump out there and start something fresh and different?

These are not new questions, and Occupy searched for answers and found them, looking for a balance between pure democracy and delegated responsibility. There were smaller working groups. (In the media center, while we were there, Reverend Al Sharpton was holding forth on a WBAI radio program, broadcasting, "live from Zuccotti Park.") I read about a kind of executive committee called the Spokes Council, composed of representatives of these working groups to undertake "legal and financial decision making." But at the center of Occupy is a commitment to democracy, and the people I saw were taking it seriously. The General Assemblies (GAs) or meetings of the people were held at the far end of the complex. There were a few people doing most of the talking—young, white, male, and female; very forthright and with authority. And everyone repeated what everybody else said because there were no microphones. Statements were always initiated by the now-famous phrase "mike check," and then their messages were carried back by hundreds of voices to those farther away from the raised platform constructed in the park.

There were drummers, constantly playing, making up riffs as they went along. Maybe that's what made me think of quilombos, because of the drumming. I imagined constant communication in the quilombos among various settlements, through the drum, an African extension of self in the Brazilian free communities of color at that time. But I saw very few people of color on the drums. And certainly there were no master drummers like those in the parks throughout New York in the summer, setting the tone with rhythmic creativity and authenticity. Not only were the drummers mostly white, so was most of the Occupy encampment.

There was a kind of post-racial quality about Occupy that I saw that afternoon. The black people I did see were comfortable with their roles and mixed in with the masses at Zuccotti. This was their land as well as anybody else's. I got the impression that color was not an obstacle per se. After all, the young people gathered at Zuccotti had earlier supported President Obama. In fact, in 2008, they wanted Obama to lead us in a new American revolution, but that didn't happen, did it? So all colors were welcome in Occupy, and in fact the participatory democracy at the General Assemblies was structured to make sure more than white men got a chance to speak. There was indeed race consciousness, but the absence of larger numbers of black people in Zuccotti (and on television in the police clashes I saw regularly on the news from all over the country) confirmed my suspicions that the call to join Occupy to take on the Empire had not penetrated to the people in my neck of the woods.

There is a lot in common between people in the Occupy Movement and people like me, working, in my case, through the Abbott Leadership Institute. I created ALI to compete for a place in people's minds. There are many people running for office, but very few who commit to creating a fabric of information and technique to make other people learn to think. Politicians explode onto the consciousness of the people momentarily, but when their term is over, they are gone from the minds of their constituencies (with a few exceptions, like President Obama, who will always be "the first"). But people who plant and cultivate ideas, and perpetually force or negotiate these ideas forward into the consciousness of the public, we last forever. Such *should be* the goal of the Occupy Movement. It is indeed my goal for ALI, and so, Occupy, let me suggest some ways in which the movement can imprint upon a larger and very important sector of the populace that I described above: young, black and brown men and women, girls and boys, at all socioeconomic levels of society, but especially those who are at the margins of society in places like Newark.

Teams of Occupy organizers should connect with black and brown youth whenever and however they can, and work with people in local leadership who are developing young people at whatever level of political development they may be. I saw people from the Occupy Movement in Newark, camping out in one of the parks. They attempted to join in the struggle of parents and community activists who were in resistance to school closings and replacement by charter schools at that time, and some other issues. At first the local elected officials were in favor of Occupy occupying the park, but at some point the cops ordered the encampment shut down, the people left, and that was the last I saw of Occupy (except for some individual representatives looking for space to set up an office at Rutgers).

This cannot be representative of the extent of the Occupy attempt at penetrating the black and brown communities in places like Newark. I am reminded again of the SDS project in Newark, which came to Newark with the intent of organizing neighborhood people around economic issues in 1964. They raised enough money to sustain themselves for the long haul, as I described in chapter 4 of this book. NCUP made an impression on the power structure because they were visibly committed and did not rely solely upon confrontations, which could not be sustained over time. The goal was to teach, and bring the people along slowly, until such time as they could build and sustain their own organizations.

NCUP didn't survive, not because of the strategy and tactics centered on long-term commitment to organizing, but because of the racial polarization brought to a head by the Newark Rebellion and the police response. Afterward, the political vacuum created by this violent upsurge was filled by Black Power organizations, pointing out, correctly, that black folks should organize themselves. Who among Occupy can and should tackle the matter of educating and organizing the youth of the inner cities? Are there sufficient black and Latino operatives within Occupy to undertake the tasks? Or should it be left to a group of black and Latino locals, as yet unformed, with experience in gang, prison, and drug culture to make the connections between education, jobs, a better life, and the acts and omissions of the 1 percent, including the government it controls? Maybe some "OGs" ("original gangsters," that is, older men and women who used to be gangsters) need to penetrate the hype, call the next truce, and start the training process for a brand new neighborhood movement that will convert the untapped power from the streets into a formidable nonviolent movement to put real pressure on the suites.

If Occupy is to be successful, they must adjust their strategies and tactics to educate, create, and sustain an inner city base. Black and brown youth (and the white youth already in Occupy) need to understand how race and class operate today, making plain the connections among poverty, racism, and the 1 percent. If they make that adjustment, Occupy Wall Street may just become the next step forward in the lives of those young people I have successfully reached with the help of my team, and those beyond our reach in the gangs, that are still missing from the table. Perhaps then we can all work together to redefine and undertake a new agenda for justice and equality in America. One that we can collectively finish!

Index

About the Author

JUNIUS W. WILLIAMS is a prominent attorney, educator, musician, and advocate. As a planner, government administrator, and nonprofit real estate developer, he is responsible for over 2,000 housing units and many community centers in Newark, New Jersey. Williams, who attended Amherst College and Yale Law School, was elected the youngest President of the National Bar Association in 1978 and listed among *Ebony*'s "100 Most Influential Blacks in America." His singing group, Return to the Source, has performed at grade schools, colleges, and other venues throughout the East Coast. He is currently Director of the Abbott Leadership Institute at Rutgers University Newark, where his free Saturday morning classes attract hundreds of parents, teachers, and students in learning how to become better advocates for public education.

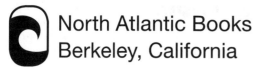 **North Atlantic Books**
Berkeley, California

Personal, spiritual, and planetary transformation

North Atlantic Books, a nonprofit publisher established in 1974, is dedicated to fostering community, education, and constructive dialogue. NABCommunities.com is a meeting place for an ever-growing membership of readers and authors to engage in the discussion of books and topics from North Atlantic's core publishing categories.

NAB Communities offer interactive social networks in these genres:

NOURISH: Raw Foods, Healthy Eating and Nutrition, All-Natural Recipes

WELLNESS: Holistic Health, Bodywork, Healing Therapies

WISDOM: New Consciousness, Spirituality, Self-Improvement

CULTURE: Literary Arts, Social Sciences, Lifestyle

BLUE SNAKE: Martial Arts History, Fighting Philosophy, Technique

Your free membership gives you access to:

Advance notice about new titles and exclusive giveaways

Podcasts, webinars, and events

Discussion forums

Polls, quizzes, and more!

Go to www.NABCommunities.com and join today.